Global Capitalism

For Turi
For my parents, Stephen Cohen and Janet Gagnon

Global Capitalism

A Sociological Perspective

Miguel A. Centeno
Joseph N. Cohen

polity

The right of Miguel Angel Centeno and Joseph Nathan Cohen to be identified as Author of this Work has been asserted in accordance with the UK Copyright, Designs and Patents Act 1988.

First published in 2010 by Polity Press

Polity Press
65 Bridge Street
Cambridge CB2 1UR, UK

Polity Press
350 Main Street
Malden, MA 02148, USA

ISBN-13: 978-0-7456-4450-9
ISBN-13: 978-0-7456-4451-6(pb)

A catalogue record for this book is available from the British Library.

Typeset in 11 on 13 pt Sabon
by Servis Filmsetting Ltd, Stockport, Cheshire
Printed and bound by MPG Books Group, UK

The publisher has used its best endeavours to ensure that the URLs for external websites referred to in this book are correct and active at the time of going to press. However, the publisher has no responsibility for the websites and can make no guarantee that a site will remain live or that the content is or will remain appropriate.

Every effort has been made to trace all copyright holders, but if any have been inadvertently overlooked the publisher will be pleased to include any necessary credits in any subsequent reprint or edition.

For further information on Polity, visit our website: www.politybooks.com

Contents

Figures, Tables, and Boxes

List of Figures, Tables, and Boxes

Box

Acknowledgments

Miguel Centeno first needs to thank his colleagues and students in the Sociology Department at Princeton. It would be impossible to imagine a better place in which to think about the sociology of economic systems or a more rewarding environment in which to work on these issues. I especially want to thank Viviana Zelizer for teaching me what I know about the topic and first thinking of this book.

Much of the writing was done while a visitor at the University of Salamanca. *Gracias a todos.*

My family has put up with the standard faults of any academic plus a few extra ones of my devising and still seems to love me. For the forbearance and patience, thanks to Deborah Kaple, Alex Centeno, and Maya Centeno.

While this book was being written, I spent a lot of time in Washington, DC, saying goodbye to my brother and lifelong best friend, Arturo Girón. There are no words to describe the wonder of his life or the sadness of his death. Debbie Anker, Laura Girón, and Carlos Girón: I hope we will always remember the holidays and the beach.

Joe Cohen would like to thank my teachers at Carleton University, the University of Buenos Aires, and Princeton University. Obviously, there is Miguel Centeno, but I also feel a great debt to Paul DiMaggio, Bruce Western, and Scott Lynch for the time and effort that they invested in me.

I am also grateful to my new department at Queens College. I have enjoyed working here immensely, am grateful for all that you have done to help me manage the first years of my professorship, and for the constant investments of faith that you place in me.

I would like to thank Galit Dadoun for being my partner in the considerable task of raising our daughter and managing the chaos of our household while this book was completed. Thank you, Galit.

For Danielle: you are the light of my life, and my reason for being. Your first two years of life have brought me joy that I could not have imagined before you were born. I love you more than anything else on earth.

For the new girl, who is scheduled to be born in a month: I cannot wait to meet you, and hope we share a long life of love, laughter, and learning together.

Introduction

On November 9, 1989, the Berlin Wall collapsed, marking the final chapter of the Cold War and its long-running ideological battle. After decades of struggle between the liberal political-economic ideals of the West and those of the socialist world, the USSR's demise appeared to resolve that conflict conclusively for experts and lay observers. Francis Fukuyama (1992) could credibly declare that the Cold War's end stood at the "end of history," the final victory in the long saga of democratic capitalism.

Capitalism's decisive victory over post-Depression, mid-twentieth-century *dirigisme* and socialism remained intact for almost twenty years. From 1989 to 2007, pro-market ideologies maintained what Thomas Kuhn (1962) might describe as a dominant paradigm, and Antonio Gramsci (1992[1927]) might call a hegemonic belief system. The superiority of free market capitalism seemed to carry the irrefutable weight of historical proof. No matter how problematic such sweeping conclusions may seem now, they were very powerful. Governments embraced and acted on the principle that unfettered, unregulated, and private sector -dominated markets were the best options for any society. This global experiment in economic reform yielded mixed results. It created previously unseen fortunes, but also new forms of insecurity and hardship. It shook societies from the stranglehold of old elites and long-running conflicts, but also gave rise to new ones.

If history ended in 1989, it may have restarted on September 15, 2008, when Lehman Brothers declared bankruptcy. This was merely a public highlight of a very deep global financial crisis that threw the world economy into a severe recession. During 2008, an astounding $25 trillion of wealth simply disappeared into thin air.[1] (Some might argue that it was thin air to begin with, but that does not make the loss any easier to bear for those experiencing it.) Economies that had been growing now shrank, ships full of new goods docked not knowing if any consumers existed for their wares, and jobs that appeared secure vanished. From celebrations of the market, the media shifted to ever more sophisticated analyses of the causes and consequences of the 1930s Great Depression.

The crisis prompted hard looks at the global economy that was created in the run-up to 2008. Did our great experiment in global capitalism ultimately fail? Why? Are we better off for all of the economic liberalization reforms that took place over the past thirty years? We offer a starting point for those interested in these questions by examining the social basis, reach, effects, and net human welfare benefits of the grand experiment of global capitalism. Our purpose is to describe what global capitalism is, how deeply entrenched it became in the world's economies, and which other societal changes ran concurrent with global capitalism's rise.

We do this explicitly using the tools available to our academic discipline. Sociologists have been interested in capitalism since the beginning of our discipline. Different authors focused on distinctive aspects:[2] Karl Marx argued that the key to capitalism was its historical development as a set of relations between those who owned things and those who had nothing to offer but their labor. For Max Weber, capitalism was defined by the centrality of exchange in a market where new spirits of rationality, asceticism, and entrepreneurship flourished. Georg Simmel was less concerned with capitalism per se and more with the central role of money in modern society. The entrepreneurial spirit of capitalism was of particular interest for Josef Schumpeter, who noted, however, how its "creative destruction" perpetually weakened the very institutions needed to maintain the system. Karl Polanyi observed that attempts at "pure" markets solely driven by interest were destined for catastrophe and that one had to understand capitalism as "embedded" in a set of social institutions which also protected what he called "social interests." More recently, sociologists have been concerned with demonstrating how truly *social* economic life is through attention to social networks (Mark Granovetter), personal relationships (Viviana Zelizer), class power (William Roy, Charles Perrow), institutions (Paul DiMaggio and Walter Powell, Neil Fligstein), and specific national settings (Frank Dobbin, Ronald Dore, Mauro Guillén).

What links all these approaches and defines the sociological perspective on capitalism used in this book is a reluctance to treat it as a categorical imperative rooted in universal scientific principles, and more as a socially and historically constructed worldview. During the last two decades, many flatly declared that "there was no alternative" to capitalism (or markets, globalization, etc.). Sociologists challenged the orthodoxy of a unified set of maxims on economic governance and economic life. As a discipline, sociology always holds that there are alternatives; our task is to analyze how one predominated and why.

Given our critical tradition, there could be a temptation to treat the 2008 crisis as a vindication of our disciplinary perspectives. In our view, this is inappropriate for a variety of reasons. First, relatively few now argue for unfettered, "self-regulated" markets as a viable principle upon which to build an economy; belaboring the point with economistic "straw men" will get us nowhere. Second, sociologists were not alone in our critical viewpoints. Many others expressed similar concerns about the net economic benefit of laissez-faire, and several countries pulled back from an embrace of free markets well before 2008. The fact that we were critical is neither distinctive nor a vindication of our analytical approaches specifically. Moreover, neither the good nor the bad of the last twenty years' economic progress can be entirely attributed to markets or the lack thereof.

This book analyzes global capitalism as a historically created social system: a structure of relationships between organizations and individuals that has evolved over time in response to challenges and promises. The global economy did not arise from a vacuum, but is the product of uncountable transactions and consequences thereof over hundreds of years. Global capitalism was socially constructed through expectations of behavior and the institutionalized rules governing it. We present the march of global capitalism as the diffusion and entrenchment of a set of authoritative, meta-theoretical principles embodied in a series of global and national institutions. We demonstrate that the result of these developments has been a global system with clear hierarchies of benefits and costs, and we propose a way of understanding how these work and the challenges they represent.

Some of the earliest commentators on the economic order that arose in the eighteenth century used the metaphor of a machine or even a clock to describe the new economy (Hirschman 1977). We believe this metaphor can provide us with a useful perspective with which to understand the creation of the global capitalist system over the last 200 years. Global capitalism was and is a spectacularly effective machine. It produces and consumes at an astounding speed. This book provides an analytical map with which to understand the inner workings of the global capitalist "clock." Like any machine it can also break down. We provide an account of how it was built and how, in this very process, the underlying reasons for its failure may be found. We seek to pull the gears apart and demonstrate how they could both produce so much prosperity and so spectacularly come close to collapse.

The global economic system is not just any machine, but a highly complex one. Complex systems consist of a huge volume of parts each behaving at least partially autonomously (even if reacting to one another). Moreover, the interaction between the various components results in aggregate activity, which is not simply a summation of the individual behaviors, but a product of their continual response to each other's action (a property known as "emergence"). These systems feature elaborate feedback loops leading to emergent outcomes; ones not necessarily linked to the characteristics of the individual pieces, but to the process of their interaction. These interactions, ever growing in scale and scope, make it ever more difficult to manage the system and ever more likely that small errors or failures can cascade into crises. From this perspective, the crisis of 2007–8 needs to be understood not as an aberration, but as the consequence of complexities and contradictions built into global capitalism through historical developments. It was, to use the term coined by Charles Perrow (1984), a normal accident: a systemic failure brought about by the inevitable (but unexpected) interaction of tightly integrated parts. The crisis of 2007–8 was a product of the belief that history could be escaped, that universal principles would never know an exception, and that we could enjoy the fruits of complexity without risking its dangers.

We now live on the crest of a roughly 250-year wave of unprecedented growth in material wealth, technological innovation, scientific advancement, and human population, but also one of severe social problems and industrial-strength oppression and violence. For its proponents, capitalism brings freedom and riches, and obeys basic natural laws. Its opponents see capitalism as a violation of human nature, which leads to exploitation. Both of these views have merits, but gloss over their own shortcomings and the potential validity of opposing views. The system is rife with contradictions. Capitalism does rely on an apparent human instinct for individual preservation and self-interest, and represents a system that does give people the freedom to pursue them. But it is also a historical creation mirroring distributions of power, implying that the system is neither wholly liberating nor a pure reflection of human nature. Capitalism does serve as magical processor of information, imposing a productive, materially enriching rationality on billions of apparently random acts, but it can also exacerbate systemic irrationalities and lead to its own crises and forms of economic immiseration.

A Look Ahead

We begin the next chapter by defining what we mean by global capitalism and providing a broad historical overview of its development. We wish to emphasize the paradoxical and often contradictory tendencies inside it. Building on an appreciation of the apparent inescapability (but not inevitability) of capitalism and its complexities, we emphasize its character as a "deep institution" – a socially constructed, politically contentious and deeply habituated way of understanding and practicing economic life.

The next three chapters delve inside the machine of global capitalism and analyze the three critical parts of the system: trade, finance, and consumption. Each part involves flows across the world: the first of goods and services, the second of capital, and the third of marketing. While treated separately, it is vital that the reader keep in mind that each of these structures is linked to the other. So, for example, without the creation of a global marketing arena, much of the trade flows would not exist; without the borrowing and lending of finance, trade would be impossible; without the movement of goods, the links between the various global economies would be ephemeral.

Chapter 2 presents an analysis of how the global trade system developed over the past two centuries, emphasizing the role of key institutions in developing its rules. We pay particular attention to the changes over the past two decades that may signal a transformation of the global economic hierarchy. We suggest that the global trade system is best understood as a network connecting nodes of production and consumption. Position in that network can be critical in and of itself, helping to determine how countries will participate and how they will benefit from that participation. We then explore three relationships within the global trade network: between a resource producer and its consumers, between a rich market and poorer suppliers seeking to profit from it, and between a global food system and those who rely on it for their subsistence.

The complex flows of money (the subject of the most recent crisis) are analyzed in chapter 3. Here we emphasize three concurrent trends: first, we track the rise of finance to fundamental importance in both individual enterprises and in systemic management. Over the past few decades, the accounting of and control over money became the center around which all other functions gyrated and on which decisions depended. Second, we analyze how the flow of money became truly global, with markets and ownerships knowing few national boundaries. Third, we emphasize that the ability of any authority to manage the system was strained by its size, fluidity, and increasing deregulation. The result of these trends was very much the same paradox we note in global capitalism in general: the production of revolutionary amounts of wealth thanks to the multiplication of exchanges and the increase in available capital, *and* an increase in systemic instability that regularly produced crises culminating in 2007 and 2008.

The social mechanism fueling the increases in both merchandise and capital flows was the revolution in global consumption analyzed in chapter 4. Modern consumer society arose in the nineteenth century, but over the last few decades this expanded to reach much larger parts of the globe in an increasingly universalized economics of desire. The rise of global marketing has brought with it new lifestyle possibilities for many, but also threats to cultural autonomy and social integration. The often hidden flows of global media created a much more global economy than had ever existed. Whether this leads to greater global integration or simply a general dissatisfaction with materialism is a core question facing global capitalism.

The second section of the book then discusses what we have identified as the three most important challenges for global capitalism: governance, inequality, and the environment. We have focused on three that call into question the survivability of the system as it stands. They do so because they defy the very ability of the system to right itself as it produces unexpected consequences. As in the case with our analysis of the three major component parts, we need to emphasize the unavoidable interaction between these challenges. So, for example, one of the problems of our common environmental future is the inequality in the degrees to which societies have abused the planet, combined with the fact that the system with which to safeguard our resources will require new forms of governance.

As recent events have demonstrated (yet again) global capitalism requires some new system of governance over and above the linking of territorial authorities. Chapter 5 discusses the challenges and promises of political control over the market. While much Cold War discourse portrayed free markets as taking place in the absence of state interference in the economy, laissez-faire is probably better characterized as a deliberate policy (and state-directed) project. The state is by far the most powerful force shaping economic life, and its active involvement is required if markets, as we know them to exist in the advanced industrial world, are to function. Global capitalism functions with a fundamental governance paradox: policy and enforcement remain within the responsibility of individual states, yet transactions occur in a space policed by none of them.

We then analyze how the fruits of capitalism are divided in chapter 6. We argue that global inequity is not merely a question of ethics, but of long-term survival. Our logic is simple: as global capitalism expands and absorbs previous non-participants, it becomes increasingly dependent on the universal acceptance of its rules and assumptions. Yet, as has always been the case, global capitalism provides many with new prosperities, but also many with the frustration of not sharing in its rewards. The global communication revolution, which is both a cause and effect of global capitalism, links us in a set of expectations and desires. Focusing on both rising inequality within countries and the continuing disparities between regions, we ask whether it is realistic to believe that the significant part of the world that does not enjoy the riches of capitalism, but is very much aware of them, will continue to stand by and accept a political and economic order that permanently excludes them.

Chapter 7 recognizes that at the very heart of capitalism there is an expectation of perpetual growth. If we are to resolve some of the inequities discussed in chapter 6 this imperative becomes even more significant. Such expectations are historical products of a millennia-long process of humans dominating nature. Yet we now find ourselves in an era of limits. We simply may not have enough raw materials to continue producing in our accustomed ways. This last chapter summarizes these limits and suggests a set of questions and issues that global capitalism must address if it is to survive the twenty-first century. In the face of this challenge, the old fights between right and left, between regulation and unfettered markets, may become irrelevant.

Having taken our machine apart, analyzed how the various

components work, and discussed the new tasks which confront it, we then conclude by trying to put all the parts together again. Each of our constituent parts is linked to each of our challenges: trade and inequality, finance and governance, and consumption and the environment. This means that to address these challenges we need to rethink at least some of the basic structures of global capitalism, and perhaps all. We do not pretend to provide solutions to these dilemmas, but, rather, no more than a guide to defining the problems we face.

Examining the march of global capitalism as involving the diffusion and legitimation of a specific, socially constructed model of the economy and its governance is critical to the future of the global economy in the twenty-first century. We may be especially well served by maintaining a healthier skepticism about how well human beings can understand, much less control, complex systems such as the global economy. Most importantly, we can begin treating global capitalism not as a completely immutable, inescapable force of history, but as something that we have the power to mould.

1

Global Capitalism

Two key institutions define capitalism: private property and market exchange. Both are historically rooted, which means that they were created and shaped by past (and, for the most part, recent) generations, and do not constitute universal, timeless aspects of human society. Private property and market exchange are social institutions, which were forged, propagated, and entrenched through numerous political, economic, cultural, and even military conflicts. What we understand as "normal" or "natural" about the way the economy works is neither, and much of it is surprisingly new.

The characteristics often associated with capitalism: commerce, money, the pursuit of self-interest, and conflicts between "haves" and "have-nots," are not defining features of capitalism or unique to it. Indeed, all were present in Soviet Russia, Feudal France, Ancient Rome, and Old Testament Israel. None of these societies would typically be described as "capitalist," and so the term must connote something more. The institutions of private property and market exchange must be distinguished from the commonplace practice of ownership or commerce. They represent what can be described as core economic rules that underlie the social pact between modern states and societies. Private property and economic markets are legally integrated into a structure of governance. Capitalism is the economic system that operates under those rules.

In capitalism, objects, money, ideas, and spaces, can be

appropriated by individuals (or legal entities like corporations). Their ownership grants them the right to determine how these assets will be used and to claim the profit or return on these activities, and any attempt to re-appropriate these assets faces legal and normative hurdles. The extent to which this marks a significant historical change merits highlighting. Not so long ago, many people could not claim ownership over their bodies or the freedom to sell their labor on a market; they literally did not own themselves, let alone other assets. Our notion of property has now grown so extensive that people own images, ideas, or even genetic sequences. Whether celebrated or bemoaned, private property is fundamental to capitalism. Without an acceptance of this tenet, the remaining economic and political structure of capitalism falls apart. As far as capitalism is concerned, we are what we own and what we sell.

Capitalist societies have developed a rich social infrastructure to facilitate and safeguard voluntary exchange through markets. Historically, most property transfers, beyond the smallest transactions of daily life, occurred by means of coercive appropriation and political patronage. In the ancient economy, most assets moved across communities by plunder, and exchanges as commonplace today as the transfer of real estate moved by grants from political powers rather than by purchase (Finley 1999 [1973]). Over time, some societies created institutions that allowed and encouraged voluntary transactions hinging on competition over price and quality. This does not imply that capitalism operates without any compulsion or violence, but serves to emphasize the extent to which individual autonomy within an explicit legal constraint is the main operating principle of this form of economic life.

In the ideal, each economic actor, whether as an owner of property or seller of labor, is free to make decisions regarding the sale, rent, and use of what they have to offer, each following no other norm than the pursuit of their self-interest. These forces come together in a market where exchanges take place that will literally link billions of offers and demands. Ranging from the face-to-face negotiations between a single buyer and a seller to the electronic auction of derivatives among millions, markets essentially match the supplies of goods and services with the demands for the same. Markets allocate the flow of goods and payments according to the intrinsic logic of a balance between needs and offers.

Varieties and Convergence

Within this basic framework, however, capitalism can be organized in a myriad of ways. Different capitalisms take distinctive shapes, and are experienced in dissimilar ways. Scholars have produced a range of typologies to describe the varied forms that capitalism can take. Some see the main distinction in the extent to which the state is involved, and, more importantly, how investment is allocated.

Peter Hall and David Soskice (1999), for example, distinguish between "coordinated market economies" and "liberal market economies." Both are inherently capitalist systems in that the rights of property and the centrality of the market are respected, but there are critical distinctions in how these two institutions are managed. In the liberal market economies, decisions are made either through hierarchies within firms or in markets between them. Relations are instrumental and calculated for the benefit of individual players. In coordinated market economies, relations exist outside of formal market mechanisms, and involve cooperation in achieving some collective goals. In this case, investment choices will involve co-ordination between owners of capital (often in the form of banks rather than individuals), labor, and state authorities

A parallel (but often related) distinction is the extent to which the two systems provide welfare provisions for their populations. "Liberal market" systems tend to have smaller safety nets than coordinated economies, thereby exposing people to more stringent hardships should they not find a productive or remunerated role in the economy. The United States is a paradigmatic example of the liberal system, in that public provision of things like guaranteed income, childcare, or health care is relatively limited compared to countries of similar wealth. Alternatively, countries like those of the European Union tend to offer a richer array of government-subsidized or -provided income or products to guarantee some level of economic safety or comfort to those who cannot (or will not) secure them through market participation. While both kinds of systems are fundamentally capitalist, they differ in terms of the degree to which people must secure "necessities" by successfully competing in markets.

William Baumol and his colleagues (2007) offer a typology that differentiates the size and monopoly of power of a country's economic enterprises, overall or in particular markets. In this case, the emphasis is on the level of what they call entrepreneurship or the creation and dissemination of new products or methods. For Baumol, the world's economies are divided into *state-guided* capitalisms (where government plays a central role), *oligarchic* capitalism (oriented toward the interests of a few players), *big-firm* capitalism (where giant enterprises predominate), and *entrepreneurial* capitalism (in which small innovative firms play a more central role). State-guided capitalism (epitomized by East Asian economies in the 1950s through to the 1970s) can have excellent success if governments can set their economy in the right direction. Some economies have experienced great development successes as state-guided systems, but this form of organization has also produced giant failures in others. Oligarchic capitalism is usually found in economies that focus on commodity production, such as the Middle Eastern oil producers, and, to a lesser extent, some Latin American countries. These economies' fortunes tend to be tied to the prices of a single commodity with the predicted boom-and-bust patterns. In big-firm capitalism, a set of predominant companies or agglomerations thereof is able to dominate. The prototypical examples are Japan and Korea in the 1980s, and, while the success of these speaks well of this model, the failure of sectors such as auto production in the United States attests to its limits. Finally, small and innovative firms characterize entrepreneurial capitalism. Rather than national examples, the economies of the American Pacific Northwest, or those of Italian Emilia-Romagna, best exemplify this type. However, a permanent entrepreneurial economy is almost a definitional impossibility and it would likely blend with one also focused on large firms.

Note again that in all these variations, the central principles of private property and market exchange remain privileged. What differs is the set of institutional provisions in which these are embedded. These arrangements in turn help define who will benefit from (and how much), and who will pay for (and how much) global capitalism.

While these differentiations help us understand the various forms that capitalism can take, it is not clear how they affect the integration of the respective economies with a world market. The term global capitalism implies much more than economic activity in different national borders. At least in theory, one could have an "international" economy consisting of autarchic domestic economies engaged in limited commerce with each other. Or one can imagine (as was largely the case well into the nineteenth century) an international economy whose connections involved luxury goods or a few "products" (sugar and slaves, for example). A global economy, however, implies one in which few if any of the domestic economies really exist separate from the planetary whole. A global economy is one that is interconnected and networked across a variety of borders, as well as including a variety of goods and services. It also presupposes a set of agreements regarding the "rules of the game," whether these involve accounting regulations or business norms.

Global capitalism arose through the diffusion and entrenchment of the twin institutions of property and markets to virtually all corners of the earth. Fifty years ago, many of the world's economies were strongly controlled by governments and existed in semi-autarchy. For many countries in 1959, the sanctity of private property was weak (if it existed at all), and the power and autonomy of private markets were more limited (if they were allowed to operate). The role of foreign markets and investors was limited. By the summer of 2008, private property and markets had become well-entrenched features of most countries' economies and the relations between them, and had expanded to an ever-widening scope of activities. Societies had come to commodify, trade, and monetize practically every social institution or human product. No economy could afford to be isolated.

The result is that we produce and trade more, and we have garnered spectacular improvements in our consumption. The global economy is now larger than it has ever been and the pace of its growth has been unprecedented over the past half-century (despite the recent shocks). World GDP increased sixfold from 1950 to 1998, with an average growth of 3.9 percent per year compared to 1.6 percent between 1820 and 1950 and 0.3 percent from 1500 to 1820. Over the past ten years (prior to the summer of 2008) the world economy has grown by more than a third and some of the poorer parts by two thirds. Each person in the world (*on average* – but many are above it and most are below) is now seven times richer than 100 years ago and four times richer than just fifty years ago.[1] Due to improvements in technology, the last fifty years have seen a fivefold increase in production per hour worked. The total amount of merchandise exports (the amount of goods that countries send out to the global market) is roughly $10 trillion per year. Annual global financial flows include over $625 billion invested across borders, $227 billion sent by migrants back to their countries, and $750 billion spent by international tourists. $1.5 trillion is exchanged in currency markets *daily*.

While global capitalism is experienced in different ways by different people at different times, it also represents a major phenomenon that all of the world's countries have felt over the past thirty or forty years. We are less interested in the varieties of *domestic or national* capitalism than in how different societies experience its *global* variant. In this instance, one can speak of much greater convergence than that found among the national variations. Global capitalism is, in some sense, a historical development with which all societies grapple in common. To a very large extent, all participants in the global capital system need to play by the same rules (some of which bind all countries, and others that can be applied or enforced more selectively). We can speak of a global capitalist order to which a very large part of the world now belongs. Unlike the situation prior to 1989, those who do not accept these rules are marginalized.

One set of rules has to do with the explicit and implicit laws that govern transnational transactions. Property rights are established and protected by nation-states. In this way, global capitalism still very much depends on the supposedly anachronistic notion of territorially defined authority. While there are global bodies in charge of overseeing and standardizing property claims (and this is particularly important for intellectual property), an individual or firm must establish its claim to any asset in a national jurisdiction. It is important to note that no global bodies exist with enough power to enforce these rules over and above the laws of national states. In one of the most interesting paradoxes of global capitalism, its own global dynamics are based on national and territorial governance.

The implications of this system are critical for a global system to work: states must recognize the property claims of other countries' citizens, and transnational payment for goods and services or contracted service of debts is demanded of all players – the transport of one's asset to a different part of the world does not imply the surrender of rights to it until payment has been received. The global capitalist system is governed by a set of rules based on those established in large parts of Western Europe and North America to manage and regulate their domestic markets in the eighteenth and nineteenth centuries. This is a central point in order to understand many of the international debates on the future of the market. Whether one treats the basic rules of capitalism as "natural" or stemming from a historical domination by a part of the world will make a significant difference in attitudes toward capitalism (Robinson 2004). In this way, the social context through which global capitalism is perceived and analyzed can make a great deal of difference.

It is also important to recognize the expected or assumed motivations of those involved in global capitalism. In the twenty-first century, the pursuit of self-interest and specifically financial profit from transactions is expected. There are some global institutional actors motivated by and acting under altruistic norms, but the global economy functions under the assumption that each person is seeking to make money on any transaction. The global food trade, for example, is not driven by a concern to feed the world's population, but by the desire to make money from selling commodities and products to consumers. As we now know, bankers were after short-term profits, and not concerned with establishing stable systems of payments, transparent economic information, or prudent allocations. This is still accepted as legitimate by the vast majority of the world's population (as long as the game is played by the minimum accepted rules). Again, perceptions of this can either involve the freeing of human nature and choice, or the enslavement of our emotions by materialist desire. Either way, it is important to appreciate how central such an assumption of self-interest is to the social underpinning of global capitalism, and how relatively new such an assumption truly is (Hirschman 1977), as well as the extent to which a rejection of such assumptions forms the basis for much of the resistance to global capitalism.

Another critical regulation concerns the freedom to truck and barter across borders. Fetters on cross-border exchanges are increasingly discouraged and sanctioned. The capitalist system is arguably more open across the globe than at any other time in history and former non-market "intrusions" on trade, such as tariffs, subsidies, or embargoes are becoming less commonplace. There are significant exceptions and these are linked to power asymmetries (as we will see in later chapters), but the percentage of global transactions of goods, services, and money that operate without significant national hindrance is ever expanding. The major exception (and a significant reversal from historical norms) involves labor. While sellers and buyers of practically any asset can utilize the global market, those who wish to sell or purchase labor cannot except in highly elite sectors (entertainment, the academy). The construction of segmented channels into the global market (a privileged one for goods and capital, a much more restricted one for labor) indicates once again how much we need to understand the construction of global capitalism as not arising from a vacuum, but reflecting underlying interests and powers.

Differing Roles within the Same System

Applying Donald Black's theories of law (1976) to the global system, we could say that the salience of these norms and regulations decrease dramatically as we approach the peripheries of the system. For capitalist relations between countries at the core of the capitalist system, regulations tend to be applied both stringently and relatively even-handedly. There is, of course, some tough brinksmanship between OECD countries, for example, but there is often a core dedication to maintaining international trade and investment and private markets.

As we move toward the external districts of the capitalist economy, the prevalence of democracy, limitation of corruption, capacity for governments to govern, and average standard of living drop precipitously. These frontiers are commonly described as the "global periphery." Transactions between actors at the frontier of the global economy – including in the business of government – are fraught with uncertainties, transparency problems, systemic instability, and a sad legacy of squandering economic opportunities. Relations between those closer to the center and those on the frontier may also deeply reflect the asymmetries of power.

What separates the core from the periphery? For Wallerstein (1996), a first-order difference is the amount of capital present in a society. Simply put, the rich are different. Just as importantly, the core is differentiated from the periphery by the former's capacity to enforce control over that capital through the capacity of the state. In the final analysis, states remain the actors of paramount importance in the global economy, and any explanation of a societies' economic character, power, or prosperity must consider seriously the role played by governments. The core capitalist countries are economically rich and powerful, but also the most politically stable and militarily dominant. Governments play substantial roles in advancing other important factors, such as technological advance, basic health, or educational levels. When we speak of the rich, we also speak of the governed. Another way of thinking of the difference is that the global economic system is capitalist because the countries in the core are capitalist. In the periphery, countries are capitalist because the global system is capitalist.

The United States stands alone as the capitalist core's first-order power, most central venue, and chief guarantor.[2] Its economy constitutes one quarter of global value-added (whether real or financial). Coupled with Canada and Mexico – two very strong allies (and, some might argue, dependents) – the North American Free Trade Association (NAFTA), accounts for 30 percent. The North American relationship with the global economy is in part dictated by its sheer enormity. First, the size of its domestic market makes it economically less reliant on trade (exports of goods and services account for only 10 percent of the American GDP as opposed to 26 percent of the French, 35 percent of the German, and 44 percent of the Korean). It is the world's principal consumer, absorbing 16 percent of global exports and providing considerable demand for other countries' output; when the US consumer stopped spending, the whole global system faced a major economic slowdown (if not outright collapse). The US is also the central destination for global financial flows, absorbing over half a trillion dollars in net transfers every year. The vast majority of international currency exchange involves the exchange of a US dollar for something else, and the world's assets are typically valued in local and US currencies. Despite their recent declines, the dollar, US banking system, and US equity markets remain the world's destination of last financial resort.

The second category consists of the other main engines of global capitalism which, in turn, could be subdivided into a European division including the UK and the Euro zone, and an Asian one including Taiwan, Japan, and South Korea (we deal with China below). Many of these are significant economies in their own rights, yet, while the EU as a whole is larger than the US, no country can individually claim the centrality of the United States (Germany and France combined represent roughly 40 percent of the American economy, Japan 30 percent). These countries, however, are much more significant players than the US in the global merchandise trade. The combination of France, Germany, the UK, Japan, Korea, and Taiwan account for almost twice the amount of merchandise exports, as does the United States or roughly one third of the global total. In some sectors of global manufacture, such as autos, steel, and electronics, they are even more significant. These countries also represent critical markets for producers of goods and particularly commodities. In the financial sector, the rise of the euro and the development of twenty-four-hour electronic markets have made these countries as central as the United States. London, for example, is possibly replacing New York as the center of global finance, if the notion of a city acting as a "center of finance" really retains so much meaning.

These two macro categories do not necessarily parallel standard ones derived from the varieties of capitalism literature. The contrast between Mexican, Canadian, and United States domestic political economies could scarcely be greater given their proximity. In the second group, the United Kingdom's form of capitalism is arguably closer to that of the United States than that of their Nordic neighbors, while Japan and Korea pioneered their own combination of state-managed and large-firm capitalism. We note, then, a clear distinction between analysis of what we may call domestic capitalism and our more focused topic of its global variant. From the perspective of their roles in a global capitalism, however, the two groups make up the central core of the system with the United States clearly still serving as first among equals. In order to appreciate the relative importance of these countries, note that while they contain roughly one sixth of the world's population, they account for over three-quarters of global income.

Three other categories deserve special attention. The first and most important for the future structure of global capitalism are the new claimants for membership in the central core. The four largest of these are Brazil, Russia, India, and, most notably and importantly, China (the so-called "BRIC economies"). Combined, these economies account for roughly 10 percent of global income (they are individually ranked 10th, 12th, 11th, and 4th in the globe, but together they are still roughly half the size of the US alone). In terms of global trade they are even more significant. China is the key player in this group, and arguably deserves as particularistic a status as the United States. These BRIC societies, however, are also what we may call bifurcated economies. In the case of China, for example, its eastern coastline clearly is at the core of global capitalism, but roughly half of its population remains marginal to that system as consumers or producers. Similar divisions plague Brazil and Russia, and even more extreme ones characterize India.

These inequalities not only represent limits on the integration of these societies within global capitalism, but also remain long-term challenges for the continued success of their economies.

Another significant category is that of commodity producers, who participate in global capitalism by providing its fuel in the form of petroleum, gas, minerals, and food. One subgroup consists of those wealthy enough to also represent important consumer markets for construction, arms, and luxury goods (the Gulf States). Others share characteristics with the "bifurcated" economies discussed above in that their output plays a central role in the global economy, but their national economies remain vastly underdeveloped (Angola and the Congo are extreme examples of these). Depending on the price of their respective commodities, these countries may also play a very important role in global financial flows.

The final category includes those countries that for all intents and purposes play a marginal role in global capitalism. Consisting of practically all of sub-Saharan Africa, and significant parts of South Asia and Latin America, these countries include roughly one-third of the global population, but only account for less than 3 percent of global production and even less of global trade. They typically sell local commodities, opaque financial systems, and/or cheap unregulated labor. They have a long history of being subverted by the world's major powers, but an equally impressive record of destroying their national economies by internal means. They constitute a massive, and massively marginalized, people. They are at once a fertile field from which economic profit can grow, and wastelands of violence, corruption, lawlessness, and exploitation.

There are (and will remain) real differences between the world's societies, and these differences are non-trivial. However, global capitalism can also be seen as a homogenizing force in contemporary global society. The scope of this change can be seen in a very wide range of international economics statistics, which we will analyze through the book. But, beyond affecting conventional macro-economic metrics, the capitalist transformation has also rewritten many of the basic cultural assumptions upon which economic life is premised. The ubiquitous spread of market logics to an ever-expanding range of instrumental transactions has transformed social life worldwide (Zelizer 1994). The *market logic* can be understood as a form of social organization premised on materialism, individualism, and rational utility-maximization. In this context, *materialism* is the emphasis of the provision and consumption of goods and services as a social goal and metric of success. The "good life" is one in which we own and consume as much as possible, and the "good society" is one that provides people with maximal consumption possibilities. *Individualism* refers to the desirability or practical necessity of organizing a society in which individuals' efforts are geared primarily toward their personal self-interests. Social demands that place community or country ahead of personal interests come to be seen as oppressive and undesirable. *Rational utility-maximization* refers to the increasing use of material cost-benefit analysis as a means of making practical social decisions. Decisions that render economic profit are seen as desirable, and those incurring economic loss are to be avoided.

Historical creation

The march of capitalism is often imagined as a unitary, unidirectional, natural, and irresistible force of history. Yet present-day global capitalism was neither inevitable nor unavoidable. Instead, it emerged from a very long and messy process that was steered substantially by struggles over material wealth, culture, institutional entrenchment, and power.

Neither the pursuit of self-interest nor the material exploitation of others was new to the capitalist era. Economic exchanges have existed in many societies without the accompanying social characteristics we associate with capitalism. We certainly have evidence of market transactions going back as far as the invention of writing (and the rise of the two social phenomena is inherently linked). We may also speak of global (or last "Old World") trade as far back as the Roman Empire's links with the Han dynasty connecting the Mediterranean to the Silk Road. By the tenth century, the Sahara served to link large parts of Africa to the remains of this system, and the Indian Ocean was a central arena of global transactions in the thirteenth century (Abu-Lughod 1989). The Spice Trade, the conquest of the Americas, and the creation of slave economies further integrated the global economy (Braudel 1982). The Imperial Age culminating in the nineteenth century created the basic political and economic infrastructure, the legacy of which still helps define global capitalism.

The political and social foundations for capitalism, however, represent much more than the mere truck and barter of a market. These include, as discussed above, the acceptance of the need for a system of exchanges and contracts in order to allow interactions between individuals. Where did these come from? The practically simultaneous establishments of the British and Dutch East India Companies at the start of the seventeenth century may best serve as the official birth of global capitalism (Wallerstein 1974). What distinguished these forms from previous economic pursuits were their ownership structure (based on equity shares), sheer size (each had thousands of employees, controlled massive territories, and was responsible for a significant percentage of world trade), and their global scope. The later development of the slave trade equally represented the expansion of a form of market transaction to a global level. Note that in these cases, the fulcrum of change was the European expansion of power and the imposition of a set of institutional logics designed to produce profit for the elites of that continent. Some would argue that these origins still characterize global capitalism.

This expansion of power combined with a technological and organizational explosion. Beginning some time in the early to mid-eighteenth century (the exact timing of both the Agricultural and Industrial Revolutions has been the subject of considerable debate), a historically bounding production ceiling was removed (Maddison 2001; Overton 1996). This allowed the expansion of, first, agricultural production, and then industrial manufacture. The latter was partly based on a slew of new innovations making ever better use of steam power and then coal, but it was also the product of a new form of organization: the factory.

The debate on when exactly the transformation began, what caused it, why (or even if) it was centered in England and Northwestern Europe is one of the longest running and most productive in academic history. For our purposes, the major debate is the one between those who attach central importance to organizational and technical innovation and those who focus on the interests of a particular social group (Landes 1999; Perrow 2005). We wish to argue that privileging one over another has more to do with a general view of capitalism (it is good in the aggregate, it is only good for some) than with the actual historical record. Moreover, from the point of view of global capitalism, its domestic roots matter less than the fact that the economic revolution was historically tied to the creation of a capitalist market in North America and Western Europe, and that the victory of capitalism to hegemony would have been impossible without the simultaneous global expansion of the "West." The central point here is that capitalism came from a place and at a particular point in time, and that has made much (if not all) the difference.

The more immediate origins of our contemporary global capitalism are in the years from 1820 to 1870, and from then to 1914. The first period established the technological and social foundation, initially in England, then Belgium, and then on to the rest of the continent. The second period saw a veritable explosion of growth and a gradual shift away from the earlier dominance of Great Britain as Germany and the United States overtook it. During those years, we see the beginning of the revolution in productivity that would characterize the long-term progress of industrial capitalism. In Western Europe, productivity increased an annual average of 1.5 percent and in the US close to 2 percent between 1870 and 1914. This meant that in the span of roughly forty years, one worker would produce twice as much as he or she had before.

The same period witnessed a dramatic growth in *social aggregation,* the process of integrating more people and territory into a single system of economic production and distribution. Many of the social innovations that can be credited for our increasing material standards of living fundamentally involve this process of aggregation, including divisions of labor, economies of scale, economic specialization, and resource pooling. In the sixteenth through eighteenth centuries, national markets and governments in Western Europe consolidated. At the same time, the countries of this region were finding ways to tap into, and eventually dominate both economically and politically, other parts of the world. European and North American goods flooded the entire planet, while commodities flowed toward the global centers to be transformed into consumer products. In this process, again, the role of the state was critical. Only the state could provide the protection and regularize standards and rules within national markets, and only the state could provide the protection to its own merchants when they ventured onto imperial shores. In this way, at least, it is impossible to imagine the development of global capitalism without the intervention and development of the state.

Not surprisingly, along with the aggregate expansion of wealth came the appearance of massive asymmetries in income across the world, as the West grew while others remained mired in stagnancy (or, in an alternative reading, were kept there by the imperial project itself). Most estimates agree that up to 1500 global economic growth was slow but equal. By 1870, global per capita wealth had doubled, and by 1913 it had tripled; simultaneously, the share of Europe to Asia came to be along the lines of 6 to 1 and that of North America to Africa close to 10 to 1. This regional wealth gap and its apparent permanence (except in the prominent Asian example) in many ways still define many of the challenges of contemporary capitalism (DeLong 1993: 4). Figure 1.1 indicates the revolutionary growth that occurred after 1820 (solid line and right-side y-axis). It also shows how the global share of Western Europe and its "offshoots" grew exponentially faster than the rest of the world from 1800 on. The reasons for this divergence remain so contested (to say the least) that any bibliographic summary would be inadequate. Suffice it that the reasons proposed have ranged from imperial perfidy to cultural superiority, and we will deal with some of this debate in chapter 2.[3] For now, two observations are critical: first, there is at least a historical coincidence between the rise of global capitalism and

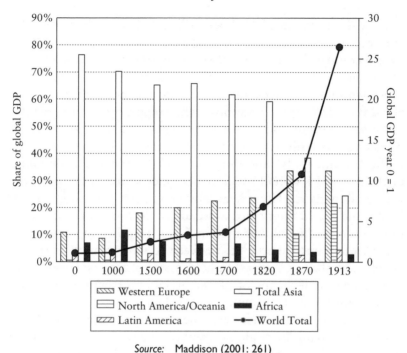

Source: Maddison (2001: 261)

Figure 1.1   Regional shares of global wealth

the expansion of Europe to global domination, and, second, as the world entered into the twentieth century, the lead enjoyed by the "West" was considerable.

Capitalism's advancement and its concurrent process of social aggregation of first national markets, and then global ones, unleashed two distinct forms of contradiction associated with "control" (Polanyi 1944). First, societies at the turn of the twentieth century became very large, and, in many senses, more difficult to control. Second, capitalism brought about significant changes in the constancy or predictability of daily life. In many ways, the advance of global capitalism stabilized material livelihood, but it also made each participant more reliant on the others, thereby reducing everyone's independence. Both mass social control and economic stabilization became serious problems during World War I and the Great Depression of the twentieth century (Hobsbawm 1994; Frieden 2006). The rivalry for markets and resources between the great powers was at least in part driven by the competition between their respective capitalisms. The rise of the new economic system produced social conflicts between those who had colonies and those who did not, those who benefited from freer trade and those who sought protection, between those who supported the dearer currency of gold and those who needed cheaper silver, and, of course, between those who worked in the "satanic mills" and those who owned them. The disruption of the pre-1914 system by global conflict shook capitalism to its core. Following the Great War, and after a few years of exuberant boom, the world then faced a decade of declining prices, production, trade, and employment. The Great Depression showed how complex and intricate the ties between economies were in the new global capitalism. Changes in the flows of money and goods from or to each one of the major players would reverberate throughout the system; no single economy was isolated.

The result of these crises was the apparent collapse of the first phase of contemporary global capitalism and the very real threat that it would be abandoned as a political and economic system. The failures of the interwar years, leading to the murderous catastrophe of World War II, did much to discredit the institutions of capitalism, prompting a popular backlash and sustained political effort to contain its effects. At this critical juncture, the path toward the contemporary version of global capitalism was defined by the actions of a single state and its imposition of a particular economic order on a significant part of the world.

Facing a largely destroyed world, in 1945 the victorious US dominated the global economy in almost every aspect. Its economy produced half of total global output, its farms helped feed Europe, and its currency ruled the world. US policymakers sought to create a more viable form of capitalism, led and maintained by the United States. After 1945, the competitions between individual countries became much more focused on the contest between the "two worlds": one "free" and capitalist, one socialist and largely dominated by the Soviet Union.

In order to triumph in this new competition, the capitalist

victors created a historically unique system. It arose from conversations in a small town in New Hampshire called Bretton Woods. The system was unique in several ways. First, it was truly global in scope, focusing on not one economy or the other, but on their integrations. Second, while the system reflected and helped support the central role of the United States, this country did not seek to create a new version of a mercantile empire, but sought collective growth. The centrality and supremacy of the US in this system would be unquestioned, but it did provide an opening for other economies and societies to rise. This was the result of US awareness of its need for partners with which to do business, and for incentives to keep communism at bay. Third, it created historically unprecedented institutions that sought to smooth out the inevitable fluctuations of the global market. The "organized capitalism" by then established in domestic economies (due to the pressures of war and depression) was now applied to the entire world (Frieden 2006: 259; Eichengreen 2007).

The system was established to provide assurance in an uncertain world and prevent the insecurity that had had precipitated the disastrous 1930s. The two major institutions of this newly organized global economy were the International Monetary Fund (IMF) and the International Bank for Development and Reconstruction (World Bank). The first would allow members to borrow whenever trade flows temporarily went into deficit, while the second provided funds to create the global infrastructure needed by the new forms of trade. Soon thereafter, with the Marshall Plan, the United States committed itself to provide the capital needed for Europe to rebuild itself from the destruction of its wars (and to be its partners in the new order) while the General Agreement on Tariffs and Trade (GATT) ensured the freest possible flow possible of goods (Bordo 1993; Helleiner 1994; Ruggie 1982).

Within countries, the new model also spurred the creation of welfare states. Government participation in the economy and social transfers practically doubled, thus assuring that many parts of the richer countries' populations could and would participate in the new capitalist order. Decolonization led to even freer trade and the possibility of millions more consumers outside of Northern

Europe and North America (but also saw protectionist policies within developing countries). Domestic and international politics lent themselves to the creation of a new capitalism that sought to combine the developmental dynamism of the market with both international and domestic safety nets to protect those for whom the market did not provide.

There are three critical lessons to take away from the post-1945 "re-creation" of the capitalist economic order. First, the whole exercise was embedded in the political struggle of the Cold War. The global economic market was meant to make money, obviously. But it was also meant to use that prosperity as a strategic bulwark against an ideological and military enemy. Second, it was based on a series of supra-governmental institutions. The overall strategy might have been dictated by a state (the US), but explicit governance of much of the global order was given over to semi-autonomous institutions. Finally, in order to protect it from some of the threats it had faced in the interwar period, global capitalism was partly transformed through the creation of domestic and international income supports. This not only broadened participation, but also reduced dissatisfaction with the system.

The results were quite spectacular. The "Glorious Thirty"[4] years following the war represented a return to the pre-1914 booms. Global per capita income increased by nearly 3 percent a year or a doubling from 1950 to 1973. In those same years, the Western European economy practically tripled, while that of the US (already dominant in 1945 and untouched by the war) almost doubled. Japan's economy was even more astounding, growing more than sixfold. Already by the 1964 Olympics held in Tokyo, Japan had begun to look not like the war-ravaged, poverty-stricken state of 1945, but a dynamic member of the global capitalist order. Ten years later, Japan could boast the same aggregate standard of living as Western Europe.

The global economy not only grew at an amazing rate, but the benefits of that growth were more evenly distributed both between and within countries than any period of human history. Thanks to these changes, daily life for hundreds of millions of human beings was transformed by the increasing ubiquity of indoor plumbing, electricity, consumer goods, and basic public health (Hobsbawm 1994; Judt 2005). Life expectancy grew by a decade (in the richer countries), or even two decades in some of the poorest regions.

The economies of Eastern Europe and the USSR tripled, keeping pace with much of the West. Yet the Socialist world emphasized a form of growth closer to a nineteenth-century model than one required by the post-war era and, despite its gains, saw the gap in productivity increase. For example, while the USSR's productivity per hour doubled, that of West Germany quadrupled.[5] The socialist world's expansion outside of Europe was an economic disaster. After some initial success, the Chinese economy was destroyed by a variety of Maoist experiments and remained marginal to the global economy, while Cuba represented a considerable drain on Soviet resources during this period.

Developing countries also experienced a post-war boom. Latin American economies tripled in real terms during these years, with particularly phenomenal results in Mexico and Brazil. Africa increased its national income by 270 percent (although its share of global production dropped). The Indian economy more than doubled, and that of the rest of Asia (excluding China and Japan) quadrupled.

Despite its apparent success, this new mixed capitalist system ultimately proved to be too complex and expensive to manage. First, due to its increasing budget and balance of payments deficits, the US found it impossible to maintain the dollar as the unshakable foundation for global trade; the US government had issued more dollars into circulation than could be redeemed by all of its gold. In the rest of the developed world, the costs of paying for the post-war welfare state were ever escalating. The integration of the global system had produced many winners, but also losers who sought to rebalance the economic scales. Labor perceived that the global capitalist surge had increasingly benefited those with money. The apparently non-zero-sum relationship between international integration and domestic benefit had broken down. The general increase in commodity prices in the 1970s and the need to recycle the dollars that now flowed ever faster across the planet encouraged greater integration, but also demonstrated its fragility.

This became clear with the unprecedented period of "stagflation," economic decline or stasis accompanied by increasing inflation, during much of the 1970s and early 1980s.

After significant policy shifts discussed in later chapters, global capitalism resolved the predicament of inflation. The accompanying policy changes generated a series of crises both in parts of the developed world and in large sections of the developing world. The socialist and developing worlds responded to it with a borrowing binge but, by the late 1980s, the debt overhangs were leading to severe policy constraints. The developed world experienced a general rollback on many of the welfare measures created during the previous thirty years and a general decline in the relative position of labor.

By the mid-1980s, the wealthier countries were able to re-start their economies and these registered a growth of roughly 25 percent during that decade. For Latin America, however, the 1980s was literally a "lost decade" in which there was less wealth at the end than at the beginning. In Africa, these years marked the end of the first wave of economic success and the beginning of continental decline. For the socialist bloc, the 1980s made its economic failures too obvious to ignore and, once the political willingness to support them eroded, the economies collapsed. The experience of some Asian countries, however, was quite different: Hong Kong grew by 68 percent, Singapore by 57 percent, Taiwan by 69 percent, and Thailand by 82 percent during that same period. The star was certainly Korea, whose GDP more than doubled. To give some sense of the shift in global hierarchy, consider that, in 1968, when it hosted the Olympic Games, Mexico's economy was three times that of South Korea's on a per capita basis. Twenty years later, after import substitution, an oil boom, with a debt crisis on the one hand, and export-led growth on the other, the Mexican economy was one half as rich as that of Olympic host Korea!

These changes, both the relative decline of Latin America, Africa, and the socialist bloc, and the spectacular rise of parts of Asia, would help redefine the world in the 1990s. The reasons for them have been analyzed and debated for the past twenty years. We may identify four leading sets of explanations. For the first category, what we may call the culturalists, what mattered was a predisposition to work and entrepreneurship. The "victory" of the East Asian dragons was, at least in part, due to a different set of values and predispositions, which promoted, for example, greater savings (Harrison and Huntington 2001). A second school argued for the centrality of trade policy. The Asian countries had sought an export-led development in contrast with the "import substitution" policies of Latin America and Africa (Haggard 1990).[6] A third set of explanations focused on the role of the state, arguing that those countries that had created effective policies and promoted them successfully had done best during this period (Wade 2003; Evans 1995). Most recently, a more sophisticated approach has developed which takes into account the best of what these theories have to offer (Kohli forthcoming). The explanation for the East Asia success begins with a more effective state and it involves trade. But the key step was specific state policies to support higher value-added industries (rather than simple extraction from the ground or minimal processing), which could create new economic niches. The critical element is a combination of economic and market logic (produce something that others want and will pay for) with a political one (create the policy space necessary for these developments).

The process of institutional adjustment during these years was also accompanied by a burst of technological change arguably as important as the Industrial Revolution. The computer not only allowed for the managerial complexity required by the global factory but, with the Internet, vastly expanded the consumer possibilities of a significant part of the global population. The exogenous technological component in the rise of the latest version of global capitalism cannot be underestimated. In the US, for example, productivity practically doubled during this period. Some of this had to do with more pro-business and anti-labor policies on the part of the government, but the role of the computer in transforming the economy cannot be debated. On the global stage, the computing revolution allowed for a level of amalgamation and integration never before seen.

The greater integration of capitalism came with the expected complexities and vulnerability. Crises that previously would have been limited to a single country could now spread like the ubiquitous viruses that haunted the World Wide Web. Mexico in 1994, Asia in 1997, Russia in 1998, the Y2K panic, the dot-com bubble, the US sub-prime mortgage fiasco, all represented significant threats to the global system, leading to perpetual analyses of crises and the ever present specter of 1929. In 2007–8, an apparent "perfect storm" involving unstable commodity prices, ever worsening credit markets, and a general ambiance of uncertainty, led to talk of a collapse of the global liberal order.

Capitalism and globalization

At the root of these dilemmas is the fact that the world is still becoming used to capitalism, and it, in turn, is adjusting to being a global phenomenon. While the roots of capitalism go back to the expansion of Northwest Europe in the sixteenth and seventeenth centuries, it is only in the past few decades that we can speak of a truly global capitalist order. The nineteenth-century global system of commodities and consumer products was only capitalist in some places; in the rest, it relied more on imperial force. Nor were vast parts of the global population as closely linked to the capitalist economy, as is the case today. Even during the years of post-war growth, significant parts of the world remained outside of the capitalist orbit either because of poverty or ideology. Today, a vastly larger number of societies interact with the world system directly through the market and not through imperial intermediaries. For all intents and purposes, we are all in the same market and in uncharted terrain.

Globalization is a much more complicated process than just capitalism gone global as it involves cultural and demographic flows (and, as increasingly obvious, climate interdependence). One of the key questions for any discussion of contemporary capitalism is its relationship to the expansion of global integration. Could one exist without the other? Which is the primal causal element? How do the different institutional forms of capitalism relate to global integration?

Globalization is not new; the very peopling of the planet beginning with the migration out of Africa was arguably the most consequential form of it and this began 100 millennia ago. Transregional and even trans-hemispheric trade is also not new; nor are massive migrations. Even the cultural imperialism of American mass media (another favourite villain of globalization) is relatively insignificant compared to prior waves of religious conquest and conversion, and linguistic domination. What is new, and the reason why global capitalism is so novel, is the level of integration of economies, and the speed and force with which previously isolated events cross borders. To borrow from epidemiology, infections can no longer be isolated; the global body of capitalism can less and less afford weak parts.

The rise and rooting of market logics in the organization of social life has created unimaginable wealth in the aggregate. But capitalism's unrelenting pursuit of material bounty has elicited a range of social and environmental strains – Thomas Malthus (1986[1798]) may ultimately be right in asserting that exponential growth cannot be sustained. The creation of media, largely established to perpetuate the consumption upon which the capitalist system depends, has also made it much more possible for those on the bottom to become aware of how the top lives, generating discontent and outright opposition against the system. The capitalist system's growth may have proceeded to the point that its size, intricacy, and interconnectedness make it less controllable, and in turn more volatile and resistant to oversight.

It is in this respect that the concept of complexity described in the introduction becomes most relevant. Recall that, certainly since 1945 and less explicitly since the nineteenth century, global capitalism has functioned with some form of state oversight and support, be it first British, or, later, American. It is harder to identify a global capitalist "policeman" for the post-1990 period. At first the US seemed willing and able to undertake this role as in the Mexico crisis of 1994–5, but the control and coordinating capacities of the global structure became more frayed. More importantly, the nature of the system was transformed by the technological revolution and the subsequent global integration.

The complexity included the simple addition of ever more actors. But it was the multiplication of interactions and their mutual interdependence that created the possibility of "emergent" properties and consequences that no one could predict or protect against. This was made clear by the "domino effect" of the financial crisis of 2008 when events in an industry on one side of the world could lead to disasters for others thousand of miles away.

The end of global capitalism?

Writing in 2009, one has to wonder how relevant all the preceding considerations will be by 2010. Will capitalism come to an end? Will the global economy collapse? The news of the past year has been universally disastrous. There is no question that this represents the worst economic crisis since the Great Depression of the 1930s. First, the financial industry was only saved from total meltdown by a very expensive intervention. Nevertheless, the IMF estimated that global financial institutions would have to write off up to $2.7 *trillion* dollars in US-originated assets alone. Add to these smaller disasters, such as the Icelandic debacle and the collapse of housing markets all over the world, and the figure is much higher. These losses led to a credit crunch, which squeezed the other sectors of the economy. Global industrial production was down by 10 percent and sales and overall confidence plummeted. For the first time in the post-war era, stock market losses (of close to 50 percent in some markets) were accompanied by dramatic falls in consumption. The automobile industry (arguably still the major manufacturing engine of the global economy) suffered enormously: 9 percent and 13 percent global declines in 2008 and 2009, and 18 percent and 24 percent respectively in the United States. Overall, global GDP declined by around 6 percent in the last part of 2008 and again by the same amount in the first quarter of 2009.[7]

Such reports make it difficult to understand what exactly has happened and what its consequences might be. On the one hand, how can there be any money left? How can any political economy lose so much and still be a viable model? On the other hand, the very fact that so much existed to be lost in the first place, and that although it is gone the world still functions, points to the incredible productive power and resiliency of capitalism. It is also worthwhile to remember that a much less sophisticated version of capitalism not only survived seventy-five years of ideological conflict with various competitors, but also a depression much deeper than anything we have seen so far.

While capitalism is in a crisis, no systemic alternatives to what is described in the following pages exist other than a return to autarchy. It is possible that some later book will recall the last two decades as the "Glorious Twenty" before a prolonged period of difficult realignment. Yet this does not mean that the overall structure will be transformed. That serious adjustments will be necessary is obvious, that the growth curve will change slope probable, but that we are on the verge of yet another undefined "Great Transformation" unmaking the past 200 years is unlikely (except perhaps for the reasons discussed in chapter 7 and generally unrelated to the housing and banking crises). Global capitalism remains the system we need to understand in order to understand the world.

2

Trade

The globalization of production and consumption has remade material life worldwide. We now design, make, sell, and dispose of merchandise and services on a global scale. These changes are quite apparent among the global rich (including the rich world's poor and the poor world's rich), where the effects of globalization can be seen anywhere from stores to homes. Globalization not only allows us to purchase and use products from distant lands, but also introduces new pressures on jobs and businesses that must compete globally. This has meant lost manufacturing jobs in some locales and the rise of factories and new economic lives in others. Despite the expansion in globalization's reach, the poor world's poor see this transformation at a considerable distance, through media depictions, remittances from relatives, or used merchandise recycled to the global bottom.

Location now makes less of a difference in consumption. Indeed, as the multinationals come to dominate retail product markets, and attempt to reap the advantages of global economies of scale and brand management, shopping is becoming more similar internationally. It is certain that anyone reading this book consumes and uses products from a least a dozen countries on a daily basis. Even if one tried to be a jingoistic consumer, the complexities of the global assembly line are such that "national" products may be a thing of the past. Production similarly links workers in much less affluent settings with their wealthier counterparts across the globe.

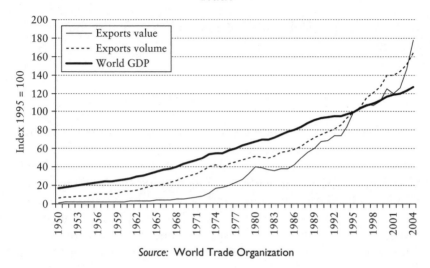

Source: World Trade Organization

Note: See the Technical Notes for the estimation of world aggregates of merchandise exports, production and GDP.

Figure 2.1 World trade

The latest *contemporary* global "take-off" began in the 1960s, but the acceleration really occurred in the 1990s. In Figure 2.1, note that, while trade has been consistently rising since 1950, the slope of the line or speed of increase picks up in the 1990s. At that point the world reached an important threshold: we started selling things to one another (dashed and dotted lines) faster than we made them (solid line).

This explosion has made it too easy to speak of a globalization of trade as if it were a smoothly accelerating process involving all parts of the world. On the linear nature of change, it is always worthwhile to remember that an equally dramatic process of globalization occurred from the nineteenth century through to the 1920s, and collapsed in blood. As to the universal nature of the phenomenon, we need to realize that the world is not flat, but really consists of a series of peaks and valleys of global integration. In order to understand both the trajectory and the distribution of trade, we begin with a historical appreciation of how this particular part of the global capitalist system was created.

Trade in History

Trade is not new. We have considerable evidence of trade in such goods as amber, incense, obsidian, and lapis lazuli existing thousands of years ago throughout the Middle East. More than 2,000 years ago, trade had already developed along the Mediterranean, along the Pacific Asian coast, and between these two centers via the Silk Road and the Indian Ocean. The Americas remained isolated, but within the new hemisphere some trade occurred within Mesoamerica and along what would become the Inca Royal Road.

The explosion of European empires transformed these relatively isolated circuits into a global system (Maddison 2007; Findlay and O'Rourke 2007). Two features of this era are important to note: first, imperial authority and attempts at mercantile monopoly largely defined it. Trade, despite the increasing importance of private companies, was very much an extension of geopolitical goals. Second, commerce was still largely dominated by the exchange of high-value goods with little (if any) manufacturing value added. Central flows included spices from East Asia to the Mediterranean, slaves across the Atlantic, and silver from America to Iberia and subsequently to Northwest Europe, and then back to Asia.

Trade grew slowly and markets remained relatively isolated until the beginning of the early nineteenth century, when it was transformed again by the conjunction of several events. The first was Western Europe's Industrial Revolution, which allowed for an explosion of production and the potential expansion of what had been a relatively small aspect of the global economy, concentrated on the exchange of a few goods, into central importance (Hirst and Thompson 1996). This was accompanied by the increasing dependence of individuals on ever more complex networks (first national and then international) to supply their needs. Third, state capacity expanded, supporting the greater aggregation of supply-and-demand transactions through, for example, the building of the necessary transport and communication infrastructure. This expansion took place in a globe where the domination of Europeans and their descendants was unquestioned. The shape of this initial global trade network was very much traced on the outlines of empire.

There is no argument regarding the extent of the global boom and transformation. There is, however, a great deal of discussion regarding trade's role within it. Was global trade responsible for the explosion in growth or was this simply a product of the Industrial Revolution? While the relative weight of trade in the boom remains disputed, there is a general consensus that it did allow for the specialization that was critical to Adam Smith's analysis of capitalism. There is much more dissent regarding the role of trade in shifting the global economic hierarchy.

Followers of David Ricardo's theories of comparative advantage argue that, while Europe benefited, trade in and of itself did not lead to the decline in other regions. The rise in trade was in part a product of the enormous increase in capacity and the decline in transport prices, both products of the technological revolution of these years. Others, such as Andre Gunder Frank (1966), argue that the growth of one side of the world was inherently associated with the decline in the other. The debate would be historical trivia were it not for the very contemporary echoes in today's policy discussions. While the argument for an inherent link between "metropole" development and "peripheral" underdevelopment has been largely dismissed, historical evidence clearly demonstrates that the growth of Western Europe and its offshoots was not without its victims. Comparative advantage led to the destruction of manufactures outside of Western Europe and North America, and imperial violence led to genocide (in the case of the Americas, and, thanks to the slave trade, parts of Africa), and the imposition of Western hegemony over the rest of the world.

Much of the debate regarding the role of trade comes down to disagreements between those who emphasize individual country attributes (from natural endowments to government policies) as opposed to those who focus on systemic-wide properties of the global system (Schwartz 2007). One assumes a significant amount of economic agency, while the other feels that the economic game is too fixed by historical legacies. The history and contemporary structure of global capitalism provides evidence for both approaches. We refuse to make deterministic choices about the development of something as complex as trade. Did technology and incentives matter? Obviously. Did these developments occur in a world controlled by a few powers and where the privilege of European descent was unquestioned? Again, obviously. We need to appreciate how individual countries have prospered, but also how some geographically defined lines of inequality persist.

In this light, there is an ongoing debate regarding the value of "free trade" and the extent to which it has dominated global commerce or should do so. The richer countries of the last half of the twentieth century exhorted the poorer ones to open up their economies to a freer global trade. Yet all of the developed countries followed protectionist strategies in *their* industrial infancy (Chang 2002). The United States in the nineteenth century might take pride of place in the extent to which it sought to limit laissez-faire. In the post-world war era, similar barriers continued to protect politically sensitive industries and often shut out competitors from the very countries the global rich preached to about freeing up their economies. When speaking of free trade it is best to think of a spectrum of grays rather than black or white. The nineteenth century was generally freer than the first half of the twentieth century, which was followed by a return to freer (but still constrained) exchanges. The global explosion of trade in the 1990s was accompanied by a general reduction in tariff barriers. But, even in this instance, it is important to always keep in mind that trade freedom often remains selective.

The debate regarding the value of trade and participation in the global economy was practically made moot during the economic collapse resulting from the "thirty years war" of 1914 to 1945 when global trade volume and value fell by half. In an echo of the mercantilist policies prior to 1800, countries sought to create preferential zones for their products. During World War II, the links between Asia, Western Europe, and the Americas, first created in the sixteenth century, practically collapsed except for military flows.

The contemporary era of global trade begins in 1945. It is difficult to exaggerate the commercial explosion that defined the subsequent decade on both sides of the Atlantic. Exports grew at an even faster pace than the underlying economies: threefold in the US and by more than five times in Western Europe. Most of these countries doubled or even tripled the share of exports in their national GDPs. Some of this had to do with the aid that the United States provided in the immediate post-war era, but more important were the structural changes in the way international trade was governed.

The General Agreement on Tariffs and Trade created in 1947 sought to dismantle the institutional and psychological legacies of the inter-war years. Over the next two decades, a series of negotiations would help lower the tariffs that discouraged flows of merchandise between the signatory countries. (Unlike in the pre-1914 world, however, capital and labor flows remained restricted.) By the 1970s, most of the Atlantic economies had cut their tariffs by at least half, if not much more. Even more important for the boom in the Atlantic economies was the creation of the European Common Market (Eichengreen 2007). Begun as an effort to coordinate coal and steel production (and as a way of buttressing the new Franco-German alliance), it grew into a continental-wide customs union, which by the 1970s included all the major economies of Western Europe and whose aggregate market was larger than that of the United States. To understand the scope of the changes during these years, consider that German trade with the rest of Europe increased by more than 18 percent *per annum* or fifty-fold. For France, the figures were 15 percent and twenty-eight-fold, for Italy 15.9 percent or thirty-five-fold (Eichengreen 2007: 25).

The creation of the post-war economy, however, was not just about inclusion, but also exclusion. In order to maintain the balance between trade openness and the social welfare expectations of its citizens, Europe's borders were partly sealed against competitors.

This included manufactured goods from other developed economies, but also the dismantling of old colonial preferences and the
protection of agricultural markets. This Janus-like behavior of
opening and closing of trade doors would remain a hallmark of the
next stage of globalization and would continue to be a challenge
for the global capital system in the twenty-first century.

The other great trade story of this period was, of course,
Japan. This island country could not hope to build a customs
union similar to that of Europe, but it did count on even stronger
American support, through both direct aid and through the
expanding US military presence in Asia. The Japanese government
was also extremely active in supporting export growth by both
subsidizing investment in key sectors and maintaining a cheap yen
that would allow for high market penetration in overseas market
for companies such as Sony and Honda. The results of these policies were nothing short of spectacular. Even more so than in the
Atlantic, Japan's growth was trade led, as the role of exports in the
economy tripled. In 1973, Japan exported to the world roughly
twenty-five times what it had sent out in 1950.

Two other parts of the globe were also being transformed
during this period: the so called "Second World," consisting of
the socialist countries, and the "Third World," made up of mostly
ex-European colonies. Literally on the footsteps of its armies, the
Soviet Union created a block of economies linked to it and (less
so) to each other as an alternative to the West. While trade grew
almost tenfold in the Soviet bloc, much of it was an attribute
of an international specialization dictated by central planning
where political and strategic considerations trumped economic
logic. Thus, for example, the Soviet Union purchased sugar from
Cuba at exorbitant rates and sold it oil on a discount in order to
maintain its ally close to the American shores.

The story in the Third World of Latin America, Africa, and
Asia was yet again different; with the prominent exceptions of
Korea and Taiwan, most of their growth was not trade-based.
Led by Latin America, almost of all of these countries attempted
import-substituting growth. The argument for these policies was
not unreasonable: given the advantage of developed countries in

manufactured goods and the declining prices of the primary products they brought to the global market, it made sense for the newly developing countries to create their own manufacturing centers to meet domestic demand. Beginning with basic consumer products through capital goods, such as steel, many of the countries attempted to re-create the Western European economies within their own borders and the share of trade within Latin American and African economies shrank, sometimes by as much as half. In East Asia, the institutional foundations of the future trade orientation were being prepared, but these economies remained relatively small.

The Triumph of Globalization

The global economy was already facing some challenges by the late 1960s and the global commodity shock, beginning in 1973, began a downward spiral (Radetzki 2006). Oil was, of course, the best-known commodity affected with a quadrupling of prices, but partly as result of this leap and partly as a result of other endogenous factors, other products such as food and critical metals witnessed a doubling of prices. For a privileged set of countries, the commodity boom paid for a bonanza of growth and consumption, but, for the majority, it meant escalating bills for anything in their national basket that they purchased on the global market. These crises and the subsequent policies designed to deal with them created the institutional basis for the next trading era.

If the nineteenth century was the first stage of the true globalization of trade, and the "Glorious Thirty" were its second, then the period after 1990 is the third and arguably the most triumphant period. Where in the 1970s many had spoken of a "crisis in capitalism," by the early 1990s others spoke of a "new world order" in which markets ruled (Simmons et al. 2007). Interestingly, in the aftermath of the boom and subsequent bust of commodity prices, it was the region with the least natural resources whose economies performed the best. While the socialist bloc and most of the "Third World" suffered during the 1980s, East Asia began to boom.

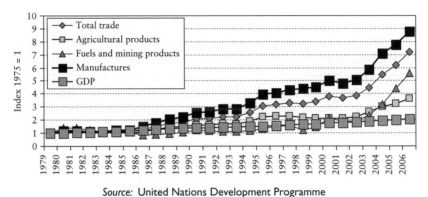

Source: United Nations Development Programme

Figure 2.2 Composition of world trade

Two characteristics distinguish this era. First, unlike either one of its predecessors, it sought to involve the entire world. While many societies' participation in the global economy is at best marginal, no country could exclude itself. Even those that rejected capitalism traded in it (North Korea, Cuba), while those who claimed autarchy actually benefited from hidden sales in the market (Myanmar). Second, the technological changes involving not just the Internet, but also much faster air and surface transport, intensified the links between the economies, made the system more autonomous from the control of any single authority, and created its own internal dynamics.

Within these global changes, we need to focus on two aspects: the composition of trade and its geographic distribution. As we can see from Figure 2.2, perhaps one of the most spectacular characteristics of global trade over the past twenty years is the extent to which it has not only increased much faster than the underlying economy, but the extent to which it has been led by manufactures; their share in global trade has steadily increased and now accounts for 70 percent of world exports.[1] Thus, trade has not only grown, but has also transformed the very structure of global production – we not only sell things globally, but we make them as well.

While global trade since the nineteenth century had largely consisted of a simple bilateral flow of manufactures and commodities, the last thirty years have witnessed the creation of a much more complex "new international division of labor" (NIDL). This involves global assembly lines with much of the manufacturing leaving the developed countries. This was initially driven by the lower costs associated with manufacturing in the developing world (resulting from cheaper wages and looser business regulations) and the simultaneous decline in transport costs. The increasing volume of trade also led to a massive development in the infrastructure required to manage it and deal with its logistical challenges. This saw the development of container shipping, the expansion of port facilities, and the increasing use of air transport.

The key actors in this process were the "transnational corporations," which increasingly had no real national home but operated on a truly global basis (Dicken 2003). Despite the rise of these new actors, and of what some consider their challenge to the salience of the state in international relations (Gereffi 2005), we will continue with our geographical focus in order to document the largest trends.

The geographic distribution of global manufacture changed with the shares of traditional powers such as the US, Germany, and Japan declining somewhat and China's share *quadrupling*. Perhaps the best indicator of this is what has happened in the steel and in the auto industries. China in 2007 produced nearly five times as much steel as the United States and accounted for more than a third of global production. This occurred in a country where, less than fifty years before, the Great Leap Forward had practically destroyed heavy industry. More important than the shift in the global rankings was the reconfiguration of the auto industry.[2] This had two broad components. First, was the elaboration of cross-border alliances between major manufacturers, ranging from equity ownerships to joint ventures. The second component was the restructuring of the components industries away from regional concentrations (in Michigan and Ohio, for example) to include truly global networks. An individual automobile may therefore include pieces from and be assembled in more than a dozen countries.

Other industries were also transformed. Since 1990, significant parts of the electronic equipment industry have moved to South

East Asia (Suzuki 2004). The trend in the production of such labor-intensive industries as clothing, footwear, and furniture was even more pronounced (Scott 2006). Beginning in 1970, the lowest technology parts of these industries began a massive shift to developing countries where labor (often the major cost factor) was often 70–90 percent cheaper. Beginning in 1990, the shift became concentrated in China. That country rose from barely exporting footwear or furniture to controlling 30 percent and 15 percent of global exports respectively. The other side of this transformation included the virtual disappearance of industrial sectors in regions where they had served as the economic base (e.g., textiles in the American Piedmont).

Another critical change occurred in the relationship between manufacturers and retailers (Appelbaum and Lichtenstein 2006). Where, previously, the manufacturer had been the dominant player, beginning in the 1980s and accelerating in the 1990s, retailers became the critical decision-makers. This accompanied the creation of "global supply chains" whereby factories were linked through their supplying particular products to gigantic buyers. In many ways, the global economy now revolves around the needs and directions of major retailers such as Wal-Mart, Tesco, and Carrefour. The concentration of this purchasing power, the extent to which decisions are determined by lowest cost, and the integration of economic activity into relatively few networks are helping to define twenty-first-century global capitalism.

Despite these changes, the *overall* geographic distribution of trade has *not* been transformed, aside from the prominent Asian exception. Even if their share has declined somewhat over the past twenty years, the North Atlantic economies still account for nearly two thirds of global exports. The share of exports accounted for by Asia has doubled since the 1970s, with the performance of China in the last decade being the most dramatic.[3] The rest of the non-Asian world has remained relatively marginal and concentrated on the export of primary products.

It is useful to think of world trade as a network, where position within a series of flows and the directionality of these makes all the difference. Being in the right place (the Dutch economy at the mouth of the Rhine valley, Singapore in the Straits) has enormous benefits, but being excluded from the network of trade, for example, will make it increasingly difficult to attract investment or to develop the logistical infrastructure required to buy and sell globally. (Thus, for example, there is a measureable penalty to being landlocked and the combination of being already poor *and* landlocked is very onerous.) Much as the best restaurant will languish if it is in the wrong location, even the most productive country may not be able to participate in a global market in a useful way if the global highway has passed it by.

Over the past two decades, several scholars have sought to better understand global trade flows by borrowing perspectives and methodologies from network theory (Gereffi and Korzeniewicz 1994; Kick and Davis 2001; Kim and Shin 2002; Mahutga 2006; Piana 2006). While some have argued that the global trade network has become flatter and more decentralized, most of the evidence points to the asymmetries first observed in the nineteenth century. With the prominent exception of those countries that succeeded in making a development leap through trade beginning in the 1970s, the global trade structure looks remarkably similar to that in the 1960s, even if its contents and micro-level geography are more complex. Those countries at the top of the heap at the beginning of the latest stage of globalization remained the ones that participated in the most profitable stages of manufacture, while those on the bottom did the literally dirtier and cheaper work. Moreover, the countries closer to the top of the network had a more diversified trade portfolio in terms of both products and partners, thus allowing them to deal better with temporary fluctuations.[4]

In network terms, the world might be described as consisting of three dominant blocs or cliques: North America, Europe, and Asian Pacific Rim. Each member of these groups deals mostly with others in the same clique (roughly 8 percent, 32 percent, and 14 percent of global trade respectively), but there is significant contact between the three groups as well (24 percent). An especially important relationship here is between the US and China. Not only are these flows significant in their own right, but the American trade deficit is paralleled by massive Chinese lending

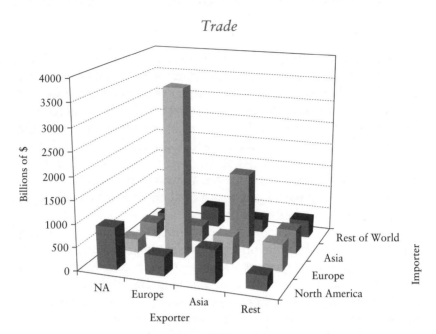

Source: UN Comtrade

Figure 2.3 Geography of trade

to the US (see chapter 3). Each clique has a set of satellite groups, which provide either natural resources (e.g., the US is mostly fueled by Western hemispheric sources and from West Africa) or privileged markets (e.g., Africa for Western Europe). Outside of this relatively small circle of cliques and hangers-on, most other countries are globally isolated; intra-Africa trade, for example, barely registers statistically.

The concentration of world trade is even more dramatic if we break it out by country. The top five countries (US, China, Japan, Germany, and Canada) account for practically half, the top ten for 66 percent, the top twenty for 83 percent and the top thirty for 90 percent of global trade. This last number is almost exclusively made up of Western European, North American, and Asian Pacific Rim countries with a few oil producers providing limited geographic diversity. The amounts traded by even the trade-oriented least-developed countries (LDCs) are minuscule. A leading new center for low-tech manufacturing such as Bangladesh exports barely $12 billion per year, half that of New Zealand, and Zambia sells 1/100th that of Korea.

If we break down trade into different sectors, the bifurcation of the global system is even more apparent. There is broad agreement that exports of manufacturers have a much better long-term payoff than focusing on commodities; a country is better off developing on the basis of factories than mines. We find that while at least three-quarters of North American, European, and Asian exports are manufactured goods, the figures for Latin America, Africa, and the Middle East are 31 percent, 19.6 percent, and 21.4 percent respectively. These regions (as well the constituent countries of the ex-Soviet Union) thus participate in the global market in an anachronistic fashion, still relying on a relatively simple nineteenth-century colonial model of selling primary materials and buying manufactured goods.

The division between the haves and the have-nots also remains the general trend in the service industry (law, advertising, accounting, tourism, etc.). The concentration of global shares of services among a small group of rich countries is even more pronounced than in merchandise trade: the top five of the US, the UK, France, Germany, and Japan account for over half of officially recorded service exports. To the extent that there has been a service revolution in world trade (e.g., the Irish and Indian cases), much less an Internet one, the leadership remains very stable.

There are two parallel networks where the poorer countries are much more central. The first concerns the "dark network" of illegal trade in drugs, people, arms, and contraband items such as endangered species and "blood diamonds." The shape of these networks tends to be much simpler as they usually involve a relatively linear flow from the source countries to the center where the merchandise is "cleansed" and redistributed. The amounts involved could reach one trillion, but the return on illegal trade for the countries involved in it is much less than one would wish. While legal services can be regulated and taxed, and workers and consumers can be provided with some guarantees, illegal ones benefit only the very few at the top and come with such uncertainties as to be closer to the world of piracy than capitalism.

A much more visible network is one in which the poor countries also have a clear commodity to offer the rich: labor. There are an estimated 200 million migrants living outside of the home country. The overwhelming majority of these are economic migrants and the flow is universally from the poorer countries to the richer ones. The US has received the most with almost 40 million (the majority of which are from Latin America), but Europe and Canada also have their millions (depending on the country, from Latin America, the Middle East, and Africa). There is a special sub-network from South and East Asia to the richer countries of the Middle East where natives are a minority in the working population. There are also significant flows inside the developing world as the bottom of the poor migrate to those above them in relative wealth (e.g., from many southern African countries to South Africa). These laborers fulfill a critical role in the economies of the wealthier countries and even dominate some service sectors. Back home, remittances from these same laborers can represent a country's most important source of foreign exchange and a two-digit percentage of total GDP (the global total in 2008 was over $300 billion). Through this export–import flow of labor, the rich and the poor are linked in a mutual dependence: the one using cheaper labor, the other receiving cash from work abroad.

To a significant extent, these trends reflect policy choices and resource "curses."[5] But they also are a product of the walls established within the leading economic blocs, which discourage imports from the bottom 150 economies. Europe and North America imported a total of less than $5 billion of agricultural goods from the least developed countries in 2006 and a little over $18 billion of manufactures (almost exclusively low-tech) for a total of less than half a percentage point of their imports. These walls consist of a variety of bricks, including tariffs, content regulations, and domestic subsidies. The most significant obstacle remains the limits on legal global movements of labor, which limits the developmental benefits of the one resource in which the poor have a clear comparative advantage. As the LDCs have pointed out in round after round of talks, the rich countries are in favor of free trade as long as their domestic constituents do not have to suffer the consequences. Consistently, the richer countries have failed to commit themselves to opening markets and have frustrated efforts to create any kind of differential treatment for poorer countries within the global trade agenda.

Global trade is therefore not a simple exchange of comparative advantages between equals. Rather, the global system is made of hierarchies and these in turn reflect both historical legacies and political realities. Patterns of trade still reflect relations established over a century ago and the flows of goods are certainly in part determined by political choices on tariffs and the like. The global trade system exists inside a historical and geopolitical context.

Dependency and Interaction

One important aspect of the globalization of production and consumption is that economic autarchy is no longer possible. If an economy participates in the global market it is, in a sense, also hostage to it. This is a perfect example of the kind of complexity discussed earlier: a society's economic well-being may be affected by decisions, and political or physical events which no one could predict, much less control.

Perceptions of this dependence are quite varied. The most optimistic reading harkens back to the first appearance of capitalism, through notions of Kantian peace, and hopes that globalization will make us all "too busy to hate" (Friedman 2005). A less sanguine perspective approaches this integration from what we may call a realist perspective (Keohane 1984). Such a view retains national interests at the center and asks how this interdependence and integration will weaken or strengthen these. A third perspective does something similar, but from the specific view of the developing world. "Dependency theory" suggests that global economic interactions invariably benefit the already rich and distort the economies of the still poor (Cardoso and Faletto 1979). Finally, "world systems" theory returns us to a global level (Arrighi 1994). Some within this perspective argue that the entire system is developed in order to benefit a new "global capitalist class" and their organizational representatives.

Within the complexity of global capitalism one may find both national and systemic forces, winners and losers. The point should not be the definition of a deterministic model, but an appreciation of how these different forces and actors engage and interact. In order to illustrate these processes we will analyze three test cases of relationships within the network of global trade.

Russian energy

Perhaps the best example of trade interactions fostering dependency involves commodity flows. These usually require a significant investment by both the exporting and importing countries in the construction of the necessary infrastructure. Because of these long-term investments, the relationships between these countries also require extensive negotiations and have all sorts of strategic implications. Most importantly, while the importer may be dependent on continued flows to operate an economy, the exporter can also become addicted to the boom times of easy money. Perhaps no better example exists of this than the energy ties that bind the European Union to Russia.

The European Union is increasingly dependent on imports of energy. It consumes 15 million barrels of oil *per day* and is the second most important market after the United States. For the past decades, Europe has been able to count on some internal sources thanks to British and Norwegian production in the North Sea. However, these reserves are increasingly becoming depleted and oil imports are expected to increase from roughly 60 percent of demand in 2000 to over 90 percent by 2020 (BP *Statistical Review* 2009). The picture is equally dire in terms of natural gas. European consumption is expected to double over the next two decades and imports will increase from less than 40 percent to more than 70 percent by 2030 (International Energy Agency 2008). The dependence on energy imports will increase in practically all forms, including coal, leading to a total energy dependence on non-EU sources of close to 70 percent by 2030 (IEA).

Some of this energy comes from Africa, particularly Algeria and Libya (crucial for Spain and Italy), and some of it comes from the Arabian Gulf. But the single largest supplier of energy for Europe is Russia. The Russian production is a particularly critical factor for natural gas where Russia currently accounts for 40 percent of imports. For countries on the eastern end of the EU, the percentage can be close to 100 percent. This dependence is expected to increase over the next two decades.

Dependence, of course, can run both ways. The European Union is much richer than Russia; Russian GDP per capita is one third of most Western European countries. Outside of Moscow and St Petersburg, the development gap between Russia and its western neighbors is even more extreme. Moreover, while the EU is the leading Russian client and accounts for over half of Russia's trade, Russia is third in line in the European trade hierarchy and accounts for a little over 8 percent of its trade. While Europe can sell Russia a broad array of products, Russia largely depends on a few commodities. As the price of oil has collapsed over the past few months, dependence on a single resource has demonstrated its ability to turn economic fantasies into nightmares. Yet the immediate impact of a decline in Russian energy exports would have arguably more immediate results on Europe than the reverse. The experience of the recent Russian shut-off of gas to Ukraine and Belarus (which then led to subsequent reductions in the flow to Europe) demonstrates that the EU depends on Russia for its economic life.

The relationship is made even more complex (and involves many more countries and untold more billions) because oil and gas need a complicated infrastructure through which to flow. Even if Europe were to diversify the original sources of its gas, the current pipeline structure largely runs through Russia and the major producer in that country (the monopoly Gazprom) has already made deals to sell and transport much of other sources of gas (e.g., from Turkmenistan). The construction of an alternative pipeline through Anatolia remains stymied by pending negotiations regarding Turkey's entrance into the EU. Alternative increases in liquefied natural gas from Africa would also require the expensive expansion of facilities in the Mediterranean coast.

What this case exemplifies is that we cannot treat global trade as a simple set of individual relationships repeated billions of times and unrelated to each other. The structure of global trade is closely linked to past commitments and strategic concerns. Many in Europe and the United States, for example, are concerned about the Soviet energy monopoly over the EU, no matter what its economic rationales (Garibaldi 2008). The creation of alternatives also implies political choices, whether greater European opening to Turkey or increasing dependence on North African sources. The fact that pipelines run through a sequence of countries mean that price disputes between one pair of governments can disrupt the entire system. The relative strength of Russia indicates that selling commodities to a much more developed customer does not necessarily involve a loss of power. But the tying of Russia's economic future to oil and gas also demonstrates how this strategy can distort domestic institutions and incentives. In all of these ways, the EU energy quandary demonstrates why global capitalism, for all of its growth and development, remains a fragile structure.

The promise of NAFTA and the Chinese challenge

China and Mexico represent two of the most cited examples of the globalization revolution of the past decade. Both countries began their greater integration with the global trade system in the 1980s. For China, this began with the return of Deng Xiaoping to power and his call for a market-oriented economy that would raise all boats. Similarly in Mexico, under Presidents Miguel de la Madrid and Carlos Salinas, the Mexican economy turned away from import substitution toward a bigger emphasis on trade. The obvious partner for both was the United States. In both cases, there was the simple reason of size, promising the wealthiest market in the world. In the case of Mexico, there was the added apparent benefit of geographic proximity.

In 1994, Mexico seemed to have struck gold by joining the United States and Canada in the North America Free Trade Agreement (NAFTA), providing it with privileged access to much wealthier countries. And, in many ways, the Mexican economy benefited handsomely from NAFTA. The institutional links with the American economy certainly provided a needed respite from the insecurity of inflation and currency failures. Following the disastrous first year, Mexico has been able to converge on OECD standards of inflation, interest rates, and even monetary stability (Wise 2007). Mexico raised the relative importance of trade in its economy from roughly 10 percent to 30 percent in the space of two decades. The composition of that trade was also transformed. Whereas in 1990 almost half of Mexican exports were primary products (mostly oil and metals), this had declined to less than 20 percent by 2005. Following the development of the *maquila* industry on the border, Mexico's manufacturing sector now accounts for the majority of its exports and includes a significant amount of high-tech goods. Disappointingly, however, these gains have not been accompanied by a surge in relative growth: Mexican per capita income *was* and *remains* roughly one sixth that of the United States.

This compares with a Chinese performance that has been astounding. From a poverty-stricken marginality in the global market, China grew at 9 percent a year for two decades (meaning a fivefold increase overall and much higher in the coastal zone), and its exports even faster (more than 20 percent a year since 2000). From almost no trade, China and the US developed a $360 billion relationship (of which $250 billion represented a US deficit). While the image of a "typical" Chinese export to the US was a cheap plastic game (a sector over which China has achieved a practical monopoly) or footwear (71 percent of US imports), that country now accounts for half of US imports in many electrical consumer products and office equipment and 33 percent of electric power machinery.

Eight years after NAFTA was signed, Chinese exports to the US surpassed those of Mexico. Of greater concern to Mexico was the Chinese encroachment in particular areas of its trade with the United States. Chinese manufactures were replacing Mexican ones in the US import of TV receivers, electric equipment, clothing, and even furniture. The share of Chinese exports to the US that are high-tech (and therefore more profitable) is growing, while that of

Mexico has stabilized. This meant that China was moving ahead of where simple issues of labor exploitation (Chinese wages being less than one third that of Mexico) could explain the competitive edge (Gereffi 2006).

Despite clear gains from NAFTA the return from Mexican participation has been disappointing. NAFTA was essentially a political economic bet that the jobs lost to any cheaper American and Canadian goods would be more than made up by gains in new employment. The losses certainly have come: beginning with Mexico's accession to GATT in 1986 and the creation of NAFTA in 1994, previously protected (and inefficient) industries have disappeared. The problem is that the jobs that were supposed to replace these have not materialized at the same rate as expected. Some of this has to do with the shift of resources such as FDI and production to China. But also some of it has to do with policy mistakes (both private and public) that prevented Mexico from making the most of its opportunities. For example, while productivity has been increasing in China, it remains flat in Mexico. Another factor in explaining the lack of dynamism of the Mexican economy is that it tied itself *too close* to that of the United States (more than two thirds of Mexican trade is with the US and American retailers have come to dominate much of its market). This was especially important in the creation of intermediate production for factories in the US. The link was beneficial in good times, but disastrous in bad (e.g. a possible shrinking of the Mexican economy by 8 percent in 2009). Whenever the US economy was in difficulty, Mexican industrial production would mirror any decline, at the same time as Mexican tourist income (also largely American) would weaken, and the northern border would be seeing dips in related businesses. In the first part of 2009, the Mexican economy was being devastated as exports to the US shrank, remittances from migrants declined, and tourists almost disappeared.

Even more dramatic has been the effects of NAFTA on Mexico's agricultural sector. The opening up of agricultural markets has provided a wonderful opportunity for Mexican agri-business selling broccoli and strawberries north. But it also allowed for cheaper (and government subsidized) US corn to flow south.

This was a disaster for the hundreds of thousands of marginal corn farmers who could not hope to compete. This has led to the virtual depopulation of large parts of the Mexican countryside with growing pressure on the already poor cities and on the (increasingly militarized) borders.

The lessons here are apparently contradictory.[6] On the one hand, China has shown that linking one's economy with the satisfaction of a richer society's needs can be phenomenally successful. On the other, Mexico has also shown us that becoming too closely integrated has its dangers. The American reliance on Chinese funding with which to pay for its consumption of that country's exports is an even more complex dependency which will generate its own moral.

The global food market

Perhaps no case better expresses the promises and challenges of the contemporary trade system than the global food network. One of the miracles of the modern, capitalist era is that the production of food skyrocketed in an unprecedented scale. Some of this reflected better yields in many places, but it also was a product of the availability of foods imported from literally thousands of miles away. This trend continued through the post-World War II era. While the world population doubled in the period of fifty years, the production of food tripled. Average global caloric intake increased by 25 percent (FAO 2004).

Over the past twenty years, long-held concerns of the ability of global agriculture to produce enough food dissipated. The yield for many of the basic grains on which much of the world depends have doubled or tripled. Even in sub-Saharan Africa, for long the one area without a dramatic increase in agricultural production, some improvement has been seen. Along with basic products, the globe has also witnessed a "horticultural revolution" with a quadrupling of vegetable production and more than doubling of fruit. The same trend can be seen in livestock and dairy products, as well as in non-edibles such as flowers. Overall, high-value agricultural exports from developing countries have also increased (Cooke et al. 2008). But the wealthier countries have also benefited; the US alone exported close to $90 billion dollars of agricultural products to countries from Canada to China and Colombia.

There has been a convergence in global consumption trends (not all of them healthy). These include a lower percentage of budgets being devoted to food (because of higher incomes and lower prices), an aggregate increase in per capita caloric consumption, and increasing shares of dairy and meat products in daily diets. The way the world buys its food has also been changing with ever increasing shares of prepared items (including fast food) and in sales through supermarkets.[7]

And yet roughly 800 million people are undernourished and many more millions live in a permanent state of food insecurity (with sub-Saharan Africa and South Asia being the worst areas). The juxtaposition of plenty and hunger is not new. Many of the greatest famines in history occurred in times and places of food surplus. The problem is not with production in and of itself. World production of basic grains is sufficient to provide more than basic caloric necessities for every person on earth. The problem is with the distribution thereof. In the same way that the global market with its diffusion of technology and specialization solved the food production problem, it has also distorted its distribution and contributed to the current crisis.

Precisely because the market rewards efficiency, it has created the potential for nutritional disasters by encouraging the concentration of production in fewer places, thus reinforcing dependence. Were it not for the fact that food is essential for human life, this would not be problematic, but by commoditizing food, the market requires that those countries that depend on purchasing nutrition be able to afford it. When millions cannot pay the price of whatever staple they depend on, they starve.

The commoditization of food was accelerated by the "green revolution" of increased irrigation and use of fertilizers, which produced astounding increases in yields. However, these innovations also led to the concentration of production in developing countries in ever larger farms owned by an ever smaller number of people. The percentage of the poor in the developing countries that were able to feed themselves through their own production declined over the past forty years. Again, this made perfect economic sense, but it also meant that more and more depended on the market for their nutrition.

The same process played out on a global scale as the most efficient economies crowded out those that could not compete. Subsidies of agricultural production in the wealthy countries have also been a factor. This is one area where the pro-market rhetoric of the OECD has been eclipsed by the political realities of electoral democracy. In order to placate a small but powerful minority in their countries, the wealthy spend an estimated $235 billion subsidizing their domestic agricultural production. Tariffs (sometimes running to 300 percent) also keep potential agricultural competitors from the developing world at bay. These policies have had a dramatically negative impact on food production in the poorest countries. First, the subsidies led to over-production in the rich countries, thus leading to cheaper prices that forced poor farmers to supply food at a price they could ill afford. Second, the closing of the wealthiest markets denied the opportunity to develop new forms of trade.

Simultaneously, the global market (and many of the leading governing institutions of global capitalism) urged developing countries to focus agricultural production on marketable commodities. Again, following the logic of competitive advantage, this made perfect sense. Why should Kenyan farmers attempt to compete in producing corn with the mega-farms of Iowa, when they could produce fresh flowers for export at a much more profitable price and thereby buy their corn on the market?

These trends resulted in an increasing dependence on the part of many developing countries on imports of basic cereals (for the poor a significant portion of their daily diet). In the developing world, the percentage of caloric intake from imports increased to roughly one third. The percentage of GDP accounted for by food import bills doubled over the last thirty years (FAO 2004).

The costs of this dependence were high: when prices of basic commodities rose faster than the wages or profits of those no longer growing their own food, disaster loomed. This fragile state was a permanent condition for many in the world, but went largely unnoticed until the price hikes of 2007 and 2008. Between March 2007 and March 2008, corn rose 31 percent, rice 74 percent, and wheat 130 percent. In some places and for some basic foods, prices skyrocketed in a matter of days. By January 2009, prices had declined, but they remained above 2006 levels.[8]

The result was the creation of a new (if temporary) set of winners (such as Argentina and Australia) and losers (large parts of Asia and Africa). Since the map of those endangered by the hike in prices closely resembled the map of those whose participation in the world market was most marginal, the specter of global famine haunted the world in 2008. Within the poorest countries, those on the economic bottom simply could not afford the new prices of goods that already consumed the vast majority of their income. The food was there, but the process of market transaction made it impossible for many to access it. The subsequent fall in prices provided a respite, but the speed of the decline also caused havoc on the previously "winner" countries who had counted on a continuing boom. The central point is not the prices in and of themselves, but the uncertainty and instability that accompanied and characterized the global food trade.

Capitalist-driven efficiencies have allowed humanity to potentially free itself from one of its worst historical scourges. But this great new plenty is only available for those who can pay for it. When circumstances change, the very poor find themselves literally locked out of the global grain bin. Emergency aid is not a long-term solution as it provides yet more negative incentives to poor farmers (why grow food when it comes free?) One of the greatest challenges for global capitalism is to balance the vast production capabilities with a more just, or at least better-functioning, mechanism by which all can be guaranteed access to the means with which to buy their daily bread.

The Promise and Challenge of Global Trade

The crisis of 2008 played havoc with what had been the linear progress of trade for almost twenty years. Arguably, the changes began in the United States. With the decline in American consumption as a result of the financial crisis, the global circulatory system began to break down. American imports declined by as much as a fifth in the last half of 2008. The repercussions were felt in and multiplied by the rest of the world. Commodity prices began a dramatic slide (with oil, as usual, in the lead). But those who depended on manufactured exports also suffered. Japan and China had declines of 27 percent and 11.8 percent respectively by the end of 2008. Since these exports helped pay for imports from other places, the contagion effect was massive and practically instantaneous. This led to the most drastic decline in global trade since the 1970s (2.1 percent globally).

The experience of the past year has, once again, taught us a few lessons. The global trade system has produced spectacular bounty. It has enabled billions to live better than our most privileged ancestors of a few centuries ago. It has enabled and supported an efficient specialization of production that allows for a broad consumption of goods. Gas from Siberia can now heat homes in Frankfurt, while (some) Russians can drive Mercedes. Inefficient and corrupt industries vanish in the waves of cheaper goods. Food of infinite variety can be available for much cheaper prices. But the system must recognize that it does not operate in a vacuum, nor is it indestructible; there are political frictions, transaction costs, and distributional failures. The global trade system is a marvelous creation, but it is also a potentially dangerous one.

3

Finance and Wealth

Much of the great economic revolution of the past two centuries would have been impossible without the accompanying transformations of finance. In recent decades, monetary institutions have assumed even more prominence and power over economic life. The global traffic of money has grown remarkably in size, reach, autonomy, and complexity. The financial sector has changed the distribution of political-economic power, redefined economic interests, and altered the prisms through which economic life is comprehended. Financial crises have devastated societies over the past forty years, but have also significantly contributed to economic growth. The finance boom helped usher in an era of unprecedented numbers of billionaires and buzzing factories, but also helped exacerbate inequality and economic hardship. Sound finance is a cornerstone of the capitalist system, and its failure poses serious problems for any activity that depends on accessing resources through markets. As markets' permeation of social activity has expanded, so have the stakes associated with the financial system's integrity.

Finance is typically explained in functional terms, as social arrangements that facilitate trade, investment, and economic risk management (Kohn 2004). For example, money, checks or charge cards provide people, organizations, or countries with tools to acquire the goods or services that they desire without the practical constraints involved in barter or holding wealth in commodities (like gold or jewels). Bank loans, commercial paper, or bond markets give enterprises access to funds for investment or to cover operating costs, or to avoid liquidity problems. Equity markets or futures contracts allow people to share profit with others who are willing to bear some of the economic risks that may arise from failed plans or adverse changes to the economic environment. In this sense, finance is an important tool that coordinates today's large and complex modern economies, including the many organizational problems associated with making payments, pooling resources, or coping with volatility, among others.

Finance should not be reduced to its functions, however, as the system we have constructed is not the only way to perform these tasks, its current development is not strictly shaped by these needs, and its effects extend beyond these services. The centrality of finance expanded over the late twentieth century. Corporate managers came to see businesses as net revenue streams, return on investment, and other purely financial terms, as opposed to seeing themselves as classical owner-operators whose business could grow via long-term internal expansion (Fligstein 1990). The language of financial accounting and investment came to pervade policymaking discussions, including areas that might not be immediately identifiable as financial concerns (e.g., welfare policy), and financial portfolios often stood as the most important and salient ministries and ministerial roles in government (Druckman and Warwick 2005). In many ways, the real economy came to serve the financial one, instead of the other way around.

Financial Markets, Systems, and Institutions

Financial systems involve a wide range of instruments, participants, and flows. Together, they form an ecology that floods or starves enterprises of resources, thereby influencing the viability of different social projects and the distribution of social power.

Instruments and prices

At their core, financial transactions involve contracts that store and transmit claims on the proceeds of some enterprise, be it a household, firm, government, or national economy. These contracts – called "instruments" – vary widely in terms of the clauses contained in them: the assets involved, the conditions of closure or dissolution, types of guarantees of fungibility, returns or minimized losses, the terms by which the invested wealth is to be used or managed, and so on. Such terms are not only determined by negotiations among these contracting parties, but also government policy, international relations, the strategic directives of this system's major players, and popular sentiment. Despite the great variety of securities exchanged in the global economy, all instruments represent contracts in which one actor transfers an economic claim (e.g., money) for another (e.g., claims on an enterprises' assets and income, or promises of repayment).

Ultimately, financial prices are determined by the degree to which actors are willing to exchange other economically valued assets for a given instrument. This is why we use the term "exchange value" – these financial instruments have no "use value" in and of themselves, but must be exchanged in order to obtain tangible benefit from them. Despite the variety of securities traded on financial markets, their value and role in society rests on faith or confidence. All instruments carry some risk that the wealth stored within them will disappear, and financial markets collapse when people are reluctant to vest their economic claims in them. Likewise, these instruments also carry the chance of growing in value, and are thus the focus of profit-seeking for many actors.

Perceptions of an instrument's risk and return influence financial prices. Such risk and return calculations are tied in part to fundamentals, which are calculable factors from financial statements or economic indicators, like the current profitability and net assets of the enterprise to which a security lays claim, or aspects of the current economic environment that can reasonably be expected to affect that sponsor's ability to meet payment or redemption obligations. However, fundamentals only predict some variation in financial prices. Factors not so easily assessed quantitatively or confidently also affect prices, like expectations about an uncertain future, privately held information or speculations about other people's behavior. To fill informational gaps, actors can turn to their impressions of other people's attitudes or actions, and such impressions might even override individual decision-making processes (Bikhchandani et al. 1992). As a result, perceptions of risk and return, and thus the attractiveness of an investment, tend to be constructed socially.

This socially constructed process of valuation can conceivably lead to stable markets. Although individuals may have partial information and unique estimates on speculative matters, their decisions in the aggregate – as transmitted by prices, trading volumes, and resources flows – can be seen as an agglomeration of their knowledge or "collective intelligence." This sentiment is articulated in notions of the "wisdom of the crowds," whereby a diverse, independent, and decentralized collective will tend to make better decisions than individuals, whose decision-making is plagued by preconceptions, limited information, and idiosyncratic irrationalities (Surowiecki 2004). Such markets' individual transactions are expected to exert a gravity that pulls prices to some "true" or equilibrium value, in which one actor's misconceived sale of an instrument is offset by another, cleverer investor's purchase of an undervalued asset. Through such a lens, one might expect markets to do a better job of resource allocation than organizations such as states, which may be more prone to group-think and dominance by powerful players.

Such a view makes good intuitive sense, and may find some support (Tziralis and Tatsiopoulos 2007), but we also need to understand that the socially constructed nature of risk and reward assessments is not independently produced. People can readily dismiss personal information in the face of public trends even when one's individual wisdom appears to incorporate solid information or viewpoints not reflected in collective wisdom (Bikhchandani et al. 1992). The intensity of peer influence among market actors can make them vulnerable to mass mania and panic (Kindleberger 2000 [1978]). Positive or negative assessments of a given instrument spur transactions that feed back to reinforce such assessments, producing "herding" or bouts of sustained buying or selling that can follow their own logic and lead to prices that dramatically depart from market fundamentals (Shiller 2000;

Hirshleifer and Teoh 2003). Examples of feedback loops include the information technology and emerging markets bubbles in the 1990s, and the mortgage securities and housing bubbles of the 2000s.

Participants

Almost any participant in an economy holds some capacity to influence prices, but this capacity is distributed very unequally. Many of the effects brought on by the financial sector's development can be understood in terms of structural change, power, and dependency.

Private actors shape financial outcomes, but their decisions are profoundly influenced by governments, and governments intervene to shape these outcomes purposively and with domestic non-economic and geopolitical agendas in mind. Governmental power over prices can be exerted in at least four ways. First, governments issue the basic constituent of financial systems: money. Manipulating the amount of money circulating in an economy influences the financial and real economy by altering prices changes, incentives, and the distribution of resources. Second, large proportions of circulating money are channeled through governments via taxing and spending, which can also be used to stimulate or dampen market sentiments or behaviors, and enrich or starve enterprises that issue or put resources into securities themselves. Third, governments regulate financial actors, mandating or restricting the kinds of instruments or contracts that can be issued or the resource allocations that can be made. Finally, they underwrite national financial systems, and jointly act as guarantors to the global economic system. They are the system's lender of last resort, and play a key role in securing basic confidence in the system. Governments can manipulate prices in a variety of ways, and often do so for political, as well as economic, purposes.

Table 3.1 compares various metrics of financial market power among the world's major countries. The central position of the US is even clearer here than it was in the case of trade.

By most metrics, the United States government is by far the

Table 3.1: Metrics of State-Level Financial Market Power, Selected Countries

	% FX Market	Gross FDI (US bil)	Public Debt (US bil)	Market Cap. (US bil)	Net Foreign Assets (US bil)	Govt. Revenue (US bil)	Trade (US bil)	GDP (US bil)	Foreign Reserves (US bil)	Global 500	Global 500 Financials	Billion- aires
	2004	2006	2006	2006	2006	2006	2005	2005	2007	2007	2007	2007
United States	88.7	392	4900	19425	-527	2285	3322	12397	75.2	153	33	415
Euro	37.2	—	—	—	—	—	—	—	—	—	—	—
Germany	—	150	1956	1637	1482	802	2124	2786	146.3	37	8	55
France	—	201	1429	2428	866	918	1131	2136	124.4	39	8	15
Italy	—	81	1969	1026	35	628	923	1769	104.7	10	4	13
Spain	—	127	486	1323	50	295	635	1126	20.1	11	3	20
Netherlands	—	54	322	779	204	250	831	628	29.6	13	4	4
Japan	20.3	57	7525	4726	486	NA	1241	4549	1004.7	64	11	24
UK	16.9	236	1015	3794	10	835	1267	2231	80.2	34	12	29
Switzerland	6.1	98	181	1212	146	68	325	365	78.4	14	5	8
Australia	5.5	50	117	1095	-159	187	268	674	35.2	8	4	12
Canada	4.2	102	858	1700	11	224	814	1131	42.6	14	8	23
South Korea	1.2	11	232	835	185	184	650	791	247.5	15	4	10
China	NA	99	555	2426	1265	215	1548	2243	1808.8	29	5	20
Hong Kong	1.9	90	25	895	396	NA	684	177	158.1	—	—	21

Table 3.1: (continued)

	% FX Market	Gross FDI (US bil)	Public Debt (US bil)	Market Cap. (US bil)	Net Foreign Assets (US bil)	Govt. Revenue (US bil)	Trade (US bil)	GDP (US bil)	Foreign Reserves (US bil)	Global 500	Global 500 Financials	Billion-aires
	2004	2006	2006	2006	2006	2006	2005	2005	2007	2007	2007	2007
Russia	0.7	56	87	1057	254	231	433	764	595.9	5	1	53
India	0.3	33	561	818	172	101	344	808	306.1	7	1	36
Brazil	0.2	47	489	711	66	NA	235	882	203.7	5	3	20
Mexico	1.1	25	195	348	31	NA	472	767	95.4	5	0	10
Turkey	<0.1	21	241	162	27	NA	228	483	79.3	1	0	25
South Africa	0.8	7	84	715	40	74	135	242	35	0	0	3

Global 500 Financials include companies in Global 500 in banking, diversified financials, insurances and securities industries.

Source: Bank for International Settlements (2005); *Fortune Magazine* (2008); *Forbes Magazine* (Kroll 2008); *The Economist* (2008); International Monetary Fund (2008); World Bank (2007); Economist Intelligence Unit (2008)

world's most powerful financial actor. Perhaps its principal source of power is its dollar, which acts as the world's money and is the instrument in which the world holds most of its financial wealth. In 2004, over 88 percent of foreign-exchange transactions involved a US dollar. The US governments' control over the dollar gives it the power to extract wealth from the global financial community by printing money, and means that the world's financiers depend on the US to protect much of their financial holdings. Fluctuations in the US dollar affect the rest of the world's trade, banking, borrowing, and many other spheres of economic concern. Ultimately, America underwrites the international financial system with its dollar, and wields considerable power as a result.

Although some of this power is attributable to US trade or foreign direct investment, one of its most exceptional qualities is its large, reasonably autonomous economy with exceptionally deep and well-developed capital markets, as evidenced by its massive market capitalization. US markets not only house American firms' securities, but also serve as a venue in which many foreign firms seek capital. Add to this a government that commands large budgets despite low tax rates, almost one third of the world's largest companies and billionaires, and a currency that has become routinized as a worldwide metric of value, and the country's status as a financial safe haven becomes comprehensible. This status enables the US government to issue Treasury bills inexpensively and in huge volumes, much of which constitutes other countries' foreign reserves. The American government can thus run large debts, marshal great spending power, run large and persistent international deficits, serve as the world's consumer, and act as the world's banker.

A second tier of actors include the governments of the world's other richest countries – such as the wealthy Anglo states, the Euro states, Japan, and Switzerland. They enjoy similar forms of monetary and fiscal power, and hold jurisdiction over several major private sector actors, but individually their power is far weaker than that of the US government. In addition to their individual forms of monetary, fiscal, and regulatory power, these states hold some formal political influence over major international financial institutions (such as the International Monetary Fund) and some degree of cooperation is probably required from them for American efforts at financial leadership to work. These countries also wield power derived from their large economies, well-resourced governments, and sovereign control over major financial havens and international economic enterprises. With the US, they serve as the primary arena in which finances flow and are stored.

Non-core powers can wield some monetary power in part by establishing large holdings of core currencies, allowing them to wield some degree of monetary power vis-à-vis these currencies' issuing governments as well as other important financial markets (Dooley et al. 2003, 2004). These have often taken the form of "sovereign wealth funds." Emerging Asian economies have used their trade surpluses to absorb the debt upon which America relies, which helps keep their currencies low and exports competitive, but also fosters US dependence on these countries' continued purchase of T-bills. Over the past few years, other countries, especially fossil fuel exporters, have also pursued the Asian reserve accumulation model.

After these major secondary states, the next class of financially powerful actors includes large and wealthy organizations with good access to international markets, such as smaller governments, multinational firms, large financial firms, major private financiers, and multilateral organizations (like the IMF or BIS). There is much variation in this group, and some of them can wield substantial market power as a result of their ability to allocate funds. This group is distinguished by its comparative lack of autonomy relative to major states, as their decision-making is subject to constraints, both by their host governments and the current geopolitical "rules of the game" for finance. While this third tier of players is constrained by regulation, their large amounts of wealth and ability to move money across borders give them some autonomy vis-à-vis regulators. If large enough, their behavior and attitudes may, in turn, shape that of the regulators themselves.

A fourth tier includes smaller, highly constrained actors, whose financial choices are structured by governments and private intermediaries – households and smaller enterprises. Although individuals in this group exercise virtually no influence over markets, their collective action can overpower other actors if strong and concerted enough. Runs on banks or popular flights from markets, for example, can inflict great pains on, if not cripple, financial institutions, economic systems, and governments.

International financial flows

Financial flows are even more concentrated than trade flows, with fewer (and sometimes different) actors acting as hubs in the international web of financial flows. This concentration can be seen when we examine two kinds of markets: *portfolio investment* (cross-border investment in equities, bonds, deposits, or other financial assets) and *reserve holdings* (governments' holdings of other countries' money). Table 3.2 depicts the geographic breakdown of the top ten economies in terms of total portfolio investment by issuers and holders for 2001. These figures are in billions of US dollars.

Approximately one quarter of global portfolio investment is destined to the United States, and roughly one fifth of international portfolio investment comes from there. In contrast, approximately one quarter of international portfolio investment is destined for somewhere other than these top ten investment destinations (which only account for roughly 13 percent of the world's population). Luxembourg and the Cayman Islands may seem like odd members on such a list, but both are examples of "offshore financial centers," small, sovereign economies that tailor their policymaking environment to be maximally attractive to capital investors. Such incentives can include lower taxes, more financial sector subsidies, lax banking regulation, or laws that obfuscate corporate ownership, which can serve legitimate business interests but also act as a conduit for tax evasion and money laundering.

Outgoing portfolio investment is also highly concentrated, with only about one quarter of the world's outgoing portfolio investment coming from outside the top ten investor countries. Of these countries, all but Italy sends more investment to the US than to any other destination. Beyond this primary attraction to

Table 3.2: Geographic Breakdown of Total Portfolio Investment: End of 2001

To: / From:	United States	United Kingdom	Japan	Luxbrg.	Germany	France	Italy	Switz.	Nethlds.	Ireland	Others	Total	%Total
United States	···	504	131	142	146	47	196	13	59	200	809	2249	18%
United Kingdom	309	···	130	131	73	91	94	22	46	15	394	1304	10%
Japan	490	110	···	176	46	34	···	46	133	22	233	1290	10%
Luxbrg.	178	60	111	···	54	47	23	103	20	11	213	820	7%
Germany	108	73	150	64	···	84	10	31	12	13	238	792	6%
France	117	69	86	13	87	···	6	106	21	4	201	710	6%
Italy	74	34	60	26	84	74	···	66	18	12	149	552	4%
Switz.	76	23	57	44	53	6	10	···	12	10	178	496	4%
Nethlds.	137	41	68	20	35	44	12	8	···	3	124	486	4%
Ireland	155	89	33	19	13	27	10	13	3	···	72	441	3%
Others	1434	277	334	170	107	128	144	113	68	29	671	3474	28%
Total	3078	1280	1160	775	698	579	533	398	398	308	3282	12613	
% Total	24%	10%	9%	6%	6%	5%	4%	4%	3%	2%	26%		

Source: International Monetary Fund (2003)

US markets, portfolio investment patterns depend on country specifics, whereby capital is often channeled to countries that share geographic, political, economic, or some other affinity to investor countries. For example, EU countries seem to invest in each other's markets, and Canada receives roughly two thirds of its investment from the United States.

The US exerts even more dominance in international reserves (and money markets more broadly). This market is important because it is large – representing $6.3 trillion of reasonably assured purchasing power at the end of 2007 – but also because reserves represent an important facet of individual governments' stored cash-on-hand, which they can use to avert crisis and maintain stability (B. Cohen 2006). America's "monetary hegemony" is apparent in this respect. Approximately 64 percent of the world's allocated[1] government reserves are dedicated to dollar holdings, with substantial amounts stored in Euros (28 percent) and a small percentage stored in British pounds and Japanese yen. However, the governments that back the currencies serving as major alternatives to the dollar invest in heavy dollar positions themselves, so that currency's central role is hard to exaggerate. In a sense, the distribution of allocated reserve holdings exhibits the broader monetary interdependencies that exist in global public finance. Everyone is, in some way, dependent on the dollar as a means of holding purchasing power.

An important issue which demonstrates both the centrality of the US and the paradoxical qualities of its position has to do the extent to which non-American institutions hold enough debt to hold that country hostage. Foreign entities own an estimated $2.2 trillion of US government debt, with China accounting for roughly one third.[2] This outstanding debt partly fueled the explosion in US consumption which in turn helped drive the trade expansion documented in chapter 2. In this way, American borrowing powered the global economy by permitting other countries to sell Americans more products than they might have been able to afford. On the one hand, this places the US in an especially privileged position. On the other hand, it implies that the American economy owes its survival to other countries' faith in it. Over and above such concerns, many continue to fear the possible ramifications of the over-saving by some and the over-consumption by others.

The Rise of Global Finance

The financial system has been shaped by social crisis and conflict, whose resolution became reified, thence falling into the background of "normal" economic practice. Much of what we take to be the financial facts of economic life were once perceived as problematic solutions to social problems that took root in historical circumstance, producing a social structure that vested particular groups with power over the world's economies.

Today's global financial markets are large, expansive, deep, mobile, deregulated, and powerful. In many respects, contemporary markets resemble their nineteenth-century counterparts, and represent a major reversal of post-Great Depression efforts to contain the power and volatility of private capital markets. Global capital markets' return followed roughly a quarter-century of chronic political and economic crisis, which set the stage for a long de-institutionalization of governments' containment of capital markets and the re-institutionalization of a system that placed the financier in a central position of economic control. From 1997 into the early twenty-first century, however, this system of financial capitalism has increasingly been seen as a cause of its own crises, and there is some evidence that states are trying to reassert some degree of financial control. The crisis of 2008 will no doubt increase the pressure to do so.

Long-run cyclicality in the financial sector's power

Many scholars believe that there is a type of long-run cycle in which the balance of power over the world economy appears to shift between domestically focused elites led by local states, and transnationally focused capitalists led by a global hegemon or clique of core countries. The best-known incarnation of this theory focuses on "hegemonic stability," whereby the edification of economic regimes that prioritize transnational capitalists both require and benefit states that rise to a position of global dominance (see Eichengreen 1999). Under a regime of free and empowered trans-national capital markets, a global hegemon pushes and guarantees an international system of free capital movement, thereby reaping the benefits enjoyed by the US today. Ruggie (1982) argues that it is not just a concentration of hegemonic power that creates liberal capital regimes, but also a shared sense of purpose among the world's major secondary powers, fortifying governments' hand against capital. Arrighi (1994: 33), in contrast, portrays the rise and fall of global financial capitalism as being rooted in changes in returns to investment, whereby societies phase through periods in which economic accumulation primarily takes place through the edification of resources within one's own territory, and periods in which countries look outside their borders to command the resources that reside outside their borders.

Whatever the causes of global finance's periodic rises and falls, these changes do appear to recur over the long run. Similar systems coalesced under the Italian city states during the fifteenth century, the Dutch-centered system of the seventeenth century, and Britain's hegemony in the nineteenth century (Arrighi 1994). Those eras shared many commonalities with our contemporary world system. Post-World War II efforts to reconstruct the international financial system took place through post-Depression financial regulation and the Bretton Woods accords. By regulating financial interme-diaries, controlling international capital flows, and fixing financial market prices, it was hoped that the financial excesses that helped cause the Great Depression could be prevented. Post-war attitudes toward capitalism had soured somewhat after the Depression, and governments sought to contain capitalism in many respects.

By the beginning of the 1970s, the Bretton Woods system faced several problems: a war-strained US balance of payments, fiscal deficit, and surplus of foreign-held dollars that were outstripping the American gold reserves (Helleiner 1994; Block 1977). The accords' 1971 dissolution marked the end of a slow process in which states' dominance over finance had been chipped away, principally through policy initiatives spearheaded by the US and the UK (Helleiner 1994), and the beginning of a period in which the institutionalized framework for interstate financial control broke down.

Just as governmental control was beginning to break down, the global banking industry experienced a massive shift. After 1973, oil-producing countries, enjoying windfall profits from high energy prices, re-channeled the proceeds of high oil prices into America's banking system. New global credit markets served to temporarily balance the petrodollar bonanza of some with the needs of others. Banks, facing the demands for interest from new international depositors, also encouraged borrowing, particularly among those countries with rich resource veins only needing extra investments to join in the boom. The result was an explosion in global debt held by many developing countries. In a period of less than twenty years, the world's most indebted developing countries went from owing 10 percent of their GDP to owing 47.5 percent. By 1987, debt service alone accounted for 25 percent of gross revenue from exports. They were joined by the communist countries whose debt rose to over $50 billion dollars by the late 1970s (Eichengreen 1999: 297).

In some developed countries, especially the English-speaking world, these currents translated into a lean government, laissez-faire approach to policy, but political polarization and gridlock often prevented developing countries from reforming their finances, and many governments dealt with this problem by engaging in seigniorage (e.g., see Morales and Sachs 1989). Seigniorage – effectively "printing money" – floods markets with a currency, making it less valuable, and hence spurs inflation. Over the 1980s, many countries fell into high or hyperinflation (Fischer et al. 2002), intensifying the breakdown of financial order.

As government debt grew to be very large and the developed world recovered from the stagflation crisis, interest rates and the cost of debt service rose. The fervor of sovereign lending began to fade, and governments' ability to carry their debts seemed unsustainable. Mexico's threatened default in 1982 sparked a panic on these credit markets, and financing was quickly cut. Many of the world's governments fell into severe liquidity crises. In this context, policy prescriptions favoring tough austerity measures, tight monetary policy, and liberalization gained much traction among professional economists (Williamson 1990a), while the established, interventionist Keynesian policies were losing legitimacy (Snowdon et al. 1994).

In financial markets, a key constituent of reforms involved the deregulation of inward foreign investment, the privatization of state-owned enterprises, and the deregulation of financial transactions. Many former government functions and enterprises were offloaded into markets. For example, pensions were privatized (Muller 2000; Brooks 2005), as was ownership of key industries and infrastructure (Megginson and Netter 2001). This amounted to a change in economic environments that gave a freer hand to finance, and put financiers in a position in which they had greater power to shape national economic fortunes. The end of the Cold War would galvanize these trends.

Financial Capitalism

By the beginning of the 1990s, financial globalization was already making clear inroads across the developing world. By the twenty-first century, international direct investment (as a percentage of GDP) increased fourfold over its median 1980s level. International capital movement and market capitalization grew threefold and almost doubled in proportion to their economies, respectively. During this decade, international capital flows expanded dramatically in size and scope of countries involved. Table 3.3 offers various metrics of financial markets' size and global reach. The figures represent the median among the relevant samples of countries.

The collapse of the Soviet system introduced a sizeable group of reasonably wealthy states to financiers. Facing many indicators that severe crisis was imminent, the former communist countries turned to the US for advice and aid, and settled on a strategy of "shock therapy," a program of rapidly de-institutionalizing former institutions of state economic control, in part in an effort to circumvent the old regime's ability to undermine economic

Table 3.3: Metrics of International Financial Development by Decade: Median Scores 1970–2005

	External Debt*		Budget Balance		Gross FDI		Gross Private Capital Flows		Market Capitalization	
	% GNI	bil US$	% GDP	mil US$	% GDP	mil US$	% GDP	bil US$	% GDP	bil US$
1970s	29.2	0.6	—	—	—	—	—	—	—	—
1980s	57.5	3.2	– 4.1	– 416	0.9	120	6.8	0.6	19.8†	13.7†
1990s	67.3	4.8	– 2.9	– 496	2	458	10.8	1.8	34.5	44.1
2000s	66.6	6.2	– 2.3	– 426	3.6	1160	14.5	4	55.7	100.1

*Developing countries only. †1988 and 1989 only
Market capitalization and budget balance figures represent a limited sample of 49 and 59 countries (21 and 19 OECD), respectively

Source: World Bank (2007)

transitions (Murrell 1993). Promises of peace dividends and the bright prospect of a future of truly global capitalism fostered much excitement among capital investors, who rushed to gain footholds in newly liberalized markets before the opportunities of early investment passed. Different countries engaged these markets with different policies and timing (Taylor 2006), but most felt the effect of these markets and their economic fates were shaped by them.

Excitement over emerging opportunities and a general environment of increased competition spurred a range of changes that saw new and more varied opportunities to invest. New pools of capital were increasingly freed to "play the markets," as the de-regulation and changes in managerial practice that took root in the 1970s continued. These introduced new, large players, such as pension funds or insurance pools, while the re-emergence of stock market confidence attracted private investors to a rising mutual fund industry (Hawley and Williams 2000). The result over the early to mid-1990s was a phenomenal increase in opportunities for enterprises and countries to finance development. Developing countries enjoyed marked growth, and arguably realized key infrastructural improvements that some consider to represent real steps forward (Kuczynski 2003).

A parallel process of making financial operations ever more central was occurring *inside* firms and governments. As outlined by Fligstein (1990), US efforts to implement stringent antitrust regulation prior to the 1970s pushed wealth-holders – large firms and investors – to find ways to accumulate wealth within the restrictions limiting power within particular markets or industries. The US government could effectively block corporate consolidation where a proposed merger involved businesses whose operations were directly tied (e.g., buying one's suppliers, distributors, or competition). These laws could not, however, block mergers across unrelated lines of business. By the 1960s, corporations were consolidating as conglomerates of multiple businesses in multiple industries.

The effect, argues Fligstein, was a fundamental change in our understanding of what a business is, at least within large firms. Whereas in earlier phases of capitalism's development, a business was understood as an agglomeration of resources, processes, and market power, designed to provide the economy with a particular product, the era of diversified mergers saw a redefinition in terms of financial concepts: return on investment, price-to-equity ratios, and other notions based on present and predicted cash flows. Businesses increasingly grew by acquiring "profit centers," rather than cultivating larger and more competitive enterprises through internal growth. The need to complete large mergers in turn created a need among corporations to raise large amounts of money, credit, and equity investment, creating the basis for an expansion of "big banking."

It was in this context that many of the key changes that created large, powerful and enormously profitable financial operations, which often seem divorced from real economic activity, took substantial root in corporate America, and in the many markets that imitated the US thereafter. This evolution arguably produced a "financial conception of control," accompanied by an emphasis on financial performance measures in the business literature and in decisions regarding compensation. In a simplified telling, this involved running firms with greater emphasis on the return to shareholders; success for a company meant what the market said it was worth in any particular quarter. On the one hand, this emphasized an ultimate confidence in the informational processes of the market to assign value and was a logical extension of the direction capitalism had taken from the beginning. On the other hand, it tended to shift attention from fundamentals of the actual business that a firm was engaged in toward the reflection of those fundamentals in the mirror of the stock market. What this meant is that beginning in the 1980s and into the twenty-first century, the successful CEO was not necessarily one who made better widgets or even sold more of them than anyone else, but one who raised the price of the shares of the widget company. Given the complexities of corporate accounting and the often "irrational exuberances" of market forces, these measures were not necessarily correlated.

Inside governments, these same years also saw the global rise of the "financial technocrats" (Centeno 1994). These leaders, often young and educated in the rhetoric of global capitalism at

US universities, replaced two different elites: one who had risen through the "smoky rooms" and ward politics, and another who had managed the resources of the state, such as oil or mining. The financial technocrats were adept at dealing with the structural equivalent of the stock market, global financial institutions, and with the equivalent of annual reports, the approval of international financial organizations such as the IMF. This trend also extended into the academy where the analysis of finance came to dominate business and economic faculties, and where whole new departments in "financial engineering" would arise.

Crises upon crises

Throughout the 1990s, the potentially negative implications of capital market liberalization became apparent. Among developing countries, these problems materialized in a spate of currency crises, in which the large funds invested in comparatively smaller developing economies were prone to flee rapidly. This behavior was true of domestic capital fleeing home as much as of foreign capital retreating to the safe havens of rich economies. Many countries fell victim to these crises, including Mexico in 1994, Thailand and Korea in 1997, Russia in 1998, Turkey in 1994 and 2001, Brazil in 1999, and Argentina in 2001 (Rodrik 2006). A particularly notable feature of these crises is that they could hit countries indiscriminately such that the developing world as a whole could see a generalized rapid capital flight to international safe havens (i.e., rich countries) when serious problems only affected specific locales (Kaminsky and Reinhart 2000; Fratzscher 2003). Worse yet, analysts began to note that panicked capital flight might flee for reasons that were less likely to be tied to any problems in economic systems' fundamentals, and more as a result of the financial community's own self-fulfilling prophesies (Obstfeld 1996). That is, the autonomy of the financial sector from the underlying economy that it was supposed to reflect increased dramatically; the tail had become much bigger and was no longer even attached to the dog.

In developed markets, loose regulatory environments created

opportunities for over-speculation and sometimes malfeasance. Despite earlier criticisms that strong government intervention fostered public sector corruption (Krueger 1974), de-regulated markets looked equally vulnerable. In the late 1990s boom, many American firms, notably Enron, WorldCom, and Adelphi, capitalized on a system that depended on for-profit private auditors that were paid by the very firms they were meant to police, to distort financial reports to attract capital. Once exposed, a general crisis of faith in financial information ensued, and investors lost billions. The losses were large and by no means unique to the modern era, but did impart a sense that more liberal markets need not result in the transmission of better information if there were enough actors to collude. Furthermore, it became apparent that the profit motive could create incentives to distort information, for example, if accounting firms were oriented enough toward the maintenance of short-term business accounts (as Arthur Andersen had with Enron, or securities rating agencies were on the companies that they monitor). In short, governance of the financial sector was in crisis.

Over the past decade, analysts have expressed a deep ambivalence about the benefit of capital market liberalization for developing countries. Soon after the 1997 Asian financial crisis, analysts began to warn countries that theories linking free capital markets to growth could be flawed (Stiglitz 2000), and countries should be advised to take a more defensive posture vis-à-vis financial markets (Feldstein 1999). Systematic reappraisals of financial liberalization's record concluded that the literature was plagued by contradictory findings and non-robust results (Kose et al. 2006). Capital controls – dismissed by some as impractical policy relics of an era gone by (Isard 2005; Dornbusch 1998) – were now being entertained as viable policy options (Montiel and Reinhart 1999). Financial globalization seems to have disappointed those who expected it to spur development (Rodrik and Subramanian 2008).

We can appreciate the possible negative consequences of the changes in financial markets by noting that between 1945 and 1971, there was only one banking crisis in the developed world, whereas fifty-four such crises afflicted IMF members between 1975 and 1997 (Eichengreen and Arteta 2002). Some notable examples in the English-speaking world include the US Savings and Loan Crisis of the 1980s (Calavita et al. 1997), the 1995 collapse of Barings Bank (Drummond 2002), the 1998 failure of Long-Term Capital Management (Lowenstein 2000), or the 2007 collapse of Britain's Northern Rock. Of course, 2008 was littered with similar cases. Pessimism about domestic market deregulation also materialized within rich countries. Some critics cited over-regulation of financial reporting as a source of problems like Enron, whereby strict codification of accounting practices created a framework that malfeasant actors could follow to the letter but circumvent in spirit, thereby hurting the underlying principle that such regulations were supposed to advance: transparency (Healy and Palepu 2003). The chief policy redress – the Sarbanes-Oxley Act of 2002 – was principally designed to improve information transmission through enhanced public reporting requirements. Critics such as Soederberg (2008) have argued that these redresses keep the practice of self-regulating financial capitalism largely intact, and still provide no strong protections for shareholders against managers.

Concerns about domestic de-regulation only intensified in 2008 with the development of the US mortgage securitization crisis and the subsequent chain reaction leading to a credit crunch and then financial and real economic collapse. In this case, participation in this crisis is so wide – and much less clearly attributable to corruption – that it evokes questions about the extent to which unfettered markets might actually result in good aggregate financial decision-making. Analyses about this crisis will certainly emerge in the coming years, but present impressions reinforce concerns that deregulated markets are not as an ideal solution as might have been assumed. Identifiable liberalization reforms set the stage for this crisis. The 1980 Depository Institutions and Deregulation and Monetary Control Act created the sub-prime debt market by removing state limits on mortgage rates, thereby creating incentives to pursue higher-risk borrowers in hopes of higher profits on interest. The 1999 Gramm-Leach-Bliley (GLB) Act repealed the mandatory separation of banks from securities and insurance companies, mandated by the 1933 Glass-Steagall Act and 1956 Bank Holding Act, respectively. GLB effectively allowed financial firms to consolidate, in effect tying multiple financial sectors (e.g., investment and retail banking, insurance) together, often under the leadership of the much less risk-averse investment bankers.

Ramifications of Finance's Rise

Socialization of risk

Risk is not a bad thing in and of itself. Arguably, any innovation carries some possibility of failure and lost resources. Innovation is often argued to be a principal strength of the capitalist system, enabling society to shed obsolete enterprises, products, or practices in favor of the new-and-improved. It was in this sense that Schumpeter (1942) celebrated capitalism as a means of forging an ever-renewing cycle of "creative destruction." While few would argue against economic dynamism, purchasing these changes through an excessive liberalization of capital markets comes with arguably excessive systemic risk.

Investment mania and panic are as old as markets themselves. Famous historical examples include the Dutch tulip bubble of 1634–7, the French Mississippi bubble of 1719–20, or the British South Sea bubble of 1720 (see Garber 1994). By many accounts, financial crises were a regular occurrence in past centuries (Hoppit 1986; Wood 1999; Braudel 1982). But, under Bretton Woods, the world system enjoyed extraordinary price stability (Fischer et al. 2002), and comparatively strong economic prosperity. Much of the post-Depression era's financial regulatory framework was intended to limit exposure to various forms of risk, by seeking to limit "riskier" actors' access to financing. For example, limits on interest rates restricted the incentives to extend credit to higher-risk borrowers, given that the potential profit payoff would be limited when compared to other investment opportunities with commensurate risk. Mid-century capital market regulations restricted investors' ability to seek high returns in many potentially profitable markets. This had the effect of restricting capital flows to less investment- or credit-worthy outlets, and is thought to have ultimately favored the financing of enterprises that were well-resourced and established. A general environment of de-regulation and private competition helped spur growth and innovation in investment fund markets in the 1980s and 1990s.

These changes gave rise to new funds that provided individual investors with a practical means of delving into traditionally opaque and inaccessible markets, thereby offering new avenues of investment to emerging firms, industries, or countries. Much of the centralized control that took place under governments was devolved to a larger, but still limited, class of financial intermediaries, whose interests could tend more strongly toward risk-taking to maximize short-term profits, rather than to guarantee stability.

This problem is most apparent, in light of recent events, with the issue of leverage. Leverage allows investors to make bets with much more money than they actually have. Purchasing stocks on margin or home mortgages are common versions of leverage. Leverage allows a possible multiplication of returns if the investment goes right, but also implies huge risks from losses. So a homeowner may pocket all the difference between his or her outstanding mortgage and the final sale price of the home (net of interest), even if they originally invested little of their own money. Conversely, in 2009, many homeowners found themselves "under water": owing more on their home than it could ever be sold for on the market.

There is nothing intrinsically wrong with leverage and, in fact, this is critical for the dynamism of global capitalism. However, leverage and agent-principal problems can take extreme forms, and did so over the past decade. Unregulated markets produce perverse incentives, whether for small investors seeking to "flip" Florida condominiums, or hedge fund managers to make bets twenty to thirty times larger than their capital.

Over-leveraged investment or short-term, high-stakes compensation schemes have brought us to the point where finance no longer involves prudent, long-term oriented resource allocation, and acts more like a casino in which players roll for massive payouts, no matter how much (or whose) wealth is at stake. The global financial system collectively gambled that growth would be eternal, so that tomorrow's earnings would always more than cover yesterday's debts. More perilously, since individuals and corporations lent to and borrowed from each other, we all became prisoners to each other's bets (e.g., A's leverage fails which means he cannot pay debts to B, but B is also leveraged and this default sends her into bankruptcy, ruining her lender C, and so on). Leverage essentially made us all hostages of the viability of the investor taking on the greatest risk. The combination of leverage and the tight coupling of global finance meant that a catastrophic "normal accident" was just waiting to happen. The bankruptcy of Lehman Brothers was merely the equivalent of the Challenger's "O-ring."

Concentrating the disposal of finance in a smaller group of institutional investors can – and has – created situations in which the public effectively subsidizes insurance for aggressive institutional investors. Theoretically, letting investors go bankrupt can discourage risky investments, but such a solution, when applied to a large firm that manages billions of dollars, can result in generalized losses of confidence, panic, and severe crisis. Other socially important institutions, like pensions or insurance pools, can collapse with markets. Often, governments bail out such risky investments, socializing the cost of institutional investors' risky moves. This creates what is often called a "moral hazard" problem – the people who move the money will not bear the brunt of a collapse, and are therefore more comfortable assuming risk in hopes of large payoffs. Even where governments do not guarantee bailouts, fund managers are often rewarded for their performance over short terms, and a trader who racks up a few years of spectacular growth before losing all of his or her client's money is likely to have already banked large management fees and bonuses before investors' wealth is lost.

The most obvious example of this social insurance is today's US mortgage market crisis, in which banks and investment houses put hundreds of billions of dollars in opaque, securitized mortgages. Intermediaries enjoyed strong returns on these securities mid-decade, and collectively allocated so much capital into them that the deflation of a long-foreseen real estate bubble (featured three years earlier on the cover of *The Economist*), posed an existential threat to the global financial system. A few years after Wall Street reportedly disbursed massive amounts of money in performance bonuses to its fund managers, the government had to absorb what has amounted to roughly a trillion dollars in loan obligations as of October 2008. Risky, aggressive profit-seeking trading has resulted in similar collapses, some of which have been borne by governments and others by individual investors.

Over and above the actual quality of the underlying investments made, many wondered if the very architecture of the system promoted far too much risk. An excellent example of this was the interlocking market of hedge funds, credit swaps, and derivatives created through financial engineering. In and of themselves, these were rational instruments with calculable risks and returns. Two dangers loomed: First, many of these were designed to survive a finite probability of events – the danger of historically unprecedented (and thus unmodelable) circumstances was not fully appreciated. Second, combined through tight coupling, these instruments produced a complex system that could and did lead to what one practitioner called a "cascade of failure" (Bookstaber 2007). Whether any regulatory scheme could oversee this with a reasonable chance of averting crisis was open to question.

More or less accountability?

One of the principal criticisms levied against interventionist state policies was that they were prone to manipulation by government officials for political purposes. While such politically motivated economic manipulations can be egregious in authoritarian states (e.g., see Acemoglu 2005), even democracies can be pushed to implement short-sighted policies that leverage long-term economic health to buy political support (Alvarez et al. 1991; Olson 1982). By leveraging the resources of the state to control prices or aggregate flows, governments are able to distort economic activity in the short term to suit their own purposes, perhaps at the expense of the long-term interests of society as a whole. Financial liberalization is believed to have had the effect of constraining government choices (Andrews 1994), thereby subjecting the state to the discipline of market forces – making capitalism the "regulator of regulators."

Liberalization does not necessarily create a wide financial franchise that would produce a truly decentralized system of independent actors. Much capital is channeled through intermediaries, which concentrates its disposal into the hands of a smaller, mutually responsive group that faces constraints that are characteristic of the institutional investor business. Financial managers face pressures to focus on the short-term, take excessive risk, and have incentives to distort commonly cited metrics of fund performance for the purposes of attracting and retaining investors (Menkhoff 2002). Institutional investors may be prone to herding, perhaps more so than individual investors (Nofsinger and Sias 1999; Sias 2004). The dynamics of institutional investment may ultimately see better returns than individual investors and do other good things, such as help corporate governance by acting as a more effective counterweight to managers or help diversity risk to individual investors, but demands emanating from the exigencies of professional investor culture and workplace incentives may not help information dissemination (Menkhoff 2002), and may help decouple financial markets from the real economy (Menkhoff and Tolksdorf 2000).

A key question here is whether, after liberalization, the gravity of control over the financial economy resides with actors that have a greater obligation or constraint to operate in ways that benefit society, and do not use their position of power for self-interest at the expense of the commons. Some of the late twentieth century's reforms have been successful in instilling sober governance into the financial system. For example, control over the monetary system has increasingly been taken from the hands of elected officials and placed in the trust of independent central bankers, which appears to have resulted in lower inflation (Cukierman et al. 1992). However, independent central banking is not a "market solution" but a Weberian-bureaucratic one. In wide measure, de-regulation has resulted in the devolution of power to an intermediate class of institutional and wealthy investors, which were described above, and who are increasingly "regulated" by markets' "self-governance" (Soederberg 2008).

"Market discipline" works by fear – that those who take improper risk will be wiped out financially. Such fear does not operate well when decisions are made by intermediaries or agent-managers, who work with other people's money and can accrue personal fortunes in a manic run-up to a tragic crisis, and not lose those fortunes when their employers go bankrupt. Furthermore, despite Adam Smith's famous equation of economic freedom with general prosperity, it now seems quite clear that a privately run financial system can leverage national economic welfare for its own benefit, particularly if it assumes risks that it knows will have to be ultimately underwritten by governments. And, as crises like Enron and WorldCom suggest, managers, companies, and private-sector auditors may see economic interests in distorting the financial information that they release to the public. Private corporations' chief responsibility is to make profit for shareholders, not take care of society as a whole.

The specters of exploitation and exacerbated inequality

One of the principal benefits of financial market liberalization is that it encourages investment in enterprises with weaker credit, which typically are poorer and/or prone to financial problems. Thus, sub-prime mortgages or junk bonds help economically disadvantaged people buy homes or entrepreneurial firms borrow money. Capitalists may be willing to bear the risk in these investments because they can earn more money or demand contracts that more strongly favor investors. The problem is that these investment outlets *are* riskier, and thus more prone to default or collapse. For the world's very poor, which comprise a large proportion of the global population, access to formal capital markets may be very limited, so that a relaxation of credit or investment may not even extend far enough to reach them (Haber et al. 2003). In this sense, capital enfranchisement may help the developed world's disadvantaged, though these people might be considered to be part of the "global rich."

But, in developed countries, individual returns on economic growth have disproportionally favored those who are already wealthy. Although wage growth has been weak over the past few decades in richer societies, returns to investment have been strong. For example, since 1980, the Standard and Poor's 500 index of US equities multiplied in value over eleven times, while wages have only grown modestly. These returns accrue to those who are "in the market," who are typically those with funds to invest – the distribution of people's assets shift to high-yield financial investments as they grow wealthier (Bertaut and Starr-McCluer 2000). As a result, according to Campinale (2005), the poorest 60 percent of the United States experienced an average return to wealth that is approximately 1 percent, while the wealthiest 1 percent enjoyed returns to wealth exceeding 4.5 percent annually, an important factor contributing to rising wealth inequality. One response to this has been a call for increased financial market participation among poorer people, but such investment would require more savings, which is difficult in an environment of stagnating wages.

Finally, there is the question of financial liberalization's effects on the provision of government services, which are often ignored as a source of sustenance for many of the world's disadvantaged. Even if private finance has helped spur incomes among the world's disadvantaged – which is by no means a certainty – governments have faced chronic financial pressure that has pushed them to cut public sector jobs and government-provided essential goods and services. A key question facing analyses of financial liberalism's benefits is whether any gains to poorer people's wages must be spent on things that might have been provided to them without direct cost under alternative economic systems.

Dangerous Money

The wealth and poverty of nations usually has been explained as a product of what happens in the real economy, and not the financial one. The 2008 crisis decisively dispelled this notion. Financial problems can destroy real economic activity, just as financial exuberance can help fuel the engine of real economic growth. The financial economy is also very much its own beast. Its role-players, power structures, and operational mechanisms differ from those in other sectors of political-economy (like trade, production, consumption, governance, or military strength). In some respects, finance appears to exert its own influence over how these other sectors operate. The financial sector is an independent force in global capitalism.

Financial instability is the cost of our pursuit of increased economic opportunity through a more aggressive allocation of financial resources. It may be a desirable outcome if it ultimately makes us more prosperous, but financial liberalization's payoff has ultimately been disappointing in many respects, particularly for the developing world (Rodrik and Subramanian 2008). There is clearly a role for private finances in the process of economic development. It helps channel capital to new and venturesome enterprises, and does so in ways that help spread risk across markets. Exposure to markets helps transmit information, allocate capital into promising sectors that bureaucrats might not recognize or understand, and provides some pressure on governments to avoid bad policymaking decisions themselves. However, when financial markets are endowed with too much power, society becomes vulnerable to this market's own excesses.

4

Marketing and Consumption

Societal changes over 200 years have brought us into an era of unprecedented material wealth. Almost ninety years ago, John Maynard Keynes (1920) celebrated the then-impressive consumption opportunities available to the rich Londoner: *"any man of capacity or character at all exceeding the average [enjoys], at a low cost and with the least trouble, conveniences, comforts, and amenities beyond the compass of the richest and most powerful monarchs of other ages."* In many respects, what was a wonder to Keynes in 1920 is much more commonplace today. A kitchen filled with imported foods, leisurely international telephone conversations, or a trip abroad is now within the means of many more people. The servant Keynes dispatched to the bank has been replaced by the automatic teller, which dispenses dollars and even exotic currencies instantly, effortlessly, and cheaply. In the United States, there was such an economic bounty that Americans not only fought several years of war without having to endure serious cuts to consumption, but enjoyed government policies (and global willingness to lend) designed to spur *more* purchasing (at least until 2008).

Over the past quarter-century, global private consumption more than doubled from $13 trillion in 1982 to almost $29 trillion in 2007.[1] These changes represent a transformation to much of humanity's material lives. Between 1990 and 2006, per capita household consumption grew in the rich world at a rate of 1.8 percent annually. The global poor's raw capacity to consume is catching up to the rich world, but very slowly.[2] Growth was fastest in East and South Asia, followed by Eastern Europe. Elsewhere, consumption growth has been weaker and in sub-Saharan Africa, many societies experienced a contraction.

Where previously consumption was done on a local or a national arena, now it takes place worldwide; not only are more involved in the consumer trade, but the potential market for any product is likely to be much broader. This has also created, for the first time in history, the possibility of global consumption classes whose lifestyles are much more similar to their income counterparts across the globe than to their own co-nationals. The explosion in consumption has occurred with the same paradoxical qualities we have already noted in capitalism. Many people live in previously unimaginable wealth, yet millions still struggle in total destitution. Some societies worry about starvation, and others struggle with obesity. This chapter examines the bounty of today's consumer markets, the means by which this abundance was forged, and the possible societal implications of its development. The implications of these advancements may go beyond raw quantitative increases in the amount of stuff consumed, affecting culture and society.

Consumption, Consumerism, and Marketing

Consumption refers to the act of using the goods and services made available by an economic system. In the aggregate, global development has meant that millions of new consumers are joining and moving up the ranks of the "shopping classes," those with enough purchasing power to acquire products or "luxuries" less directly tied to basic survival. By some accounts, our cultures change with such newfound abundance. One of these changes is said to be associated with *consumerism*, a fixation or preoccupation with the acquisition of material goods as a means of seeking satisfaction or fulfillment in individuals' personal or social lives. Questions about consumerism often involve suggestions that there now exists an inordinate, if not detrimental, obsession with material acquisition in society.

What does consumerism have to do with capitalism per se? Some accounts of the modern consumer society stress the role that businesses have played in cultivating our consumer desires (e.g., Ewen 1976). In their quest to compete, survive, and prosper, businesses have developed sophisticated repertoires of techniques designed to collect information, organize production and delivery systems, and to manage people's worldviews and opinions. These activities represent some of the basic tools of *marketing*, the organizational function of planning and administering the development, production, distribution, and public image of products and brands. Marketing is a substantial presence in contemporary society, which attracts many societal resources, exerts a profound influence on managerial decision-making, and may play an important role in cultural change. There is little doubt that marketing – particularly advertising – is prevalent. In the United States, a typical urban-dweller has been estimated to see 5,000 advertising messages daily, up from 2,000 thirty years ago (Story 2007). Although the saturation of advertising is less obvious elsewhere, it has been growing globally. This kind of prevalence is bound to evoke questions about the practice's ultimate effects.

Consider the changes in the provision of venues for social interaction in modern life. Liz Cohen (1996) has stressed the increasing prominence of commercial spaces like shopping malls as physical venues of congregation in American suburbs, a change that appears to be taking place elsewhere (Abaza 2001; King 2004). According to many observers, the provision of public space has been in decline and appropriated by private interests (Cybriwsky 1999; Kohn 2004; Mitchell 2003). When the basic physical infrastructure of social life is built and operated by profit-seeking enterprises, we can expect the environment of social interaction to be replete with opportunities and subtle pressures to buy. Even in physical spaces provided or subsidized by government or non-profit enterprises (such as universities or parks) or virtual spaces of interaction (such as broadcast media or websites), financial strain can lead these proprietors to sell space to advertising, which reinforces our submersion into an environment with messages designed to induce consumption. At the same time, one could argue that the profit potential of commercialized space creates profit incentives to invest in space. The profit motives help create bright, shiny new malls where empty fields once existed.

Despite the aggregate effect, the effectiveness of *individual* marketing efforts are likely to be limited. Audiences are likely to avoid paying attention to the vast majority of messages to which they are exposed, be skeptical about the claims made by the messages they do absorb, and run into a variety of intervening factors that will prevent the path from advertising exposure to purchasing from being consummated, especially if they did not have a prior predilection to purchase the product. Studies suggest that other sources of information, chief among them a consumer's personal contacts, are much more valued by potential customers (Katz and Lazarsfeld 2006 [1955]). Despite anecdotes of wildly popular marketing campaigns that successfully spurred purchases of particular products, it is important to remember that millions of similar attempts, some of which are highly sophisticated and well-financed, are pitched to consumers daily, and most of them fall flat.

Furthermore, marketing can be seen as a means of creating products that better meet consumer expectations, and inform them of products that they might need or want. Most modern marketing techniques begin with research on consumers' desires, and, in so doing, they are helping create an economy that is responsive to popular demands – at least those that can be served profitably. As such, one can portray marketing as a force that makes influence run from society-at-large to industry, rather than the other way around. Furthermore, advertising may help inform consumers about innovations from which real benefits could be realized. Advertising about medications may help make people aware of potential cures to their ailments. New gadgets may provide people with valued convenience or enjoyment. Advertising can be portrayed as a form of consumer empowerment, insofar as it alerts people to potential consumption opportunities and equips them with information to better use their money.

One criticism of marketing's role in society merits additional consideration: manipulation. Manipulation involves systematic features of marketing practice or media content that spur people to make consumption decisions that neither reflect their endogenous preferences nor benefit them. Examples include deceptive advertising, the stimulation of unfounded fears or insecurities, or attempts to influence vulnerable people. It is easy to condemn egregious and clearly harmful cases of manipulation, such as encouraging children to smoke, and regulating and rendering liable marketers who engage in such practices is less likely to be controversial. The problem comes in navigating the subtleties of most practical cases, where the line between real and manufactured want is fuzzy and subject to debate. Manipulation is, however, not strictly a by-product of capitalism; it has been present in decidedly non-capitalist authoritarian states, and is a potential problem in any system in which the media is beholden to particular interest groups.

Under capitalism, the question of media manipulation by private business interests often evokes concerns about the effect of constructing a general media system that is financed by advertising. Some commentators have argued that the media's dependency on advertisers may foster a proclivity to convey, and a disincentive to criticize, representations of the world that value material acquisition and consumerism positively (e.g., see Shanahan and Morgan 1999).

One recent American example of marketing with potentially dire consequences is clearly relevant to our discussion of global capitalism. Over the past decade, the insistent deregulation of US financial markets has prompted financial firms to sell credit aggressively. The first widely accepted credit cards were developed by American Express and Diners Club in the 1950s, but the provision of consumer credit was tightly regulated in a variety of ways. Beginning in the 1980s, credit cards became ubiquitous, and by the twenty-first century over 160 million Americans owned at least one credit card and they charged close to $2 trillion annually (creditcard.com). More than half of these cardholders (or "members") carried a debit balance on their cards and the average debt per person was over $5,000. Overall, the average American had over $16,000 in consumer debt (excluding mortgages). These numbers were the product of an intense campaign meant to obtain a historically new type of mass consumer: not a purchaser of things, but a borrower of money. The search for profits by banks and the arguably manipulated consumerist desires to Americans (and to an extent all members of the developed world) produced both a buying frenzy and a mountain of bills. But, even here, any ethical condemnation must take into account how the creation of mass credit democratized consumption, and that the ultimate choice to over-borrow is the consumer's to make.

The Rise of the Modern Consumer Society

The modern consumer economy is the product of changes to technology, business practices, government policies, and social mores that have been occurring since the Industrial Revolution. Together, they formed part of a massive transition from societies that were rooted in rural living, local community, self-subsistence, and small-scale enterprise to complex, global, highly specialized, and highly productive (in an economic sense) social systems. A virtual spiral of growing production capability and aggregate consumption appetites led to the massive, commercial engine that is now an integral part of global society.

Antecedents

The Industrial Revolution led to societal changes that dramatically expanded our ability to extract and acquire resources, and manufacture and distribute products. Manufacturing, resource extraction, and transportation sectors came to be concentrated under large firms, although other sectors – like retailing – often remained populated by small enterprises during the nineteenth and early twentieth centuries (Strasser 1989). The revolution reconfigured material life in a variety of ways. First, it enriched large numbers of people in industrial countries. In the rich world, urban worker's wages began to rise by mid-century, and in turn their consumption rose rapidly (Feinstein 1998; Haupt 2004; Martin 1999). Outside of the rich world, the benefits of the global economy's development accrued to a more narrow class of elites. Concentration, mechanization, and increased productivity helped producers move large volumes of products over greater distances at lower costs (Tedlow 1993), creating an increasing abundance of cheap, standardized goods for markets.

These changes not only made more products affordable to larger cross-sections of society, but also acted to homogenize within product-class choices by populating store shelves with more products made by national or regional producers. While industrial concentration exerted a homogenizing force within specific product classes, the Industrial Revolution also fueled an economic growth and investment that led to the development and commercialization of a wider range of products. Box 4.1 offers a list of the major consumer product innovations of the pre-war era, many of which continue to be major industries today.

Expanding consumer choice also occurred as a result of improvements to distributional infrastructure, and newfound ways to source foreign products affordably. In this first wave of globalization, when these changes to production took place, non-industrializing countries supplied many of the inputs or commodities that made up the growing basket of goods in the rich world. Per capita sugar, tea, and coffee imports to Britain almost doubled over the nineteenth century (Mokyr 1988). Silk imports, principally from Japan and China (as well as Italy), tripled from 1870 to World War I (Federico 1996). Per capita exports from South America quadrupled over the second half of the nineteenth century, and rose as much as sixfold in Argentina (Bulmer-Thomas 1995).

There were social changes that occurred with this industrial transformation. At the beginning of the nineteenth century, material life was sustained largely by the home and local community. Food and clothing were often home-made, and many of life's amenities that could be acquired in markets were limited by what could be extracted and produced by hand and moved by a meager transportation infrastructure. Industrialization brought several changes in the organization of societies, such as urbanization and economic specialization. One of the principal ways that the Industrial Revolution purchased its prosperity was by streamlining

Box 4.1: Selected major consumer product innovations of the pre-war era

- Gas Stove (1802)
- Tin Cans (1810)
- Bicycle (1818)
- Refrigerator (1834)
- Revolver (1835)
- Sewing Machine (1836)
- Typewriter (1843)
- Telephone (1849)
- Light Bulb (1860)
- Pasteurization (1862)
- Roller Coaster (1865)
- Chewing Gum (1870)
- Jeans (1873)
- Phonograph (1877)
- Electric Fan (1882)
- Automobile (1885)
- Dishwasher (1886)
- Camera (1888)
- Zipper (1891)
- Radio (1893)
- Disposable Razor (1901)
- Vacuum Cleaner (1901)
- Television (1923)

individuals' productive activity, in the sense that a given individual would dedicate the work day to producing a single product or service. A household member who was employed by industry or commerce represented lost household labor and hence a lost capacity for self-subsistence production. This loss would be compensated by purchasing products in markets, thereby embedding households' subsistence into the web of commercial relations.

By the early twentieth century, further technological advancements, most notably the spread of assembly-line production, greatly expanded manufacturing output, creating a need for more consumer demand to absorb it. For observers like Ewen (1976), America's economic need to stimulate consumer demand was compounded by political needs to contain emerging power struggles between capitalists and working classes over control of production relations. Both the need to absorb a dramatically increased capacity for economic output and a need to gain support for the capitalist system were compounded by the events of the Great Depression and World War II. These events shook faith in the market system (Hobsbawm 1994) and left the industrialized countries with the need to convert massive wartime production operations to peaceful purposes. The redress was an intensified development of a consumer economy rooted in the logic of "mass markets," spurred in the pre-war era by private sector innovation and post-war government intervention.

Aided by ever-improving transportation infrastructures, manufacturers strove to extend their reach into markets across their countries and expand the size and scope of their operations, thereby enabling them to raise volumes, lower margins, and compete on cost (Tedlow 1993). Manufacturers engaged in struggles to control distribution chains, and started to wrestle consumer fidelity from the hands of local shopkeepers through the nascent tools of modern marketing. Marketing itself is argued to have developed an identity as its own field of practice, and its basic theoretical precepts were first developed then (Bartels 1976). Advertising and sales gimmicks had been in use for a long time (Stearns 2006), but became professionalized, systematic, and intensive. Firms began to develop elaborate forms of consumer research to refine their plans and sought to cultivate customers' insistence for particular brands, a change that undercut retailers' ability to influence consumer purchases and hence economic power (e.g., see Strasser 1989). An emerging financing market also helped by providing consumers with the ability to make big-ticket purchases through installment payments, and helped consumers acquire products that they might not otherwise have been able to buy (Calder 1999). These innovations would prove successful, and, by the post-war era, major manufacturers not only commanded power over consumer markets by virtue of their impressive productive capacity, but also by their wide recognition and ability to count on legions of brand-loyal consumers.

America's post-war era brought government into the business of spurring consumer markets. Then-reigning economic ideologies came to favor governments' intervention in markets, and the cultivation of robust consumer demand was seen as both a key impetus for post-war prosperity and a means of "winning the peace" (Cohen 2003; Viser 2001). This combination resulted in government efforts to purposively cultivate broad consumer markets, for example, through redistribution (Piketty and Saez 2003), subsidized home buying (Cohen 2003), and the expansion of consumer credit (Logemann 2008). Not all Western governments followed a similar path to developing mass markets. For example, Germans were reluctant to expand US-style consumer credit and both West German policymakers and unions acquiesced to restrained wage growth and inflation in the 1950s (Giersch, Paqué, and Schmieding 1992). There, as in Britain and probably other parts of Europe, the post-war recovery helped spur productivity, wage growth, and increased purchasing power, all of which spilled over into fast consumption growth by the mid-1950s (Kramper 2000). Despite these national variants, post-World War II changes to political economy gave rise to various government policies whose ultimate effects were increased resources channeled to middle and working classes, which helped spur mass markets. This group provided much stimulus to the producers and retailers who served them, and consumer markets underwent rapid growth.

More countries began to pursue industrialization actively over the mid-twentieth century, in part because the war destroyed former commodity exporters' foreign markets and worsened the prospects of commodity export-led development (e.g., see Rock 1987: 238–49), and partly as a result of new, highly influential economic policy ideologies that saw capital accumulation and the reinforcement of domestic demand as key means of enrichment. In some states, such as the Soviet Union or China, this industrialization was done coercively. The centrally organized Soviet system often neglected the development of consumer riches, although some awareness of the abundance offered by Western lifestyles remained. In China, the Maoist revolution had similar effects of suppressing consumer society, and the country's people were often pushed into material deprivation (Stearns 2006). In other developing countries, industrialization was an outgrowth of a policy logic that pursued national self-sufficiency, creating privileged classes of workers in protected industries and newly expanded public sectors. Whatever its roots and means of installation, industrialization meant that the world's stock of machines pumping out consumer goods increased, and more stuff was potentially made available to a wider range of societies. Policies emphasizing trade protectionism, however, limited the degree to which this enlarged pool of products was shared across borders, and the global consumer economy remained balkanized among states that often restricted consumer choice to national producers.

The immense economic prosperity of the post-war years brought many people further away from early nineteenth-century concerns about not being able to meet the basic necessities of life. In Japan, the early entrenchment of Western goods and some facets of Westernized lifestyles developed more haltingly until World War II, after which the influence of American culture and consumerism spread rapidly: "By the 1950s and 1960s, Japanese referred to the three Ss as major life goals: *sampuki, sentakuki* and *suihanki* (fan, washing machine, and electric rice cooker). But this soon yielded to the three Cs, derived from words meaning car, air conditioner and color TV, and then even the three Js – jewels, jetting and a house" (Stearns 2006: 96). In the United States, spending on non-necessities (i.e., other than housing, food, and clothing) had been rising as a proportion of household budgets since World War I, from around 21.8 percent in 1918 to 36 percent in 1960, to roughly 50 percent by 1984 (and remaining steady thereafter) (United States Bureau of Labor Statistics 2006). During the post-war era, car and home ownership increased markedly, people ate a wider variety of foods and frequented restaurants more often, purchased vacations and recreational vehicles, and spent more on entertainment, clothing, and personal care items in proportion to their fast-rising incomes (United States Bureau of Labor Statistics 2006). Similar gains in disposable income have been noted in other industrial countries (Kramper 2000). People were getting richer and shopping more in wealthier parts of the world.

Growing domestic markets meant that an expanding group of diverse customers were entering the shopping classes in well-to-do societies. This change prompted what Tedlow (1990) counts as one of the post-war era's great advances in consumer marketing: *market segmentation*. With segmentation, producers increasingly engage in the practice of breaking down mass markets into smaller sub-groups according to product preferences, and offering slight variations in product features, image, prices, etc. across these different groups. Marketers learned to identify differences in consumer demographics, lifestyles, motivations, morals, and decision-making processes, and devised ways to fine-tune different aspects of their strategies to suit these segments. Offering different product variations to different people made sense for several reasons. Broadcast media were proliferating, and different people were "plugging into" different aspects of national culture. Our expanding production capacities meant that we were probably able to produce too many units of basic products to be absorbed by consumer demand, and segmentation and product changes could help stimulate new businesses and lengthen the lifecycle of industries. It represented the continuation of unified national markets' breaking down, a process that would accelerate in the late twentieth century (Weiss 1994).

At the very time that consumption markets were segmented, they were also increasingly homogenized globally. Different marketing approaches could be used to appeal to different classes and "lifestyles," but these might be used in more than one country or even across the entire globe. Advertising slogans or symbols that had previously been part of a national culture could become part of a global idiom. Segmentation, which had been done "naturally" by cultural, social, political, and economic boundaries, now shifted to unite people across territorial lines, but also to divide them within these.

The post-1990 global consumer economy

Globalization and political-economic liberalization introduced millions of new participants into the global consumer economy. The Western lifestyle had offered Soviet-allied society an alternative social identity to emulate, and may have influenced economic transitions there (Stearns 2006). China has also experienced the rapid development of consumer abundance, as rising wages and international integration have helped foster an emerging class of Western-style consumers. In the Middle East, newfound wealth helped form demand for Western (or Western-style) products, but also ignited disaffect over perceptions of cultural invasion from a part of the world with whom many had long experienced tensions. Trade barriers were reduced worldwide, and many people gained better access to imports and new markets for exports, while everywhere local businesses faced international pressures. Products, firms, and domestic industries that managed to survive often adopted international orientations to procurement, production, and selling, and doing business meant surviving on an international stage. Internationally oriented firms were able to serve more markets, choose among a wider range of suppliers, enjoy larger economies of scale, more bargaining power, and marshal more resources to invest and market. Consumer choice was expanded by the introduction of new products, but was tempered by big businesses' absorption or forced dissolution of smaller firms.

A second important force shaping the global consumer economy has been the advancement in information technology, which created new means of communication and information exchange, with new venues for shopping and selling. The rapid proliferation of media outlets has not only meant that people in a given country now access different media outlets and are less exposed to a common national discourse, but has also eased people's access to foreign culture. Table 4.1 presents median media penetration scores across global regions. It shows how these technologies have made major inroads in the wealthy world, but still exert comparatively minor impact on poorer regions. This media furthered the consumption integration discussed before.

Table 4.1: Median Media Penetration across World Regions

Year	Telephones per 100 people				TV % households				Cell Phones per 100 people				Computers per 100 people				Internet Access per 100 people			
	1990	1995	2000	2005	1990	1995	2000	2005	1990	1995	2000	2005	1990	1995	2000	2005	1990	1995	2000	2005
E. Asia & Pacific	3	5	8	12	64	70	54	64	0	0	2	27	0	1	2	5	0	0	2	8
Eastern Europe	16	24	32	31	65	75	92	97	0	0	17	81	1	2	9	21	0	1	6	27
Ex-USSR	9	12	12	15	--	78	88	94	0	0	1	26	0	1	2	4	0	0	1	6
Lat. America & Carib.	7	12	17	16	73	67	76	82	0	0	8	46	1	2	5	8	0	0	4	16
Mid. East & N. Africa	5	8	11	15	52	82	87	92	0	0	7	47	0	1	4	6	0	0	2	12
OECD	46	51	55	50	87	89	97	98	1	7	65	98	9	20	36	60	2	2	30	53
South Asia	0	1	2	4	11	23	22	32	0	0	0	7	0	0	0	2	0	0	0	3
Sub-Sah.Africa	0	0	1	1	11	10	14	16	0	0	0	8	0	0	0	1	0	0	0	2

Source: World Bank (2007)

Whereas national markets might have been unified by shared consumption of their limited choices in radio or television programming decades ago, we now access a much more personalized mix of cultural content, and could have more in common with foreigners who share our own idiosyncratic tastes and interests. It may have also contributed to productivity gains that could theoretically drive down prices. Studies suggest that the positive productivity effects of information technology investments have occurred in rich countries, but not necessarily in developing ones (Dewan and Kraemer 2000).

Changes to purchasing power

Globalization and liberalization have had mixed effects on incomes. Typically, those who sat at the top of their societies' wealth pyramids, and those who lived in fast-growing economies, saw their purchasing power expand, while societies' disadvantaged – unskilled workers in the rich world and the global poor – often stagnated (Firebaugh 1999; Wood 2002). These trends suggest a basis for a growing market in luxury goods, whether they service the world's very rich or emerging economies' privileged customers. These markets have been the targets of global brands (Hassan and Katsanis 1994) and may be a key reason for Western brands' global success (see below). For lower-end customers in rich countries, stagnating wages can be expected to help producers who compete on price and low-cost structures. The global poor often lack strong purchasing power and have been experiencing weaker gains. In a sense, the global market became broadly segmented into three broad categories: luxury goods (e.g., Lotus or Maybach cars) for the top level, "first-world" consumables for the next (Fords or Fiats), and first-stage items for those on the bottom rung (motorcycles). Note, of course, that the majority of humanity was not a marketing target except at the most basic level.

With respect to prices, humanity's increasing aggregate production capacity is expected to lower them, to the extent that production growth outpaces population growth. Over the long run, this seems to be what has happened (e.g., see Firebaugh

2003: 59), but it is uncertain whether global liberalization has accelerated this process. Theoretically, reductions in trade barriers, global economies of scale, enhanced competition, and the cost savings from global sourcing are expected to further drive global prices down. Offsetting these gains is the potential for global price fixing, which has been observed in some markets (Connor 2001). Furthermore, consumers' purchasing power is mediated, and perhaps dominated, by exchange rate changes (Goldberg and Knetter 1996). By the early twenty-first century, at least, rising commodity prices, notably in fuel, food, and metals, offset some of the purchasing power gained by falling global prices. Given the importance of commodities to the prices of finished products (especially with increased costs of transporting products over the long distances often traveled in a globalized world), potential costs savings elsewhere may be imperiled. Inflation had been an ongoing policy concern before 2008, alongside the prospects of fuel crises and heightened food insecurity among the poor.

Global retail and global brands

As has been the case in production markets, retail has been in the process of concentrating globally, in which small retailers are often being displaced by cost-competitive, high-volume retailers. Two developments are particularly noteworthy: big box stores and Internet retailing. Big box stores – like America's Wal-Mart or France's Carrefour – are large retailers that economize on labor and storefront costs, secure inexpensive foreign supplies, and attempt to profit by selling at high volumes and low markups. Internet retailers do away with physical stores and much personnel cost. The effects of these new forms of retail competition are mixed. In one sense, they release consumers from the need to finance more expensive retail operations through higher prices. Furthermore, they have the capacity to increase the choices available to consumers. There are at least two potential stressors associated with these changes. First, these new forms of retail pressure traditional ones, and may hurt the jobs and profit recirculation which local retailers once may have provided. Second, big box stores may wield monopoly powers once other retailers are priced out of markets. Furthermore, powerful retailers like Wal-Mart may exert inordinate influence upstream on suppliers. Once these retailers gain power, it is unclear whether or not they abuse their economic position.[3]

The migration of manufacturing to the developing world led many firms in the rich world to understand themselves as managing brands rather than making products (Klein 2000). A firm focused on brand management will outsource the physical production and distribution of products, and instead concentrate on product design, promotional campaigns, customer relations, and supply chain management, with the ultimate goal of cultivating consumer demand that is willing to pay a premium for products bearing one's brand. A plain T-shirt may command eight or ten dollars on the US market, but, with a Nike swoosh or Lacoste alligator embroidered on it, can command three times such a price. This willingness to pay brand premia can represent a major profit center for a firm, which, given the cheap manufacturing options offered by developing countries in a globalized world, enables companies to expand their profit margins and release themselves from the economic burden of maintaining factories and employees.

Table 4.2 lists the twenty most valuable global brands, according to Interbrand (2007a). Under the march of globalization, many well-known firms have sought to shed physical production, and compete on the basis of brand strength. The late twentieth century marked the rise of the global brand, and multinational firms sought to capture markets by wielding the weight of the cultural prominence of their internationally recognized symbols.

These are brands with strong purchase on international markets (but "Citi" may no longer be after 2008–9). Some domestic brands in developing countries can also become quite valuable. For example, China's top two brands – China Mobile and Bank of China – were valued at roughly $35 and $10 billion, respectively (*Interbrand* and *BusinessWeek* 2007b), which places them in the company of these major global brands. Typically, however, developing countries' brands tend to be weaker, low-cost competitors that do not command strong trade-name premia.

Table 4.2: World's Most Global Valuable Brands 2007

Rank	Brand	Country	Brand Value (US bil)
1	Coca-Cola	USA	65.3
2	Microsoft	USA	58.7
3	IBM	USA	57.1
4	General Electric	USA	51.6
5	Nokia	Finland	33.7
6	Toyota	Japan	32.1
7	Intel	USA	31
8	McDonald's	USA	29.4
9	Disney	USA	29.2
10	Mercedes	Germany	23.6
11	Citi	USA	23.4
12	Hewlett-Packard	USA	22.2
13	BMW	Germany	21.6
14	Marlboro	USA	21.3
15	American Express	USA	20.8
16	Gillette	USA	20.4
17	Louis Vuitton	France	20.3
18	Cisco	USA	19.1
19	Honda	Japan	18
20	Google	USA	17.8

Source: Interbrand and BusinessWeek (2007a)

Dilemmas of the Modern Consumer Society

Humans like consuming products, and society is providing more stuff for us to consume. If we take a strong view that equates more consumption with a better life or society, it is easy to celebrate the increasing material comforts and amenities of modern life. However, this growth in human consumption need not deliver such unambiguous benefits, and some observers see much of our increasing consumption as being dedicated to superfluous or even damaging ends.

Proclamations, if not lamentations, of some societal preoccupation with material acquisition are a mainstay of social commentary. Plato's *Republic* impugns the masses *"who spend their time banqueting and similar indulgences"* and who, if not controlled by a non-acquisitive ruling class, will *"kick and butt . . . till they kill one another under the influence of ravenous appetites"* (Plato 1908: 326). Joan Thirsk (1978) (quoted in Campbell 1987: 28) notes that the taken-for-granted household goods of Adam Smith's day "had been condemned in the 1540s as childish frivolities or unnecessary, even harmful, indulgences." Consumerism has a long history of being construed as an abandonment of some popular spartanism that prized some set of non-material values in favor of satiating one's worldly appetites. Treating contemporary consumption in this way, as the product of modern people being non-ethical material *gourmands,* clearly runs the risk of value introjections and idealizing the past.

While there is little doubt that people now shop, own, and consume more than at any other time in history, a productive engagement of the modern consumer society requires us to go beyond simple concepts of "greed" and "materialism." They obfuscate the sociological mechanics of what is happening. The products that we consume are the material artifacts of broader social practices – the behavioral and cognitive scripts that we use to navigate the complexities of everyday practice (Warde 2005). Our consumption is often not oriented toward the specific utilitarian functions of the products themselves, but rather the role that they play as tools or props in activities oriented toward other goals. The salience of such an insight is that many changes in consumption may be by-products of wider changes in society at large. They are part of a broader package of economic and social transformations, and concerns about consumerism may signal an observer's stresses about such changes.

Take, for example, humanity's departure from small, tight-knit communities to social contexts that require interaction with strangers. As more of our interactions are with people whose reputations do not precede them, we are often forced to use other sources of information to determine the identity, status, and character of those with whom we interact. One way we do this is by using people's possessions as such a cue. An early study in this tradition was that of Thorstein Veblen (2001 [1899]), who highlighted an emerging class of nineteenth-century nouveau riche's overt display of material wealth as a means of broadcasting social status. Pierre Bourdieu (1984) suggested that social class is not simply transmitted through cues that suggest a raw ability to acquire expensive goods, but rather through consumption choices that suggest that a person has a particular *savoir faire* – a knowledge of which goods, services, interests, or tastes suggest a better "inside" knowledge of, and by implication stronger connection to, more elite cultures. All of this suggests that consumption choices are deployed in ways that signal identity, an activity that would probably be less necessary in social communities where individuals were well known to each other and where social status was already known by those with whom they interact in everyday life. In this way, capitalism has replaced complex, personally rooted means of forging status and identity with the more impersonal capacity to consume products. Some see this as a horrific depersonalization of human relations, but others see it as freeing us from the constraints of birth and making possible a world of choices.

When appraising the role and net benefits of global capitalism per se in this process, it is important to differentiate it from the effects of investment, technology, peace, or good governance, which are not necessarily implied by the presence of a more liberal economic system and greater material consumption. Unfettered markets provide no guarantees of things like technological advance or peace, nor are they the only means of securing them. It is also unfair to equate many problems – such as environmental degradation or the erosion of traditional values – to laissez-faire alone; government and popular sentiment also play important roles. The question at hand is whether economic liberalization and globalization help accelerate or retard these changes, or ultimately help or hurt other facets of our quality of life.

Consider the role of consumer society in creating demand that can sustain economic enterprises. Consumers' desires for what seem to be trivial purchases, such as video game consoles or ever-changing clothing fashions, mobilize global commodity chains that can enlist the services, and hence channel wages and profits to, producers across the world system. Video games sustain enterprises across the world, from chip manufacturers in China to programmers in India, to oil exporters who provide crucial inputs to plastic production (see Johns 2006). The prospects for profiting from consumers' propensity to regularly replace wardrobes can serve as an impetus for investment in Bangladeshi textile factories, Chinese sewing machine makers, or Brazilian cotton exporters (see Gereffi and Korzeniewicz 1994, for extended expositions of global commodity chains). In the absence of such industries, we might expect countries to lose opportunities to develop.

Beyond strengthening the economic bases for development, one might also consider the role that increasing consumption plays in fostering political stability. The link is tricky here, because the materially rich are not necessarily less inclined to political rebellion. Instability appears to materialize when economies are less prosperous than usual (Alesina et al. 1996), although it is a matter of debate what the specific reasons are for voters appearing to respond to macro-economic variables (Dorussen and Palmer 2002). What does seem clear is that political support appears to be responsive to people's sense of their prospects for continued and increasing material abundance, and the behavior of politicians in almost any democracy suggests a sense that voters are responsive to material inducements.

The link between consumption and prosperity and governments' re-election prospects creates incentives to spur consumption. Satisfying such demand can be difficult to accomplish to the extent that consumers' satisfaction is a matter of beating their expectations. If the goal is to improve consumption opportunities beyond what people typically expect, or to which they have become accustomed, then a society is faced with pursuing a moving target, trying to satiate an unquenchable appetite. At least two concerns with this persistent need to spur consumption merit mention. The first entails potential strains of ever-increasing consumption on natural resources or the environment. Human consumption uses natural resources and creates waste, which can present serious environmental concerns. If our consumption exhausts non-renewable resources or causes lasting damage to the world's ecosystem, our habits may damage our future material welfare and overall quality of life, not to mention the potential harm done to other living species. The price we pay for many of the goods we consume, and the profit we make from selling them, often do not consider the long-term natural costs of our choices. Indeed, we may be racking up large charges on an environmental credit card that may one day have to be settled. These issues are discussed at length in chapter 7, but are pertinent when evaluating the net benefit of the modern consumer economy.

Another concern involves using policies that over-stimulate consumer purchasing in untenable ways as discussed above. Relying on high consumption to spur domestic prosperity is used with particular intensity in the US, where relatively low taxes, interest rates, and fairly loose credit provision have led to near-zero national savings rates and mounting debt. America plays a similar role in the global economy, in which US imports drive much of the world's industry, but at the expense of chronic US trade deficits and foreign borrowing. In this way the structures of trade, finance, and marketing are clearly interlocked. Yet neither individuals nor countries can borrow forever, and overzealousness in bolstering consumer purchasing can run into excesses that lead to problems like today's global financial crisis and emerging recession. It may be that relying too strongly on aggressive consumption can help prompt boom-and-bust cycles, exacerbate instability, and cause much hardship. These are concerns that should be considered by any country that seeks to emulate the US consumer-driven economic model, or rely on a world system that depends on such high American demand.

Just as the formation of national markets created commonalities in the everyday life of people within countries, so have today's global brands become artifacts of an increasingly interconnected globe, and perhaps a force of worldwide social homogenization (Mansvelt 2005). The visible penetration of foreign products and brands into new markets has been seen as a kind of invasion into the cultural fabric of societies. The sight of old, national brands being purchased or displaced by foreign multinationals can reasonably evoke sentiments of lost national autonomy, with concerns that these rich world's products and marketing may also be covertly transporting cultural changes that will "Westernize" societies and import what are perceived to be the social ills that plague countries.

Global brands not only populate the shelves of the world's stores, but also fill informational flows through marketers' efforts to transport messages and promotional techniques across borders. In an effort to economize on international marketing expenditures, producers have sought ways to standardize their market offerings across countries. This kind of strategy runs against traditional notions of tailoring one's marketing strategy to local tastes, and can amplify the sense of international marketing as a form of foreign cultural invasion. However, a sense of "foreignness" is desirable in many markets and to many consumers, and may contribute to the formation of transnational similarities in material lifestyles. Given that most of these brands are Western, some observers see the transportation of products and advertising across countries as agents of cultural change that cause a loss of local culture and tradition. The emergence of global consumer economy can be seen as a force that homogenizes material life, though the intensity of this homogenization should not be exaggerated. Scholars have had different expectations of how culture might react to these changes, with some expecting a global homogenization of consumer tastes, others a balkanization of global markets into transnational segments based on region, demographics, psychographics, lifestyles, and attitudes, and still others maintaining that national differences will continue to be a dominant means of sorting customers (Hassan and Katsanis 1994).

Despite the fact that we now live in an era of unprecedented flows of symbols, products, and people, Held and McGrew (1999: ch. 7) offer a strong case for tempering expectations that Western culture is reaching out to absorb the world's people. First, the trans-community spread of culture is nothing new. Past eras have seen attempts to spread religious, national, or imperial (like Roman or British) identities and practices, and did so when the sponsors of such efforts had the means and inclination to propagate culture coercively combined with better methods of excluding alternative informational flows. Today's societies face any outside cultural forces armed with resources to counteract their influence, such as culturally protective government policy or an information technology infrastructure that eases grassroots cultural production and transmission. Even without these resources, past efforts at cultural assimilation did not succeed in erasing local culture. In fact, they often needed to afford space for local culture to continue in order to avoid outright rejection, and current marketers' practices in national market segmentation operate in similar ways.

Furthermore, one might reasonably question whether concerns about the effect of global-reaching, Western-rooted cultural imperialism is really replacing true "grassroots" culture, rather than some other agents' means of cultural domination. For those who live under political or religious regimes that systematically disempower the cultural practices of one's personal status groups – e.g., ethnic minorities, women, homosexuals, secularists, liberals, and so on – the fraying of old dominant cultures can be seen as something that affords social "breathing space" in which one's personal worldviews, beliefs, and activities can be represented, shared, and perhaps less stifled. Indeed, culture exists through reproduction, and perceptions of Westernization can be understood as the product of some degree of acceptance and contribution among those in the receiving culture.

Consumer satisfaction and well-being

Perhaps the ultimate question facing a critical analysis of the modern global consumer society is whether our lives are better for these changes. This question requires us to develop some metric of quality of life, which can be bound up with a range of analytical difficulties and value judgments. To the extent that our quality of life is determined by the products we consume, increasing consumption can be seen as part of building the "Good Society," and a noble project that releases us from the specters of want and discomfort. Beyond the satisfaction of basic needs essential to survival, however, appraisals of rising consumption run into philosophical questions about what constitutes the "good life" and the relationship between material and non-material aspects of our quality of life.

Some criteria can be taken as objective, such as longevity, health, or literacy, although most observers would maintain that these are very minimal standards for measuring quality of life, and it is difficult to determine the independent effect of the consumer economy net of things such as infrastructure development, good governance, or general prosperity. Alternatively, we could consider people's sense of satisfaction with their lives. If we do, how should we approach the prospect of such measures being plagued by methodological concerns and possibly influenced by low expectations or non-consumption factors? Beyond these basic metrics, we venture into quagmires. In assessing the "good life," to what degree should we consider the availability of luxury and comfort, fidelity to and strength of nation or religion, maintenance of morality, ability to meet personal aspirations or realize personal potential, or to engage in truly meaningful pursuits? How would we even define these things, let alone agree on their importance to standards of living?

Research suggests that richer societies are, for the most part, more satisfied and healthier, but a closer examination of the data evokes important questions (Pew, World Bank 2007). First, recall that consumption is closely related to general economic wealth. A wealthy country can use its resources to channel more consumption products to people, as is done in America, or it can use some of these resources to create well-financed public goods and services. For its impressive levels of private consumption relative to other wealthy countries, America does not appear to have similarly impressive levels of subjective satisfaction or longevity. This suggests that wealthier societies may enjoy better quality of life, but, beyond some particular threshold of consumption, the rate of return in satisfaction per dollar declines.

The benefits of enhancing consumer opportunity are most apparent when we consider differences among developing countries, but it is still not clear whether it is the effect of more consumption or more wealth in general. Very poor countries appear to be plagued with severe health problems and less satisfaction with their lot. The contrast between China and other developing countries is striking. Despite the fact that per capita Chinese consumption is only a fifth of the typical middle-income country, its quality of life indicators appear somewhat comparable. This may be an artifact of methodological difficulties, but could also suggest that non-consumer market factors, such as governance or a general sense of societal advance, may be important to welfare. Likewise, the high degree of reported satisfaction in countries like Mexico or Venezuela suggests that there is more to being at peace with one's life than satisfying consumer appetites.

Costs of Desire

We live in an age of unprecedented material abundance. Some of this abundance seems to be a product of global capitalism's march, but other forces are at work. Private enterprises' search for profit fueled the great technological advances that help fill our material lives, but so did the advance of literacy, science, and government investment. Modern marketing is impressive, but is its influence really about the techniques of advertising or the raw power of modern media technology and infrastructure?

Private property and free markets are not the only way to feed the world's desires for products. Government can also invest and finance innovation, and many of today's most successful consumer markets have some roots in state-sponsored technology and public contracts. Human nature might be such that we are prone to huge appetites without the inducement of well-financed private marketing. Still, global capitalism has produced an independent effect on the evolution of global consumption. It provided incentives for private investment, helped industry develop its presently massive economies of scale, and it opened the doors to foreign resources and foreign markets. It may also have created a lifestyle with perpetually unsatiated needs and wants. In comparison to all other forms of organizing a society's economy, no system has produced as much wealth as has been produced under capitalism, but this does not mean capitalism has made us happier.

5

Governance

Economic governance refers to the formal and de facto rules that politics and governments impose on other actors' economic activities, and how the state uses its capacities and resources to shape economic life. Although governments can try to manipulate almost any sphere of the economy, there is often considerable disagreement over whether they should do so. Debates concentrating on the trade-offs involved in government interventionism versus laissez-faire are a recurrent feature of contemporary policy debates. Although some researchers deride such debates as simplistic and dated (e.g., Block 1994), public sphere perceptions of this trade-off do impact policy. In periods of widespread political, scholarly, or popular antipathy toward markets and private enterprise, governments have been elected on platforms that propose using the state's power to check business interests or correct their failings. Where government corruption or incompetence is blamed for problems, political power can be gained by taking anti-government stances. While social scientists can reasonably question the validity or usefulness of seeing economic problems as the result of bad balances between states versus markets, the influence of such discourses is hard to deny.

States and Markets

We often discuss markets and governments as analytically distinct or even antithetical spheres of society, yet this sense that states and markets are separate is relatively novel in the history of human civilization. Over much of our history, politics and economics were fused (Finley 1999). Trade was a subsidiary activity in a global system largely rooted in serf, peasant, and slave agriculture. Resources moved between societies more by military conquest than by free exchange. Labor was rarely free and land rarely for sale. Markets came to be a way that we organize economic activity in large measure over roughly the past two centuries. Rather than being an intrinsic feature of human economic organization, the free market system is a novel human construction. Markets' power is a product of our collective choosing, rather than a force of nature. In many respects, this choice has been made by states through the institutions they create (such as money, property rights, contracting law, and so on). As the capitalist system depends on these state-created institutions to exist, we may ask whether it makes sense to see markets as existing apart from government and society.

In some respects, conceptualizing states and markets as independent, antagonistic forces is a by-product of how these arguments are principally employed in political, rather than scholarly, discourse. In its crudest form, partisan discussants mount stock arguments favoring the disempowerment of the public or private sector by postulating that the same sector is prone to self-seeking or ineptitude that sacrifices national economic well-being. For example, mid-century interventionism was often framed as a means for politicians to accept bribes, secure their power, or act out narcissistic fantasies of being able to steer capably something as large, complex, and unwieldy as a national economy. Likewise, an opposing position characterizes de-regulation as enabling capitalists' malfeasance, and portrays globalization as an invitation to exploitation.

Those who evoke such arguments almost invariably deny the fact that basically *anyone* in a position of power – in either the public or private sector – can abuse their influence for personal gain. Even moderately sized social systems will ultimately have to endow someone with such power (Michels 1999 [1915]). Corruption is always a threat. Likewise, a simplistic portrayal of public or private sector (or foreigner or domestic elites') incompetency and malfeasance misses the fact that, over the past century, both kinds of actors have run economies into the ground, but have also overseen moments of great prosperity.

Karl Polanyi (1944) famously argued that market systems are "embedded" in society. The concept of *embeddedness* denotes a kind of primacy in determining how social systems are organized, and to say that markets are embedded in society suggests that non-market factors will shape how markets are organized and determine the limits of markets' influence over society. Polanyi's *Great Transformation* illustrates this point by showing how extramarket concerns shaped the institutionalization of the market system, and ultimately led to its breakdown in the early twentieth century. This particular notion of embeddedness can be contrasted with perspectives that see markets as autonomous organizational entities, whose inner workings dictate changes to other spheres of society.

"Society" is a residual category that includes almost any social movement that can materialize to uphold or disrupt the market system. Such movements have rallied around innumerable causes – class, occupational status, nation, race, ethnicity, religion, gender, or some other status demarcating a sense of shared social, political, or economic interests. At particular points in time, status groups that have previously championed liberal economic principles have sought to squash it in others. For example, the bourgeoisie that contributed to economic emancipation from landed nobilities in the late eighteenth century later worked against political movements that sought to give laborers the right to walk away from employment contracts before their expiration (Hobsbawm 1969, 1975). Likewise, the Roman Catholic Church, which acted as a conservative force against liberal reforms during the nineteenth century, played an important role in emancipating Eastern Europeans from communism in the late twentieth century. Capitalism has always been fraught with social conflict over its extension or scaling back, and the focal issues and participants of these debates change continually. What does not seem to change is the importance of the state, which acts as an arena for these conflicts and ultimately puts their resolution into action. Economies are shaped when coalitions successfully grab the levers of state power and use them to redefine production, consumption, and ownership. The country-specific idiosyncrasies of these conflicts help explain why specific forms of capitalism vary comparatively and historically.

The influence, of course, runs in both directions. We know that the presence of prosperity or crisis in markets influences state and society. Democratic governments tend to be re-elected when economic growth is strong and inflation is contained (Chappell and Viega 2000; Lewis-Beck, Nadeau, and Belanger 2004; Lewis-Beck and Stegmaier 2000). Economic crises often de-stabilize social order and political regimes. Particular interest groups' fortunes in markets endow them with resources and power to influence government policy, and others find that their lack of fortunes can render them more politically inert. Markets do exert some kind of societal influence, even when they take the shape of black markets under regimes of hard market suppression, as under Soviet communism during the mid-twentieth century or in drug, prostitution, or weapons markets today. Some observers even see private economic enterprise as having played a role in the institutionalization of the modern state (Tilly 1990; Weber 1978), meaning that markets helped construct the modern state, just as the latter helped build the former. These institutions not only exert mutual influence, but also share a history of mutual construction.

In the end, governance is important because states are the most influential actors in the global economy. Not only do they tend to marshal more money, personnel, or property than any other kind of actor, but they also create and guarantee the basic institutions upon which markets depend in order to work as intended. Even resources that are not directly allocated by the state are still influenced by the laws that governments impose. And even where states fail to do things like provide fungible money, guarantee private property, enforce contracts, or impose regulation, their influence is still felt by the possession of coercive power, which helps guarantee a basic set of rules and level of social order upon which capitalism depends. When states are unable to impose even such basic order, or abuse this power, economies on any basis other than barter or piracy may simply disappear. Whether they are strong, benevolent, feeble, or abusive, states exert a profound influence over how capitalism works.

World Governance?

In this chapter we will largely focus on governance within states as opposed to global orders. This merits some explanation and also provides an opportunity to establish critical aspects of the governance of capitalism. Simply said, there is no global governance. With some exceptions noted below, governance of capitalism is constrained by the same territorial limits of all law. Capitalism may be practiced globally, but it is ruled nationally.

Despite significant convergence on some aspects of corporate governance and even more technical agreements on accounting rules and the like, there are no consistent and uniform rules presiding over global transactions. In the end, the vast majority of disputes must be settled in the national courts of a country. This means that the failure of any single state to enforce its own rules (or to reasonably match the rules established by other states) can easily de-stabilize the system. So, for example, the failure of Liberia to impose any kind of control over the ships officially registered with that country means that a significant part of global transport operates without any regulatory oversight. Similarly, the lack of oversight over some financial institutions in the US made the global financial system much more fragile even in countries whose institutions worked under stricter regimes.

Governments exercise sovereign power over their jurisdictions, which is to say that they are the ultimate legal authorities within their countries. They guard this authority jealously, often accountable only to those who keep them in office (e.g., voters, domestic elites, or foreign sponsors essential to maintaining power). During the twentieth century, there emerged a wide range of highly visible organizations whose purposes were to direct governments' use of their policymaking power. In the realm of economic policy, some of the better-known organizations include the United Nations, Organization for Economic Cooperation and Development (OECD), World Bank, World Trade Organization (WTO), International Monetary Fund (IMF), Group of 7 (G7), and Bank for International Settlements (BIS), but many more exist. Often, such agencies are portrayed as agents of economic globalization and liberalization, which forced unwilling or unknowing governments to adopt laissez-faire reform. Such a characterization may be fair only in a very limited set of circumstances and in a highly simplistic sense.

An alternative way of understanding international governance organizations is through the lens of the practical challenges and complexities involved in making policy. Governments make their own policies, and in large measure they choose to participate in these organizations and follow their dictates. Where IMF or OECD directives are being institutionalized into law or policy, what we are seeing is an example of institutional isomorphism (DiMaggio and Powell 1983). The impetus for following these directives can be as varied in economic governance as in any isomorphic process. Understanding these different impetuses can help us move past simplistic depictions of these agencies as US or Western cronies who propagate economically liberal ideologies.

Often, governments participate in international governance organizations, and take their directives seriously in the policymaking process, because they help countries overcome the economic costs and practical difficulties of not cooperating with each other. These agencies can act as facilitators that help countries develop policies that make it easier to trade or invest in each other, or coordinate action to realize collective goals. For example, EU or WTO policy that harmonizes government regulation in food content or labeling means that a food producer can enjoy economies of scale by producing a standard product that can be sold continent- or worldwide without being forced to tailor its production process or repackage its goods for particular markets. Likewise, G20 negotiations can serve as a venue in which the world's major economies can develop a coordinated, non-contradictory response to a crisis. These are examples of *rational isomorphism*, policies that spread because they save economic costs or waste, and could reasonably be expected to raise economic efficiency. Such cases of isomorphism suggest that the influence of governance organizations exists because national governments see a clear economic benefit to following their agenda.

Under some circumstances, these agencies can push policy changes coercively, but these influences are rare. *Coercive isomorphism* involves policy changes that occur because governments are pressured with negative sanctions if they resist. The paradigmatic case of coercive isomorphism under global capitalism[1] via these agencies is IMF conditionality, in which the IMF demands policy reforms from a government afflicted by financial crisis. IMF conditionality is visible in part because it is an exception to the rule. In reality, governance organizations rarely have the resources or power to coerce governments alone, unless they are acting on behalf of or in concert with other powerful governments or financial institutions.

We should also note a hybrid form of isomorphic pressure combining elements of rational and coercive. If we consider the pressures on some economies in the 1980s and 1990s, and the need to satisfy the strictures of global capital in order to obtain financing, the line between these two is blurred. Governments were rational in that they accepted measures in order to obtain the necessary capital, but given the absence of alternatives (once the socialist bloc could no longer play geopolitics with subsidies) there remained a coercive or at least monopolistic element that could not be ignored.

Mimetic isomorphism is a third potential way in which international governance agencies can influence policy, although their role here can be portrayed as merely facilitating an outside source of policy change. This type of isomorphism occurs in contexts where governments cannot define or agree on how to engage and resolve a pressing policy problem. Despite their vast investment in economics research and the apparent sophistication of our knowledge, economies are tremendously complex, and our ability to comprehend them fully and steer them precisely is very limited. Often, problems materialize that cannot be solved easily by existing policymaking models. Under such circumstances, organizations (including states) often try to mimic the behavior of similar organizations that seem to be faring well or appear to know more in the face of common difficulties.

One can see the broad embrace of free trade in the early 1990s in this light. Those who portray free trade as simply imposed by capitalist ideology or US policy directives, pushed via agencies such as the World Bank and IMF, often neglect the context in which these policy changes occurred. Developing countries' economic interventionism was premised on the idea that such interventions would enable them to develop globally competitive economic enterprises after some period of incubation. By the 1980s, not only was it patently clear that economic insularity did not produce globally competitive enterprises, but it may have created a policy environment that triggered government bankruptcy and massive financial collapse. Only the export-oriented emerging economies of East Asia bucked this trend, thereby serving as a real world alternative policy model of how poorer countries could develop.

One has to wonder whether failed import-substituting or socialist economies would have reformed in this direction had they not been so desperate and had a policy success story that did not involve exporting been available. Trade (particularly export) liberalization was among the few unambiguous, truly global policy changes realized in the 1990s (see Cohen and Centeno 2006), despite the large chorus of voices expounding other forms of liberalization. This reinforces the sense that many of the policy changes attributed to force or manipulation from agencies such as the IMF or World Bank may have been derived by developing country governments' own desperate attempts to emulate Taiwan or Korea. Under these circumstances, one might wonder whether the IMF or World Bank were creating policy directives that swayed governments, or whether they merely discussed real world policy successes that other governments may have been inclined to mimic anyway.

This is not to suggest that the recommendations of economists at the IMF, World Bank, or anywhere else do not exert an independent influence on governments' policymaking. A fourth form of isomorphism is *normative isomorphism*, which is a form of policy diffusion that is sanctioned by social authorities that are taken to hold authoritative knowledge about best practices. In economic policy, such authority figures are almost exclusively professional economists,[2] and many of these international governance organizations operate as economic research institutes in addition to acting as brokers or facilitators for intergovernmental negotiations. There is little doubt that major organizations such as the IMF and World Bank house economists of strong professional stature, and that their voices are heard in the policy analysis community. What is unclear is whether the collective voices of the economics profession have provided a substantial part of the impetus motivating globalization and liberalization.

Governance in the Twentieth Century

Perhaps the most important contradiction facing global capitalism is that it operates in the paradoxical legal space: transactions are global, but laws are not. Many of the problems discussed in this book – from capital flows to cultural diffusion, from inequality to environmental limits – may require a very different form of governance. For now, however, we are stuck with the governance of capital through the nation-state.

Over the twentieth century, global capitalism is often understood to have passed through three distinct "regimes" of governance, in which the relationship between states and their economies have differed in clear, identifiable ways. The century began as a continuation of nineteenth-century patterns of governance, in which states were smaller and operated within a narrower sphere of operations. Economic governance was more "hands off" compared to today, in the sense that governments purposely left much of society's economic activity to be determined by private actors.

Until World War I, governments spent little compared to the overall size of their economies. Even under severe wartime conditions, such as the US Civil War, government outlays generally did not breach 10 percent of nominal GDP. These low spending levels are indicative of economic systems in which governments provided relatively few goods and services, and employed relatively few people. Economies were dominated by private enterprise.

An enduring structural shift in economic governance occurred after the Great Depression and World War II, events that foreran dramatic expansions in the size and scope of government operations (as suggested by the growth in their expenditures relative to the overall economy) and in turn the degree to which they influenced the overall economy. The reasons for this shift are complex, but can be reasonably synopsized as involving a profound, broad-based loss of confidence in the benevolence of free market systems, a political shift in which governments deemed it desirable to micro-manage their economies, and the experience of wartime mobilization that made the state's tight orchestration of economic production and distribution seem practical.

This style of post-war governance is often known as *interventionism*, a means of economic management in which governments "intervened" in private economic activity with the intent of pushing the economy toward state-defined goals. Interventionism would take many concrete forms, including Keynesian-inspired macroeconomic management, more stringent and actively enforced government regulation, major expansions of the welfare state, the provision of new government-backed economic insurances, and increased public sector employment, investment, and goods and services provision. In many ways, today's economies still operate in the legacy of these post-Depression changes. In the United States, for instance, agencies such as the Federal Deposit Insurance Corporation (1933), Tennessee Valley Authority (1933), Securities and Exchanges Commission (1934), Federal Communications Commission (1934), Federal Housing Administration (1934), National Labor Relations Board (1935), the Social Security Administration (1935), or the Civil Aeronautics Authority (1938) were formed in this period.

Much like the Great Depression led to a broad-based backlash against then-reigning classical liberal (or laissez-faire) paradigms of economic governance (Dobbin 1993), a period of protracted and severe global stagflation set the stage for the displacement of government interventionism during the 1970s and 1980s.

Government over-reach came to be seen as the root cause of economic stagnancy and instability, and the apparent failure of then-traditional economic policy redresses to that period's chronically slow growth, high inflation, and high unemployment helped fuel a broad-based doubt, if not antipathy, toward interventionism. This resurgence and re-legitimation of laissez-faire governance paradigms, often termed "neoliberalism" to denote a sense that it resuscitates the principles of pre-Depression economic liberalism (Portes 1997), made early inroads in the English-speaking world and then in other wealthy countries.

The combination of changing economic-theoretic currents, the continued spectacle of failing governments, the collapse of the Soviet Union, and prominent interpretations of export-oriented Asian countries' economic successes, hardened attitudes favoring free market reform among outside observers, including some elite and mass constituencies in developing countries (Armijo and Faucher 2002; Bruton 1998; Snowdon, Vane, and Wynarczyk 1994; Williamson 1990a; Yergin and Stanislaw 1998). These reforms were further advanced (but not totally forced) by financial help offered by rich governments that was made contingent on liberalization reforms, notably the 1989 US Brady Plan (see Edwards 1995) or IMF conditionality in their loans (Dreher 2008).

During the 1980s and 1990s, the world economy underwent clear changes that scaled back governments' economic control and released private enterprise from many of the post-war regulatory and policy practices that had previously constrained them. Over the past quarter-century, countries embraced many, but not all, forms of liberalization. Between 1985 and 2005, societies appeared to scale back the size of their governments aggressively, and their engagement of a range of market reforms designed to increase the influence of market forces is well established (see Bruton 1998). This occurred at slightly different times in different regions. The contours of these developments can be illustrated with references to data that attempt to create broad liberalism indexes, such as the Economic Freedom Network's *Economic Freedom of the World* (Gwartney and Lawson 2007), presented in Figures 5.1 and 5.2. These measure the degree to which a country's government:

Governance

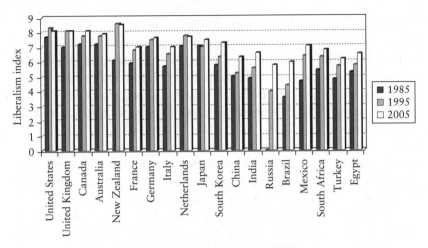

Source: Gwartney and Lawson (2007)

Figure 5.1 Liberalism by country

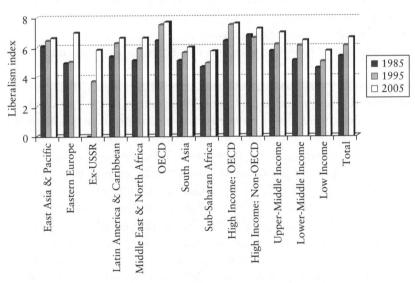

Source: Gwartney and Lawson (2007)

Figure 5.2 Liberalism by region

(1) maintains small and limited government; (2) imposes low taxes; (3) offers secure property rights and rule of law; (4) presides over a stable monetary system; (5) refrains from regulating or taxing trade; and (6) refrains from regulating credit, labor, and business markets.[3] Although any index is quite rough, it is a reasonable proxy, and demonstrates marked changes over the twenty years depicted.

The United States is often taken as a bulwark of global economic liberalization, due to its immense political, economic, and intellectual influence, and the importance of libertarian-influenced economics in its history. America positioned itself as a champion of capitalism in the Cold War, and acted as a force that conditioned interventionism among its mid-century allies. The Soviet Union's collapse seemed to vindicate market-based organization, which, coupled with perceptions of America's economic resiliency under Reaganomics, endowed any American-led liberalization effort with much credibility. Transitioning economies from Latin America to the former Warsaw Pact not only turned to America for advice, but also for direct funding.

American attitudes toward non-interventionist economic policies in many ways reflected a quarter-century of strong Republican rule and "Third Way" Clintonian liberalism (Weir 2001), which embraced free market tenets. Yet American antipathy toward, or reluctance to engage in, government intervention appears to be partial, variable, and relative rather than wholehearted, unanimous, and absolute. Polls show that a wide range of Americans have viewed some government attempts to manipulate markets favorably, for example, in welfare provision (Hasenfeld and Rafferty 1989), trade (Mooney 2008), or perhaps banking regulation today. Even US economists almost universally (97 percent) see government intervention as playing *some* potentially positive role, and, if any bias among them exists, it slightly favors intervention (Klein and Stern 2007). Notwithstanding these qualifications, the American political process has resulted in substantial moves toward market liberalization over much of the last thirty years.

Britain's role in laying the groundwork for global non-interventionism trends was substantial. Most obviously, there is the significance of the Thatcher Revolution, which first put liberalism at center stage of global political culture (Harvey 2005; Yergin and Stanislaw 1998). The other English-speaking major economies quickly followed the Anglo-American non-interventionist model during the 1980s under the governments of Canada's Brian Mulroney, New Zealand's David Lange, and Australia's Bob Hawke. Together, these countries formed a powerful and influential clique in the international political economy. In terms of formal power within major international organizations, they occupied three seats at the G7, a guaranteed presence in the IMF and World Bank directorates, and, most importantly, the threat of governmental non-cooperation from a bloc of large economies with unquestionable power (if not dominance) over global financial markets. This sway influenced the practicality of any effort to coordinate international economic policy.

The European and Asian OECD, alongside developing countries, exhibited more reluctance to liberalize their economies across the board.[4] Continental European governments, for example, have a clearer propensity to insulate the labor and business sectors from market forces, but embrace free trade to the extent that the rich Anglos do. Asian OECD countries seem reluctant to liberalize labor or financial markets. Developing countries are generally more interventionist, though Latin American countries show some proclivity toward liberalization, a view that concords with Rodrik's (1996) characterization of that region as having embraced the "Washington Consensus" with much gusto.

Eastern Europe stands as the world's most aggressively liberalizing region from 1995 to 2005. In part, this is due to the rejection of its own pre-1989 order and the desire to move away from it as much as possible. We also need to take into account the European Union's influence. Clearly, EU integration requires releasing at least some fetters on international trade and capital movement, because other EU members are still foreign countries. Furthermore, wealthier countries tended to be generally more liberal from the outset, and any harmonization between Eastern and Western Europe's policies involved the former emulating the latter. Eastern

Europe's continued momentum toward labor de-regulation may be at least partly attributable to harmonization.

Rethinking orthodoxy

Since the mid-1990s, questions about the net benefit of liberalization reforms writ large began to percolate (e.g., see Rodrik 1996), and developing countries showed some retreat from liberalization in capital and business markets, though overall government reduction continued. The specific reasons for this waxing and waning momentum are uncertain, but several credible speculations can be made.

Perhaps the most important factor in explaining this dissipation in liberal enthusiasm involves waning perceptions about the direct payoffs of embracing raw capitalism, even before 2008. Many of the reforms that took place near the Cold War's end occurred in a context of high enthusiasm about the market's capacity to spur prosperity. This enthusiasm was partly based on the firmness with which prevailing economic opinion had established a link between market liberalization and on the resolution of economic problems that had plagued countries during the 1980s Debt Crisis and the Warsaw Pact collapses (Sachs 1989).

In a sense, the successes experienced under liberalization also abated some of the needs that drove countries to liberalize. For example, liberalization made great strides toward quelling the hyperinflation that plagued much of the developing world during the 1980s (Cohen and Centeno 2006). By the end of the 1980s, developing countries were desperate for financial help to quell inflation, and there are some indications that inflation-related concerns helped tip developing countries' politics in favor of free market reform (Armijo and Faucher 2002). Without the strong impetus to meet conditionality demands for financial lifejackets, selling further liberalization to a polity that had always had reservations became more difficult.

In the early twenty-first century, interventionism seems to have regained traction in trade and business sectors, which may be partly explained by political factors. The two forms of de-regulation can be slowed for at least two reasons. First, very poor countries often rely on trade tariffs for state revenue, which may explain why the world's poorest countries seem so inimical to free trade. Second, trade and business regulations are bound to affect powerful political constituencies, who may be better equipped to combat particular regulatory changes. Power politics may also explain variation in government reduction or labor de-regulation across countries. For example, where unions (including public sector ones) are strong and garner public support, repealing mid-twentieth-century labor and union protection laws may be difficult.

There is a sense of history repeating itself in 2009, as the financial crisis of 2008 and its resulting economic contraction mark the climax of a roughly decade-long erosion in the credibility of laissez-faire economic governance. Concerns about the failures of free trade and capital flows, privatization, de-regulation, and so on – basically, concerns about excessive market power in organizing the economy – are now resurfacing, and governments seemed poised to retake control over the economy. The potential for a return to interventionism is palpable in identifiable debates over public banking insurance and banking nationalization, controlling global financial markets, closing borders to foreign finance and migrants, reforming public education and social services, or bailing out bankrupt businesses. From today's vantage point, these new governance models appear to be grappling with two key issues: (1) the desirability of reintroducing government interventionism; and (2) the importance of improving the degree to which government officials use their power well and in the service of public interests.

What are the "Right Policies"?

Can differences in interventionism or liberalism be shown to have generalizable effects on society? On any specific issue, the winners and losers of a particular proposed policy intervention can be relatively easy to identify. Considerably more intricacy is involved in developing aggregate measures. It is very difficult to unwind empirically the role that government intervention, or the decision to avoid intervention, plays in creating specific political or economic outcomes (such as economic growth, inequality, democracy, or standard-of-living improvements) and, as mentioned earlier, many question the validity of any such dichotomous comparisons. Each "all-encompassing" theory has had its fifteen minutes of fame (Wacziarg 2002: 907) and then faded away.

There are several problems with assessing real world cases as examples of interventionism's benevolence or harmfulness. One difficulty involves outside influences. For example, in societies with rampant abuse of public office or a crumbling state, it is hard to determine whether economic problems are rooted in intervention itself or are the product of a context that would also lead non-interventionist policies to fail as well. Likewise, it is hard to say whether a stable, rule-bound market system is prosperous because it is liberal, socially stable, or governed by laws. Laissez-faire is only one factor that has shaped our political-economic systems, and it is hard to identify, schematize, measure, or assess its impact net of the many other factors that could be leading to economic changes. Dozens of other factors could conceivably be at play in questions about economic growth alone. If all of these factors are potentially relevant, all must be controlled for in an experiment that assesses the effect of interventionism on economic growth. These difficulties may make arriving at a single answer to the question of "right policies" analytically impossible.

More profoundly, people are going to have non-resolvable disagreements about the ultimate goals toward which policy should be oriented, which is likely to be an insurmountable barrier to reaching consensus conclusions on the net benefit of interventionism. In a large number of policy debates, there are many raw emotions and value judgments involved, and science is not equipped to provide definitive answers to value-related questions (Weber 1949). These problems in reaching definitive conclusions may help explain why political economists have been grappling with these questions since the days of Adam Smith. They will never be resolved entirely. At best, we can enumerate some of the potential benefits and drawbacks of government interventionism, assess these relationships empirically as best we can, and leave individuals to make their own judgments.

Three fairly non-controversial goals

Below, we provide very rough assessments on the coincidence of government interventionism and three relatively non-controversial societal goals: economic growth, longevity, and literacy. These outcomes were chosen because they are relatively non-controversial, not because they are many people's policy priorities. Voters and policymakers may have other principal concerns. Table 5.1 compares societies' performance toward achieving these three goals against the degree to which they liberalized from 1995 to 2005. These sector-specific liberalization indices are drawn directly from Gwartney and Lawson (2007), who outline the specific metrics used to discern these scores. In any given sector, countries that moved further toward limited government, deregulation, private property, and market-determined outcomes were considered to have liberalized more.

The data suggest that countries with the largest and most influential governments (i.e., least liberal in terms of "size of government") are the richest, longest-living, and most literate, and have realized the strongest gains over the past decade on the first two goals. Large governments and regulated labor markets are common features of rich democracies.[5] Here, we have an example of societies' appearing to benefit from initially being interventionist, but it is unclear from this comparison whether it is interventionism itself that steers certain forms of development or whether we are seeing the effects of being wealthy or democratic. We could, of course, control for these factors in a regression model, but, in so doing, we introduce new questions about the effects of wealth or democracy per se, or factors that tend to be present in these types of societies, such as high value-added industry, productivity, diversification, education, control of corruption, infrastructure, and so on. We could regress infinitely in this way. The same uncertainty exists when we consider the relationship between trade, capital market, or

Table 5.1: Growth, Governance, Life Expectancy and Literacy by 1995 Deregulation Score Terciles

Sector	Tercile of Liberalization, 1995 – 2005†	Per Capita GDP 2005	Δ	Life Expectancy 2005	Δ	Literacy* 2005	Δ
Size of	–	$5,230	2.5%	74	0.3%	93	0.4%
Government	0	$2,444	2.3%	72	0.3%	81	0.8%
	+	$1,765	1.7%	68	0.4%	85	0.6%
	–	$4,981	2.4%	74	0.3%	NA	
Trade	0	$16,054	2.3%	79	0.3%		
	+	$21,515	2.0%	79	0.3%		
	–	$5,714	3.0%	75	0.4%	NA	
Capital	0	$23,788	1.9%	79	0.3%		
	+	$16,054	2.0%	78	0.3%		
	–	$24,324	2.7%	79	0.3%	NA	
Labor	0	$14,593	2.2%	78	0.3%		
	+	$4,496	2.0%	73	0.3%		
	–	$8,986	2.4%	76	0.3%	NA	
Business	0	$23,151	2.3%	79	0.3%		
	+	$8,094	2.3%	78	0.4%		
	–	$2,107	2.7%	71	0.4%	88	1.0%
Overall	0	$3,994	1.8%	72	0.3%	81	0.8%
	+	$4,403	2.0%	74	0.3%	89	0.3%

†Interpretation of tercile symbols: (+) = largest positive change in liberalization index from 1995–2005
(0) = middle tercile of change magnitude,(–) = smallest positive/largest negative change
*For literacy, all change scores between 1990 and 2005 due to data availability. Trade, capital, labor and business regulation were generally assessed after 1995, and are not included in literacy assessments due to inadequate data. NA = estimates not available due to missing data.

Sources: Gwartney and Lawson (2007), World Bank (2007), Kaufmann, Kraay and Mastruzzi (2005).

business liberalization, all of which appear to be a rich country's game.

What about *changes* in relative liberalism? The data suggest that the aggressiveness with which liberalization was pursued also varies with the degree to which countries were already rich, democratic, and developed, but questions about the direction of causality remain. Countries that scored well on our policy outcomes in 2005 also scored well in 1995, and it is unclear whether their initial conditions bore effects that override the effects of changes in interventionism and liberalism. Disentangling these relationships requires more sophisticated analyses, which lie outside of the scope of this chapter, but some observations can be made. First, countries that were wealthier and better developed tended to eschew reductions in the size of government, and realized the strongest economic growth in this period. They tended to realize the smallest gains in longevity and literacy, but also had the least room for improvement. Life expectancy did not differ by the degree to which countries liberalized in this or any sector. Labor liberalization also appears to have been embraced by poorer countries, while the wealthy countries that avoided such reforms grew at a significantly faster rate (according to pairwise t-tests for differences in group means).

Trade liberalization was most enthusiastically embraced by wealthier countries, but countries that resisted trade liberalization grew marginally faster, though not significantly so. Countries that eschewed capital market liberalization enjoyed more economic growth and faster democratization, but it is important to remember that these inferences are drawn from small samples. For labor markets, wealthy countries resisted de-regulation, and enjoyed a marginally insignificant faster rate of economic growth. Business de-regulation did not appear to impact these policy outcomes.

The economic crises of the 1970s/80s and of 2008 suggest that both interventionist and more liberal systems are vulnerable to catastrophic shortcomings, just as the great advances realized in the 1950s, 1960s, and 1990s suggest that either organizational configuration can be beneficial. If twentieth-century economic history offers any clear lessons, it is that both governments and market forces are powerful organizational mechanisms. It is impractical to try to suppress them entirely, and somewhat mindless to try to stamp them out in any form in which they might appear. The task at hand is to harness their capacity to do good, but, at the same time, contain them, lest those who wield power over these mechanisms abuse it to profit at the expense of society at large.

Focusing on state capacity

Indicators of economic policies not only contain measures that suggest governments' degree of permissiveness granted to private business, but also institutional factors such as judicial independence, court impartiality, or the subjugation of the military to civilian rule. Like large governments, regulated labor markets, or de-regulated business markets, these characteristics are generally present in rich democracies. We thus need to be careful about conflating good government with good policy. Bolstering rule of law or court impartiality are policy directives whose linkages with free market economics are tenuous at best – perhaps limited to the latter's reliance on the former – and presenting these former factors as somehow being constitutive measures of "economic freedom" in some "free market" sense is a total misread of what such measures actually say.

Containing governmental power was an important sentiment motivating many of liberalization's proponents in the 1970s and 1980s. The basic idea underlying this sentiment was that interventionism concentrated too much power under the control of state institutions, presenting a tempting opportunity for public officials to reap personal political or monetary benefit (Hayek 1944; Krueger 1974), or delusions of *grandeur*. Those who subscribe to these lines of reasoning certainly have many real world examples at their disposal. At the same time, the behavior of private sector elites, from Russian oligarchs to Wall Street bankers, has demonstrated that government service does not have a monopoly on rent-seeking, corruption, or opportunistic malfeasance.

Hopefully, policy is exercised by prudent, competent, and professional practitioners, using sound, consensus policy practices with society at large's best interests at heart. Arguably, post-war interventionism and neoliberalism were the formulations of well-reasoned policy professionals, but their actual implementation may have ultimately been plagued by political conditions that took intendedly modest policy directives to places its original architects did not foresee. For example, theorists might have envisioned post-communist Russia as benefitting from a robust private sector, but might not have expected a rushed, weakly planned transition to such a privatized economy (Stiglitz 2002). Laissez-faire was often proposed out of a sentiment favoring the relinquishment of an over-burdened mid-century system of government micro-management, but relatively few serious scholars considered that the need for regulatory oversight should be ignored. Many of the neoliberal experiments' failings are likely to have been a product of their implementation, leaving us with questions about how much of the late twentieth century's economic problems are the result of poor execution. For many observers, answering these questions involves looking at how governments work, including how specific policy decisions are reached and implemented.

Those who emphasize the effect of politics and the government's organization on the actual effects of policy often focus on aspects such as political accountability, political stability, rule of law, control of corruption, or bureaucratic professionalism. Kaufmann, Kraay, and Mastruzzi (2007) offer a well-known empirical index of these factors, which is derived largely from meta-analyses of surveys in which experts, policymakers, and international businesspeople subjectively assess political-institutional conditions across countries.[6]

Voice and Accountability suggests the degree to which a political system makes governments subject to popular oversight, for example, through the presents of democratic elections or guarantees of civil and political rights. Presumably, such accountability pressures governments to placate the populace, forcing them to engage in policies that benefit large portions of society at a minimum. Where such accountability is absent – for example, in authoritarian or franchise- or rights-restricted regimes – officials face fewer barriers or risks in enacting policies that are widely seen as undesirable by the public. Voice and accountability is strongest in the rich world, although some variation exists within this group. Denmark , Finland , New Zealand , and Norway register scores suggesting the most accountable governments of the rich world, while countries such as Japan, Italy, Spain, and the United States have voice and accountability scores that are commensurate with some countries at the next income level such as Chile or Hungary. Overall, developing countries are substantially less accountable and democratic, with the Middle East/North Africa and ex-USSR being the most authoritarian regions in the world. Authoritarianism and poverty seem to coincide, although the causal relationship is unclear given the fact that East Asian countries are generally less democratic and more prosperous. The relationship between democracy and development, independent of effects related to corruption or lawlessness, is a matter of longstanding, unresolved debate (Przeworski and Limongi 1993).

Political stability and the absence of violence suggests a situation in which a political system is not vulnerable to extra-constitutional rebellion or overthrow, or a disintegration of its ability to maintain societal order. Again, rich OECD countries are the most stable, while South Asia, sub-Saharan Africa, and the Middle East/North Africa are the least stable. Stability can benefit a country's economy in at least two ways: by creating an environment that is amenable to long-term planning and investment, and by creating a system in which the transfer of political power is a lower-stakes endeavor that does not make political regimes more desperate to maintain their rule at any cost.

Long-term planning and investment suffers in politically volatile countries for many reasons. Because of this, investors are generally reluctant to invest in unstable countries unless these investments can be withdrawn quickly and easily. Unfortunately, longer-term investments are important to help poorer economies develop. In more extreme cases, severe instability can put states into a position where it deems it fit to destroy parts of its own economy. Acemoglu (2005) calls these "winner-take-all" systems, whereby political systems offer nearly unlimited power for leaders to profit and punish their competitors. Competition in such systems can be aggressive to the point that those in power face incentives to destroy the economic bases of their competitors.

Finally, fragile governments often lack the ability to secure general order, enabling crime and violence to become a problem.

Even when crime does not result in the destruction of human and physical resources, it can lead to the diversion of resources away from production toward expenses such as the financing of private security or payment for extortion. All of these outlays are resources that are lost in the pursuit of building a greater economic capacity.

Rule of law and *control of corruption* are similar concepts, and their scores are highly correlated. A strong rule of law denotes a situation in which impersonal law takes precedence over rules derived at the discretion of powerful people. When law is not well codified and its application not highly proceduralized, economic life suffers from a form of uncertainty associated with the personal whims and agenda of society's powerful actors. This not only makes long-term investment less attractive, but also opens a door to corruption, which is public officials' use of their status for personal gain. Corruption can result in severe resource drains as a result of direct embezzlement, as well as policies designed to help politicians' clients, even at the expense of general welfare. Rule of law and control of corruption is strongest in the rich world except perhaps in Greece and Italy, whose scores are commensurate with better-governed developing countries.

Finally, *governmental effectiveness* refers to the "competence of the bureaucracy and the quality of public service delivery" (Kaufmann 2007). Such competence is highest in the OECD, Eastern Europe, and East Asia. Clearly, any country would like to have an "effective" government, but conceptualizing good governance in this way does not offer clear reform prescriptions that a country can pursue to reach this goal. One promising take on this problem is pursued by Evans and Rausch (1999), who assess states by the degree to which their governments resemble the Weberian ideal-typical bureaucracy. Weber (1978) postulated that governments could be organized in forms that structure bureaucrats' behavior in ways that would direct their decision-making toward a sound pursuit of public interest, such as meritocratic hiring, the professionalization of public officialdom, lifetime employment, subjugation to government superiors, and the dominance of impersonal rules. Their results suggest that "Weberian" bureaucracies generally preside over faster-growing economies. Unfortunately, their study is limited in its coverage of countries and has not been collected longitudinally, but more research along these lines could be helpful.

Rule of Rules

The 2008 credit market crisis is the apex of a roughly fifteen-year period of chronic outbursts in financial instability attributable to free markets themselves. What is special about this crisis is that it has affected almost everyone, and appears to have triggered major economic problems that may be of long duration. Perhaps most importantly, its effects are being felt among neoliberalism's chief architect and proponent countries, and, at present, there appear to be no actors of serious consequence that are not poised to pull back from the economic liberalization of the previous two decades.

The extent of the pendulum swing that will follow depends on many factors, especially the length and depth of the upcoming recession. Even if the worst of this crisis has already passed, it has already affected politics and popular perceptions – and probably scholarly perceptions as well – and we are likely entering a period of new, deep economic reforms. These reforms are probably going to involve at least two agenda: reintroducing government controls over the economy and perhaps reforms of governments themselves.

If the crisis exerts strongly negative effects for a long time, we might expect mounting animosity toward the previous thirty years' free market reforms, and may see more governments yielding to demands to contain capitalism's destructive effects. There is also the prospect of markets or sectors collapsing (as in America's auto industry), which may require governments to step in and assume greater economic control. Without doubt, there will remain a chorus of voices opposing more intervention as governments over-reach (as there were during the Great Depression), pointing to the problems of the 1970s and 1980s as cautionary tales. The influence of these dissenting voices will be determined by the many factors that shape politics on almost any issue. Whatever happens, however, public sphere discussants would serve their societies well by steering clear of simplistic state-versus-markets framings of these issues. Their usefulness is limited, and there are better ways to think through these policy dilemmas.

Finally, it is important to recall that most of the discussion on the governance of global capitalism retains the territorial basis of the nation-state. One point that became clear throughout 2009 was that policing one's own finance sector may provide little protection from the effects stemming from the failures of a neighbor to do so. One of the central challenges facing global capitalism is to design new forms of governance to function on the same scale and scope as the transactions they are supposed to be policing.

6

Inequality

From its very beginnings, the question of fairness has haunted capitalism. Did it reward the worthy, the lucky, the powerful, or the unscrupulous? Many of the debates regarding the last twenty years of globalization and the future of the system come down to the same old questions of inequality: how much of it is acceptable and to what extent is it a tolerable product of global integration?

In its simplest terms, *inequality* denotes unevenness in the distribution of resources, wealth, or opportunities. Although the meaning of the term itself is rather straightforward, debates concerning its necessity or desirability are more complicated. Observers can have very different views on whether the world is becoming more unequal, whether inequality is avoidable, or even whether we would want to do away with it (Held and Kaya 2007). On the one hand, there is the classic liberal argument that reducing government barriers to global integration, or reducing opportunity for government patronage, results in equality of opportunity between people regardless of their political identity. According to this view, by creating an unfettered and global market of individuals we enhance the aggregate probability of each getting what he or she merits. On the other hand, opponents of globalization claim that the equality of opportunity in a free global market is a fiction, that these changes have only benefited the wealthy, and that the very process of linking economies and societies has actually produced a more unequal distribution.

Can both sides be right? Can the spread of global capitalism both enhance and retard economic inequality? Precisely because inequality is a relational concept, the answer may be yes. For example, freer trade flows may decrease between-country inequality (by allowing workers in poorer countries a chance to compete), but increase within-country inequality (by decimating wealthier countries' labor opportunities and by creating pockets of prosperity within poorer countries). In order to better address these issues, several important points regarding inequality must be clarified.

First, although pure equality is an absolute concept, it exists nowhere and is probably impossible to achieve. As a result, this issue must be addressed comparatively. The burning questions are not whether or not we are or should be equal, but rather how unequal our economy is in comparison to others, how satisfied we are with prevailing trends, and how much we should invest in trying to engineer a more equal society (if at all). This is an important consideration, as we cannot practically use notions of perfect equality to guide our thinking, but must always place it into a context of rules, expectations, and other conditions.

Compounding these difficulties is the fact that equality is also very much a matter of perception, and bound up with (if not conflated with) discussions of fairness (see Firebaugh 2003). What differences in status or resources are significant? What distinctions are legitimate? What sources of inequality are acceptable? To argue that equality is in the eye of the beholder is not to dismiss its importance. Recent evidence, for example, indicates that our sense of happiness and well-being is closely tied to comparisons with those around us, and that, past a certain level, more riches do not result in greater happiness if all others obtain them as well. Similarly, studies of rebellions and mass movements long ago discovered the critical importance of "relative deprivation": it is not how badly off you are that matters, but how poorly you feel about how you fare compared to your reference group.

Most importantly, we need to distinguish inequality from poverty. The latter is a social fact that can be measured by the absence of basic goods (but the definition of "basic goods" is in itself very technologically and socially elastic). Inequality can exist even within a world in which all are provided with at least the minimum, or even in a society of the hyper-rich. The complaint that "your yacht is bigger than mine" may sound absurd, but it is nevertheless a perfectly correct expression of inequality. This distinction is particularly important in the debate on globalization and the consequences of globalized capitalism. Many times, advocates of the different sides speak past each other by talking of prosperity and inequality simultaneously. We need to separate these two. As we have seen in previous chapters, global capitalism has brought many rewards for large parts of the world. Yet this may have actually worsened the realities and perceptions of inequality, and it is this debate that may present the most serious political challenge for the current system.

Such a perspective invites another round of questions. What weight do we assign to differences in well-being as opposed to the absolute measures of economic bounty? If all are getting rich, how much does it matter that some are getting richer, faster? How to take into account the psychological dissatisfaction of comparison? To what degree should we be concerned with domestic inequality when a country has so little wealth that even a perfect redistribution would leave everyone quite poor?

If these issues were not difficult enough, there is also the old debate regarding opportunity versus outcome. Many might be willing to accept some inequality in the latter if assured of equality in the former, and argue that de-prioritizing inequality actually enriches everyone more quickly in the long term. Others reject such distinctions and contend that significant socio-economic gulfs between populations or even individuals are illegitimate in and of themselves. Within the debate on globalization, we find parallel debates on whether the fate of individual economies reflects their particular endowments and efforts, or is more a product of historical legacies and injustices.

Yet another critical question concerns what is to be distributed or measured (Therborn 2006). The largest part of the inequality debate deals with the distribution of economic resources, whether as wealth or income (an important distinction). Thus, much of the discussion regarding the effects of globalization analyzes relative prosperity using a variety of measures. But there are other possible measures of material inequality. Years of life are perhaps the most basic currency we can compare, as are causes of death (e.g. cancer vs diarrhea), or the probability of surviving infancy. Our chances of achieving a defined level of material or physical well-being are also not just a function of our economic position or role, but include the heritage of our race, ethnicity, and gender. In a global world still defined by national jurisdictions, one's citizenship or residency may be one of the most important forms of distinction and one of the most significant determinants of life outcomes.

When discussing inequality and globalization, the unit of analysis is critical. First, it is important to distinguish within and between country inequality, and global capitalism has arguably affected both. The first refers to differences within a specific national, or regional population – for example, have some Americans become richer or poorer faster than others? The second compares the relative position of different countries within a global spectrum – for example, have Nigerians become poorer compared to the French? While we will address some aspects of within-country inequality, most of our emphasis is on the still much larger element of between-country inequities.

Second, there exists another major debate in the field of global inequality between those who focus on the distribution between societies and those who emphasize distribution across the 6½ billion individuals in the globe irrespective of where they live (Milanovic 2006). Basically the debate comes down to whether we "weigh" the income figures by population or not. For the latter, Firebaugh (1999, 2003) argues that global inequality is diminishing as a result of the rapid growth being experienced in China and India; since these two societies represent a third of humanity, their rapid economic improvements mark an equalization of economic conditions on a person-by-person basis. However, one can look at the same set of facts and ask whether the world is indeed become more equal if this robust growth is not really occurring outside of China or India, or if some countries (no matter their populations) are falling behind others. Despite the predictions that the world would converge on a more equal spectrum of income, it has actually become more polarized and there is increasing inequality between countries (Firebaugh 2000; Korzeniewicz and Moran 1996). There also exists a technical debate regarding the measurement of income between those who favor the use of simple dollar values and those who argue for figures adjusted to the relative purchasing power within specific countries (PPP). (The latter usually results in higher income figures for poorer countries and thus lower global inequality.) For our purposes the unadjusted dollar figure provides a clearer picture of global gulfs.

A Pyramid of Money

Our discussion begins with the simplest level of analysis, comparing the relative economic performances of societies (Held and Kaya 2007). Note that much of the discussion has to do with income as opposed to wealth. In general, there is a wider gulf in the latter given the distribution of capital, factories, research facilities, and communication centers in a few countries.[1] Because of the problems with wealth data, however, we focus on the amount of money generated per year, per person as the best means to compare distribution. We will then analyze differences within these societies and welfare measures. Using that base, we can then discuss the role globalization plays in defining these outcomes.

At the crudest level, the world is a very unequal place.[2] There is a general consensus that the global Gini index[3] (the most used measure of inequality) is above 60 and many say it is closer to 70, higher than that found in even the most unequal countries (Milanovic 2006). Expressed another way, one sixth of humanity receives more than three-quarters of all the income.

We can crudely divide the world between haves, have-nots, and some societies in-between. As before, we will focus on geographical divisions. This is not to deny global class divides, but, as should be clear from the material below, geography still accounts for a large part of our economic destiny. Of course, national income numbers hide many things. Per capita figures are nothing more than aggregate estimates and do not take into account internal distributions within their respective societies; income is not perfectly distributed by country, but through individuals and households. Despite these cautions, there is a clear gulf between societies that make it to a pre-defined floor of income and those far below it.

At the very top we have the twenty-five wealthiest economies, whose per capita national incomes were above US $20,000 in 2005. This group consists almost exclusively of countries in Northwest Europe and its predominantly white colonial offshoots in North America and Oceania. Of the top twenty-five richest countries in the world (with a total population of around 880 million), the only exceptions to this geographical pattern are Japan, the island economies of Hong Kong and Singapore, and Qatar and Kuwait. With some variations, these countries have achieved a level of material wealth unimagined by our richest ancestors. For those at the economic bottom of these countries (again with important variations and exceptions), the basic conditions of life are guaranteed and even the middle sectors lead what can only be called luxurious existences.

The next twenty-five countries (or the global upper-middle) have a population of roughly 300 million and GDP per capita of $7,000–$20,000. Many of these countries share the same basic material assurances, but with greater economic pressures on those on the bottom and middle sectors. Because of the lower income and the (often) higher inequality, those on the bottom in these countries live more like their counterparts in poorer societies than like their own co-nationals. This category consists of several ex-socialist countries, some Latin American ones, and a few oil producers with larger populations. With these two categories we account for only 20 percent of humanity, but over 80 percent of the annual income generated.

Another billion people live in the next fifty countries in what may be called the global middle (with incomes ranging from $2,000 to $7,000) where a small percentage of the population can enjoy the same qualities of life as in the richest countries, but where the majority live with material deprivation and, more than anything else, insecurity. The main source of poverty in these countries is not their relative global position, but their internal distribution of income. Most Latin Americans live in such countries, as well as the populations in richer African states and poorer oil producers.

With the inclusion of this class, we now account for one third of humanity, but 90 percent of the income.

China is immediately below this category (with a 2005 GDP per capita of US $1,700 or PPP $7,000), adding a further 1.3 billion people. The inclusion of China in any geographical category is fraught with problems. The Chinese boom has had truly incredible effects on the global distribution of income by individuals. Treating it as an aggregate country, however, ignores the dramatic regional inequalities that define the Chinese society. In fact, we may find gulfs as wide inside China as exist in the globe altogether.

The other half of the world's population lives in the remaining eighty-plus countries and shares the remaining 5 percent of global income. In this last category, we can witness the greatest disparities in internal distributions, with the urban upper class of say Bolivia or Pakistan (with a GDP per capita of US $1,000 or PPP $2,500) being able to enjoy the lifestyles of the rich in the wealthiest countries, while the vast majority of their populations live in serious hardship. Towards the low end of this group (the poorest 700 million people in the world), only a few thousand or even hundreds in each country can be said to enjoy an approximation of the global lifestyle and many live each day on less than what the average person in the wealthy countries pays for a cup of coffee (Collier 2007). In sub-Saharan Africa, 78 percent live under the international poverty line of $2 per day, and 46.6 percent live with less than $1 per day. For the poorer countries in Asia and Latin America, the numbers can be as high as 80 percent and 37 percent (Nepal and Nicaragua). India (accounting for 1.2 billion people, including a vast majority of poor) includes regional and social examples of all of these categories and would perhaps be best not treated as an aggregate.

A more challenging (but arguably less precise) method with which to measure global inequality is to create a truly global sample, taking into account external *and* internal inequalities. From this perspective, the distribution of income in the world is shaped like a sharply sloping hill with a small percentage at the top claiming the best view: the richest 10 percent of the world has 53

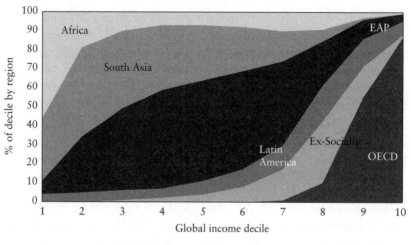

Source: Dikhanov (2005)

Figure 6.1 Where the poor and rich live

percent of the income and the richest 20 percent, 73 percent. The regional distribution is also quite skewed, with the richest concentrated in the wealthiest countries and the poorest in sub-Saharan Africa and South Asia (Dikhanov 2005). In the graph in Figure 6.1 we try to take into account both domestic and international income distributions to give a sense of how the global pie is cut. It is clear that while regions have a variety of levels of income, the global poorest (the bottom decile) consists overwhelmingly of Africans (56 percent) and South Asians (33 percent), while the global rich come overwhelmingly from the OECD (87 percent). Inversely, most Africans are poor (67 percent are in the bottom two global deciles) and most of those living in the OECD are rich (94 percent are in the top two deciles). Overall, there is no doubt that one's basic life chances are to a significant extent determined by where one is born. No matter the rise of some of the poorer societies, the gulf between nations explains roughly 70 percent of global inequality.

Despite these global divisions, however, a significant amount of inequality comes from differences between those that share a country or origin or residence (Milanovic 2006). Put another way, the richest of the poor countries may still be better off materially than the poorest of the richest countries. Thus, relatively poor countries can have their billionaires (at least until 2008): according to *Forbes Magazine* in 2007, Mexico had 10, Brazil 18, India 53, Hong Kong and China 67, and Russia 87. The United States had the most billionaires with 469. As this list of countries demonstrates, inequality is not only a function of the gulf between countries, but the manner in which wealth is distributed within them.

The global distribution of domestic inequality to a large extent parallels that of income, but conforms to the general pattern of the Kuznets curve.[4] The line in the figure below represents the relationship between development broadly understood (the UNDP's HDI[5]) and Gini. The rich countries of the OECD (with some exceptions such as the US) tend to be the most domestically equal. In such places, the richest fifth of the population will make anywhere between three and six times that of the bottom fifth. The next group of middle-income countries tends to have very high Ginis. Latin America as well as many of the most recent commercial boomers such as China dominate this group. Ginis here can approach or even surpass 50 and the ratio of the richest to the poorest is in the mid-teens. Towards the bottom of the scale, measurement of both development and inequality become increasingly problematic, but the latter seems to go down somewhat. At the very bottom are countries where absolute poverty *and* inequality go hand in hand.

One further unit of analysis provides a useful and revealing perspective on how geographical and individual factors combine to help determine a person's place inside the global pyramid. Regional inequality within countries is a pronounced characteristic in every part of the world. In the poorest countries, the contrast is between the small islands of plenty in the best neighborhoods of the capital and the rest of society. These isolated territories of wealth are often surrounded by walls and private security and in many cases can be literally next to appalling slums. The different fates of children living on either side of the walls serves as a perfect illustration of the tensions and challenges associated with inequality.

Inequality

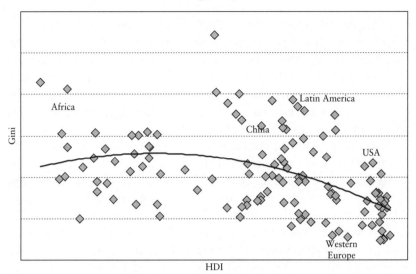

Source: UNDP (<http://hdr.undp.org/en/statistics/data/>)

Figure 6.2 Development and inequality

As we move up the economic ladder, the zones of distinction grow larger (Kanbur and Venables 2007). In Mexico, the north and the south of the country represent two different economies, while in Brazil the south is vastly richer than the northeast. Perhaps the most dramatic case is that of China, whose coastal regions and cities can boast "first world" living standards, while the farms of the interior remain mired in poverty. Regional contrasts may also be appreciated by citizens of the rich world: between northern and southern Italy, between the environs of London and the Midlands, between the Northwestern Pacific coast of the United States and the region around the Great Lakes.

Inequality and Globalization

What has been the role of globalization in the contemporary development of both the divergence and convergence of economic and social well-being? The link between globalization and inequality

155

is a matter of intense debate.[6] A recent survey of the massive literature on this topic argues that it is impossible to accurately ascertain the direction of change (if any) in global inequality (Anand and Segal 2008). Even if, however, we cannot provide a blanket answer to the question of how much better or worse the globe is in this regard, we can provide some indications of trends within and between some regions.

First, there has been considerable movement between countries. If we compare the countries of the world to the United States in 1950 and 2005, we note that, while the US is still the dominant economy, several nations have significantly narrowed the gap since 1950.[7] Some made the greatest advances between 1950 and 1973, such as Western Europe, Japan, and Taiwan. Most countries (with the important exception of Korea) lost ground during the long adjustment that took place between 1974 and 1990. Over a period of fifteen years, from 1993 to 2008, there was dramatic growth (relative to the US) in India, China, and other South and East Asian economies. Some geographical-historical patterns are also important. While the socialist bloc gained some ground during the immediate post-war years, they had their lost decades during the late 1970s and 1980s. Latin America had a mixed record during the "Glorious Thirty" but stagnated during the 1980s, then realized some improvements between 1993 and 2008 (note, however the consistent, and sometimes precipitous, decline of Argentina). The most dramatic pattern, however, is the general decline of sub-Saharan Africa during the last half-century. Overall, this region's income is (at best) one-twentieth that of the United States.

Over and above income, many of the gaps between countries in basic welfare measures have actually shrunk since 1960. On the most aggregate level, life expectancy in the low-income countries has risen from 62 percent to 75 percent of that of the high-income countries. For those in the middle, the numbers are 78 percent to 90 percent. Overall, there has been a remarkable convergence in global patterns of some aspects of human development, but, obviously, some countries have progressed more than others. In both Asia and Latin America, life expectancy grew around twenty years; in Korea, the increase was from fifty-four to seventy-eight

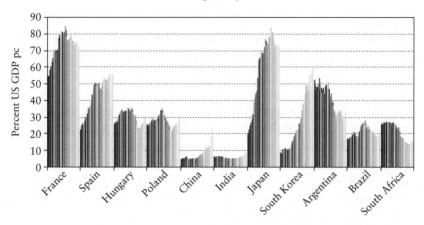

Source: The Conference Board and Groningen Growth and Development Centre, Total
Economy Database, September 2008; <http://www.conference-board.org/economics/>

Figure 6.3 Growth relative to the US 1950–2007

years! While Africa did see some improvement (especially before
the AIDS epidemic that intensified in the early 1990s), it remains
the region that has progressed the least in both absolute and relative terms.

While there is every reason to welcome narrowing gaps between
rich and poor countries in nutritional levels, infant mortality, and
access to sanitation, other data indicate that there exists a glass
ceiling of improvement. First, some of these aggregate figures
disguise structural differences in the underlying societies. For
example, the improvement in life expectancy in developing countries has come largely from declining infant mortality. In and of
itself, this is an obvious social good, but also obscures the lack of
progress in improving access to health for adults, the scourge of
many diseases, and the existence of a very real longevity ceiling
of sixty if not fifty years (Deaton 2006). Second, the gap between
global rich and poor is widening in figures that would indicate
potential for future growth and development, such as measures of
education, number of scientific personnel, and access to computers
and the Internet.

What if we disaggregate the data or take into account

populations? Obviously, given China's and India's 2.5 billion inhabitants and their economic boom over the past twenty years, weighing of populations will produce less drastic gulfs in global inequality. Experts such as Firebaugh (2003) see the trends in these two countries (as well as in others such as Vietnam and Brazil) as signs of significant improvement. Others have argued that the decline in global inequality also reflects a general reduction in the percentage of people living in poverty and that we can speak of a global convergence in income levels (Sala-i-Martin 2007). For all of these analysts, the reason for this shift over the past twenty years has been precisely the diffusion of globalization and the greater integration of the global market.

Others, such as Wade (2004), argue the opposite, claiming that not only is inequality getting worse overall, but that globalization has much to do with it. The data on *within*-country inequality over the past twenty years indicates that it has been rising in all regions with the exception of the richest countries (Cornia and Kiiski 2004; Birdsall 2005), and we will look at this trend in greater detail in the case studies below.

Many studies that have tried to combine the within- and between-country measures indicate that, even without the "China effect," there has been some reduction in overall global inequality over the past decades (Chotikapanich et al. 2007). The major exception in this trend is that the distance between the rest of the world and sub-Saharan Africa has been increasing. In general, while there has been a widening of the middle of the *between*-country distribution, the distance between the very rich and the very poor has increased dramatically (Sutcliffe 2007; Collier 2007). That is, as we discussed in the beginning of the chapter, global inequality has both increased and declined, depending on one's set of references.

Domestically, globalization appears to have hit the middle of the *within*- country income distribution the hardest. There is no question that globalization has shifted the returns to particular forms of labor, skills, and capital over the past decades. In some parts of the rich world, this has led to a virtual de-industrialization, as many manufacturing enterprises have moved abroad. This trend, coupled with technological pressures that automate jobs and release employers from the need to hire people, exerts a tremendous pressure on laborers. The fate of the displaced workers contrasts deeply with the much more pleasant outcomes for the high-tech professionals managing the new computerized economy. In poorer regions, the increased availability of foreign products has often decimated previously protected industries, leading to the erosion of these countries' former middle classes.

Yet the same shift in production has theoretically reduced the prices the working class all over the world pays for consumer products. The integration of global manufacturing has created new jobs for millions of people in impoverished countries, and may represent a substantial enhancement of the economically disadvantaged's economic opportunities. The integration of financial markets has made investment capital more available, but the regimen dictated by the global markets has also led to reductions in welfare safety nets and government employment.

All sides agree that globalization has had its winners and its losers. The lingering question concerns the reasons that some have won while others have lost.

There is a clear positive relationship between trade and relative growth. The countries that trade are more likely to be richer and have the highest levels of general welfare. The question here is one of causal order: do the rich simply trade more or does trading make you rich? With all due caution, the evidence does seem to say that, for those countries that were in the process of development in the 1960s, an integration with the global commercial network was beneficial. Certainly the different fates of East Asia (particularly China), as opposed to those of Latin America, would indicate that globalization is not only compatible, but even necessary for economic development.

There are several important caveats to any simplistic "globalization is good" argument, however. The first has to deal with the obvious fact that not all integration is the same. So, for example, while there is a positive relationship between the role of trade in an economy and its economic performance, there is an almost equally strong negative one between focusing on primary goods and the same outcome. Practically all commodities have their booms, but also their busts. Moreover, economies based on primary commodities (such as those in Latin America) often fail to develop the domestic dynamism necessary for long-term development. The same argument can be applied (but with less certainty) to the so-called "race to the bottom," where countries compete by offering the lowest possible labor costs in manufacturing the simplest products. The return on global integration unquestionably increases with the sophistication of what is offered to the world market. It is equally undeniable, however, that autarky does not work. The countries at the very bottom of the global pyramid cannot be said to have been placed there by globalization (or at least the contemporary version of it – the historical roots of the current hierarchy of global income is another matter). They are too marginal to the world and the world is too distant for most of its inhabitants for that to be the case.

If participation in the global network is generally positive (again depending on how it is accomplished), the role of domestic institutions is also critical. Here the emphasis has to be less on the global aspects of interaction and more on the "capitalist" aspect of global capitalism. To argue that capitalist-defined integration is solely responsible for the East Asian boom, for example, is to neglect obvious evidence. To begin with, the role of the state in fostering the growth of the East Asian economies is undeniable. These were not products of a pure laissez-faire, but very much of managed development. Second, the returns on growth (and thus the relative position in the distribution of well-being in the world) clearly depend on the kinds of institutions created to protect the population from the vagaries of the market. This point will become clearer when we discuss inequalities within specific countries below.

The increasing integration of the global economy has clearly benefited those who are best able to participate in it and this is highly related to one's a priori class position. How does one benefit from globalization? By possessing either skills that can be offered to the global market place or capital resources that can achieve better returns in a global bourse. The vast majority of the winners of globalization are in the former group. This so-called "knowledge class" has grown wealthier by being able to manage the information systems of globalization. These individuals can be found everywhere in the world, from Indian programmers to millionaire American lawyers, but because of the distribution of education, they are concentrated in the already wealthy countries. A much smaller group possesses enough capital to use the competitive financial markets to make more and more money. The roughly 10 million "high net worth individuals"[8] in the world can use the integration to make ever more from their money and, increasingly, the hyper-rich have become the object of greatest marketing desire. The empirical data indicate a positive relationship between increases in within-country inequality and the degree of financial integration.

In the end, the debate on globalization and inequality may rest on an as yet understudied phenomenon: mobility as opposed to structural inequality. Given that the world is a very unequal place, to what extent does globalization provide opportunities for some individuals to move up a given hierarchical ladder? The answer is mixed. Michael Hout (2006) indicates that social mobility anywhere remains slow and difficult and has as much to do with politics as with global inequalities. The effect of globalization will be determined by the extent to which it merely serves to consolidate the already advantaged position of some. In order to better understand this phenomenon, we need to move away from simple accounting of income and take into account some other means of categorizing individuals into unequal segments.

According to the classic liberal notion of market integration, the need to compete globally should lead to a decline in any kind of discrimination based on race, gender, or any other category (Centeno and Newman forthcoming). The logic here is simple: in a competitive market place where production and consumption are increasingly atomized and where there are few if any social links between consumers and producers, allowing traditional biases to play any role is simply counterproductive. Thus, we would expect that globalization has helped dismantle traditional divisions. A very different perspective comes from those who view globalization as actually supporting these traditional barriers. The argument here is that, much as we have seen in the case of the geographic distribution of income, globalization tends to reward those who are already ahead. Thus, the rich (and often white) societies benefit more than the poor and darker-skinned ones. Similarly, inside every society, those who already have privileges (men, lighter-skinned, higher caste) will not only benefit more from the growth and wealth that globalization might bring, but will then use this differential success to further legitimate their position. For those on top, globalization even provides an ideological justification for their rise as now it can be attributed to a global meritocracy.

The effect of globalization on this kind of traditional discrimination may be the most important question in our analysis of its role in global inequality. Unfortunately, we have relatively little empirical data on this phenomenon. The area where most of the work has been done is in gender, given that the male–female divides are a universal source of inequality. In the aggregate, statistical evidence indicates that global integration actually reduces gender inequality in a variety of measures (Black and Brainerd 2004; Gray et al. 2006). This is not to deny the sexist practices women may find on new factory floors, the discrimination they face, or the exploitation of their social position. However, in terms of relative inequality, globalization seems to help. We have less evidence on other forms of categorical discrimination such as caste and race. There have been newspaper articles detailing how Indian *Dalits* (untouchables) have used economic liberalization to escape from the horrors of caste, for example, as well as some statistical documentation of improvement (Munshi and Rosenzweig 2006), but other studies indicate that the most important progress has been due not to global integration or market openings, but to the government policies of affirmative action (Attewell and Madheswaran forthcoming). The discussion on racism can be divided into two separate issues. First, to what extent has globalization led to a reduction in racist practices against minority groups native to the relevant countries? Unfortunately, we have relatively little data on this. The more relevant question regarding globalization and new forms of racism and xenophobia will be discussed in the section on migration below.

It is undeniable that a great deal of inequality exists across a wide array of categories. That globalization has exacerbated the distance between its winners and losers is also clear. But it is also important to recognize that many have used market integration as a way of improving their lives and coming closer to the standards of the global rich. Since one's view of globalization and inequality will depend a great deal on where one is and was standing, the next section of this chapter looks in greater detail at inequalities in the rich countries (focusing on the contrast between the US and Western Europe), the poorer nations (with special emphasis on China), and on the global population that links these two worlds: immigrants.

Inequality among the rich

The range of internal inequality found among what we may call the "traditional" global rich is astounding. While the Nordic welfare states have Gini indices in the mid-twenties (meaning that the top 10 percent earn four times what the bottom 10 percent do), in the United States the Gini is above 40 and the same ratio is doubled. In general, inequality in Europe increases as we move east, but never reaches an index of 40 (by contrast, Canada's is 32). In contrast, the US appears as relatively equal compared to Latin American countries that have Gini indices of above 50 and sometimes approaching 60 (meaning that the same ratio of top to bottom is 20 to 1). The differences in wealth distribution are even more dramatic. Comparing the US to Spain (in the middle of the European income distribution), a recent study showed that the wealth Gini for the US was 80 as opposed to Spain's 56. While the top 10 percent and 1 percent of the US wealth distribution held 69 percent and 32 percent of all the assets, the numbers in Spain were 41.8 percent and 13.2 percent respectively (Bover 2008). It is too early to tell how the 2008 crisis will affect the wealth and income distribution. On the one hand, the wealthiest with investments to lose will also lose the most in absolute form. On the other hand, the poorest are least likely to have any financial back-up if they are laid off.

To what extent is this difference in inequality connected with globalization? In order to answer this question, we need to look at the historical pattern. Among the rich countries, the US, the United Kingdom, and other "Anglo-Saxon" rich countries have seen increased inequality since the 1970s, while the rest have either remained static or have declined (Weeks 2005). Piketty and Saez (2003) suggest that the United States since 1970 has had a different pattern of income inequality from European countries. First, inequality has increased much more rapidly, and, second, it has been more concentrated on the very top wage earners (what they call the working rich).

How much of this pattern does globalization explain? According to a recent study by the Federal Reserve, the increasing income inequality in the United States is a reflection of the "skill biased technological change" we have witnessed over the past thirty years from the 1980s onwards. Part of this is due to the simple advancement in technology, which has placed an even greater premium on education. The return on schooling has been increasing during this period. The combination of this trend with the market integration and phenomena such as outsourcing has hit the working class in already developed countries particularly hard. Not only are they earning less than before in both relative and even absolute terms, but they are also experiencing greater job insecurity (Yellen 2006). In a particularly perverse effect, technological development and market integration have led to great improvements in productivity in general. These same trends, however, have narrowed the social sector that receives the benefits from these improvements.

Rather than focus solely on globalization, we again need to analyze domestic policies. No matter how globalized an economy, the state still matters and, as Larry Bartels (2008) has demonstrated, inequality is partly a political creation and the effects of aggregate economic cycles are tempered by who is in power. For example, some of the difference in inequality between the US and other advanced economies (most have much higher levels of trade as percentage of GDP) is the relative small extent of state assistance for those on the bottom; while in other societies the state's role serves to significantly reduce inequality, in the US it plays a much more ambiguous role (Neckerman and Torche, 2007; Smeeding 2002). Again, there exist a variety of forms of managing capitalist integration with the global market.

Inequality among the poor

What is the relationship of inequality and globalization within the poorer countries? One problem is that, as we go down the income ladder, the kind of data needed to make any judgments regarding internal inequality declines drastically. Nevertheless, the trend is fairly clear. Latin America experienced a significant increase in inequality, as did the countries of the ex-Soviet bloc. The Asian cases are more mixed. In Africa, the data problem becomes more acute, but evidence indicates a rise in inequality across the continent (Cornia and Kiiski 2004).

The inequality in Latin America is notorious. The top tenth of the income distribution takes nearly half of the income, while the bottom tenth doesn't even get 2 percent. The continent has also been historically tied to the global markets. These two observations have led many to use the region as a perfect example of the distributional distortions of globalization. To an extent, the last twenty years of globalization have worsened the distribution of income in many countries because states have been forced to reduce welfare protections and public employment in order to meet international commitments. But the vast majority of inequality in the region is better explained by the historical legacy of racial and ethnic barriers and the associated misdistribution of access to natural resources. Moreover, the continent has lagged far behind other developing regions in creating the human resources prized by market integration (de Ferrari et al. 2003), as well as the infrastructure needed for global commerce. It is important to note, however, that government policies combined with the appropriate interaction with the global market could begin to reverse this historical legacy: over the past fifteen years, Brazil has managed to both lower inequality (still one of the highest in the world) and the percentage of the population living in poverty.

In the countries of the ex-socialist bloc, comparisons with pre-1989 are made difficult by the fact that many pre-existing inequalities were not monetary, but based on party rank and status, and were often hidden in the mostly fictionalized statistical reporting. Certainly, the imposition of tighter budget standards and the elimination (by fiat and by inflation) of the old support system contributed to the increase in inequality (and poverty) (Rands and Centeno 1996). But, while many of the new rich obtained their wealth through corruption and thievery, the liberalization of markets also allowed others to flourish in more legitimate ways. With regard to other cases, we also have to keep in mind the distinction between those countries integrating via some form of manufacturing output (Bangladesh) and those relying on pure primary exports (most of Africa). Finally, many of these countries were suffering from considerable violence during these years due to both civil and international conflicts, and this appears to increase inequality.

Due to these issues, we are better off focusing on a single case in order to appreciate the dynamics of globalization and inequality, and no other is as well suited for this as China. This country is the most extreme example of the promises and challenges brought about by global capitalism. On the one hand, the liberalization of the market has reduced the poverty rate in China remarkably: from an estimated 64 percent to 10 percent twenty-five years later (Dollar 2007). This was not the exclusive result of global trade (well-developed human resources and initial diaspora investment were critical), but there is no doubt that China has played the globalization game well. On the other hand, however, China has seen inequality increase from an estimated Gini of 31 to 45 during the same period. As in a microcosm of the broader terms observed across the globe, China became richer, but less equal.

How was Chinese inequality related to increased globalization? In many ways, China shares the same pattern as that seen in the US: the economic shift drastically increased the return on education and skills. Second, the urban-rural and coastal-interior gap in productivity and investment added a geographical aspect to the inequality distribution. City-dwellers, for example, make roughly three times more than those in the countryside, while those on the coast make more than twice those in the western provinces (Young 2007). These territorial differences were not just in monetary terms, but by the twenty-first century were reflected in standard measures of well-being. Perhaps more worrisome, access to education (and therefore to the possibility of higher income) was also increasingly associated with parental wealth and residential region. A World Bank study has shown that the tremendous success that China has had in generating trade surpluses may actually also be making the inequality worse (Dollar 2007).

But, as in all the cases above, domestic policies and government institutions manage the link between international interaction and domestic inequality. The restrictions that the Chinese government has placed on migration from the countryside have resulted in both a perpetuation of the inequality and the creation of millions of "illegal" undocumented internal immigrants without any semblance of labor rights. The fiscal decentralization of the Chinese government has allowed many of the regional differences to be perpetuated. Finally, the combination of the Communist Party's political monopoly and the fantastic degree of economic change has created a massive potential for corruption. This same corruption of party cadres has also produced myriad other forms of inequality, from environmental dangers to shoddy construction of public infrastructure.

Immigrants

Globalization and global inequality have combined to point out a new form of categorical discrimination – that of citizenship. As we have seen, where one is born makes a major difference in determining how one lives. It is in the accompanying movement of people between zones that we can best appreciate the complexities of globalization's effects on inequality. The global integration of labor has allowed millions to drastically change their living conditions by moving from poor zones to the rich. This has occurred both on a global basis and also within regional networks. The movement is always in the direction of higher income: from Latin America to the United States, from North Africa towards Europe, from southern Africa to South Africa, from South Asia to the Middle East, and from Eastern Europe towards the West.

This shift in population towards higher wage markets has both reduced inequality (by increasing the wages of those immigrants), but also increased it (by creating new categories in the origin countries between those who have families abroad sending back money and those who do not). In the destination countries, the influx of immigrants has also created new lines of stratification between those who are citizens, those who are not but have official permission to reside there, and those who are there illegally. Everywhere critical lines separate the legal working poor from the undocumented.

We saw in the chapter on trade that the poorer parts of the world did much of the dirty work of extracting the natural resources and manufacturing the basic goods. With global immigration, the richer countries have been able to "export" the dirty domestic work of their societies onto the immigrants from the poorer countries. There are roughly 100 million immigrants in the rich countries of the OECD, making up anywhere from 2 percent (Japan) to 22 percent (Switzerland) with most ranging around 10 percent of the population. While many times these include highly skilled personnel (e.g., 25 percent of US doctors are foreign born), the majority is engaged in those jobs that the natives of the destination countries would rather not do, or which they would require a higher wage to perform.

The most extreme example of using migrants to do the dirty work, while citizens can enjoy wealth, has to be in the oil-producing countries of the Middle East. In the United Arab Emirates, 71 percent of the population is foreign born, in Kuwait it is 62 percent, in Bahrain, 42 percent, and in Saudi Arabia, 25 percent. Some of this number includes expatriate engineers and other professionals, but all of these countries feature a huge underclass of servants whose basic rights have no legal protection. Showing that all is relative in inequality, the flow also marches across borders where the difference in economic opportunities is not as drastic. Malians seek to go to the Ivory Coast, Mozambiqueans to Zambia, Salvadorians to Mexico, and Paraguayans to Argentina (where the colloquial term for maid for a time was a *paraguaya*). Whenever local economic conditions worsen, these immigrants are given cause to suffer, whether by official governments as in the case of Italy or by mobs in the case of South Africa. The post-2008 crisis will no doubt exacerbate anti-immigrant sentiment and policies.

As the world becomes increasingly integrated, the distribution of wealth by passport appears less and less natural. Why should someone born on the northern side of the Rio Grande have a few more years to live and many more dollars to spend than their counterpart born to the south? The same question could be asked of the different shores of the Mediterranean or the Indian Ocean. Again, the importance of the state in determining one's global status is startlingly clear.

Does it Matter?

Is it unfair to ask that globalization resolve inequality? Perversely, globalization might exacerbate inequality precisely because it works so well and because it does reward merit. Globalization rewards those who do what they do very well. In what Walter LaFeber (1999) calls the "Michael Jordan effect," the best at what they do are able to attain rewards from global as opposed to local or national markets. But this might also mean that those who are good, but not exceptional (at least as judged by the global marketplace), lose out. So, for example, the wider availability of NBA games on global television undermines attendance at local events. The global migration markets are another perfect example of how this works. Many areas of the poorer parts of the world are experiencing a debilitating drain of their most talented and better trained, as they can achieve a better premium on their skills in the rich world. The individuals involved move up, but their origin societies move down.

We should recognize, however, that the reward system of globalization is anything but neutral and that the globe is hardly a level playing field. One of the characteristics of inequality is that it is "durable" (Tilly 1998) and the global distribution of wealth certainly proves it. We should note, for example, the global distribution of wealth to a large extent reflects the geopolitics of previous centuries. Is it an accident, for example, that the countries joining the rich of Europe were either populated by their descendants (North America and Oceania) or were not colonized by them (Japan)? Is it an accident that a paler complexion has become an almost universal standard of beauty?

Even forgetting about pre-1945 history, economics increasingly recognizes that the rules of the market do not completely reflect innate and universal properties, but are the creation of power hierarchies at the time of their design. So the rules of globalization invariable favor those who wrote them (Pogge 2007). No better example of this exists than the division between legal and illegal products in the global market place. Prestige liquors and tobacco products (almost exclusively a province of Europe and the United States) can be bought anywhere. Prestige narcotics such as cocaine, however, which happen to be produced in the poorer parts of the world, cannot benefit from legal global markets. Similarly, the barriers to the movement of labor, largely established by the richer countries, ignore the massive and critical migration from Europe for three centuries prior to 1945. Perhaps even more incongruously, the richer countries increasingly demand of the poor that they respect new environmental standards so not to worsen a situation first created by the already wealthy.

Internally, inequality also reflects pre-existing power structures. Considerations of caste, race, and gender may be partly offset by globalization, but success in this new arena is also strongly determined by those characteristics. As in the globe, so in the nation: where one stood at the moment of economic liberalization makes a difference. This applies whether one was white (South Africa), whether one owned land (Brazil), or whether one was a party member (the former socialist bloc or China) *before* globalization.

The crises and tremors of globalization also tend to affect the weakest involved. While the rich can adjust to momentary price increases, these can decimate the poor. Even with all the talent in the world, these differences will play out. Countries where the average household spends roughly 10 percent of their income on food (OECD) will survive a dramatic rise in the prices of basic cereals more easily than those where the figures is closer to 65 percent (Bangladesh). Similarly, countries that have a broad portfolio of exports will survive the ups and downs of markets better than monoculturalists.

Why is this a challenge to global capitalism? Some would argue that, given the very clear evidence that globalization is reducing absolute poverty and improving aggregate living standards, issues of inequality are in the end irrelevant (Bhagwati 2004). Others respond with more ethical concerns, pointing out that as long as the bottom is so poor, and as long as the top is so rich, neglect of these issues is indefensible (Singer 2002; Sen 2001).

These persistent inequities can lead to what Nancy Birdsall (2005) calls "destructive inequality." In these instances, rather than fostering competition and assuring the benefits of an invisible hand, inequities skew market performance and reward precisely those who have already have power, while driving those without it to despair. The benefits from greater equity are significant, above and beyond any moral satisfaction. There is a strong relationship between equity and development: the most consistent socio-economic explanation of success in the global market is a level of internal equality. Only those societies that have limited domestic inequities and that have provided for their populations are able to make the leap into the form of global integration that can guarantee long-term development as opposed to the enrichment of a few. Thus, in order for globalization to grow in any long-term way, equity is not only preferable, but also required.

As discussed in the beginning of this chapter, it is also imperative to remember that inequality is a product of perception. Even if poverty is being reduced, what matters to those on the wrong side of the distribution may be the gulf between them and those above. The desperately poor of urban slums may not so much appreciate the electricity and the television that allows them to watch images of the rich, as resent the gap that separates their reality from the flickering images on their screens. As the world is more and more integrated, and as the capacity of rebellion becomes more democ-ratized (due to the complexities of the system, its subsequent fragility, and the low cost of weapons and explosives), the needs (no less real for being perceived) of the wretched of the earth are very much the concern of the rich.

Liberalization and integration have created and expanded what we might call a global "sushi class" of close to 1 billion. This fortunate one sixth of the earth can enjoy the now omnipresent raw-fish delicacy while sipping imported beer. They can fly practi-cally anywhere at least once in their lifetimes, if not much more often, and use their credit cards to access local currency through global ATMs. They are much more privileged than the residents of any noble castle or palace a century ago. But if they wish to live without ramparts and if they wish to continue safely walking the streets of the new global village, then they have to pay attention.

Equity for Stability

There should be no question that the world is not a very equal place. Perhaps the best rule for measuring inequality is the oft cited 20/20 rule: the vast majority of the wealth of the world is in the hands of the top 20 percent of economies and the top 20 percent of the individuals in the rest of the globe. The global 80/80 has been essentially left out.

The evidence for the role of globalization in creating that inequality is ambiguous. On the one hand, since the early 1990s we have witnessed dramatic gains in income and other measures of well-being in large parts of the world. On the other hand, the distance between those on top and those on the bottom, both between and within countries, has also appeared to increase. In any case, there is also little doubt that many (especially on the losing side of change) *feel* that globalization has changed their lives for the worse. Whether by displaced workers in the richer countries, or by desperate farmers in the poorer ones, increasing global integration is blamed.

The real dilemma for global capitalism may not simply be

taking the "losers" of globalization into account, but determining which "losers" take priority. Allowing greater penetration of rich markets by poorer exporters benefits them, but may harm domestic interests in the importing economies. More open frontiers help migrants, but again lead to possible displacement of low-income workers in destination countries. The divide between the territorially defined space of democracy and the increasing integration of an unregulated global economy will remain a critical challenge.

7

Living with Limits

This chapter is concerned with the environmental limits that are unquestionably facing us over the long march of global capitalism's evolution. Why a chapter on the environment in a book about capitalism? In part, because the environmental challenge is a product of particular characteristics of capitalism, what one scholar has called "the treadmill of production," of ever more and ever faster (Schnaiberg 2005). Moreover, we may be encountering physical limits that will inherently challenge the very assumptions and institutions on which capitalism has been built. Finally, the environmental challenges are not distributed evenly, and global capitalism needs to confront the specific problems of this asymmetry and what it means for its expansion and political survival.

The challenge of the environment is especially daunting because it, like global capitalism, is a complex system. As such, it is subject to emergent properties (the unexpected results of interactions between its parts) and is very sensitive to small changes. Moreover, as with all complex systems, these two characteristics make turning points essentially irreversible. Easy solutions to current environmental problems elude us in at least two ways: (1) undoing the environmentally damaging aspects of modern human economy is technologically and politically complicated; and (2) changing capitalism to address environmental concerns may be similarly difficult, and may involve very uncertain payoffs. Furthermore, complex systems often have internal self-reinforcing mechanisms, which means that marginal changes in our interaction with the environment or in the workings of capitalism may be insufficient to address these problems. Ultimately, we might need to experience one of two deep systemic changes, either (1) a collapse in the possibilities of human production afforded by the environment (e.g., if degradation gets so bad that activities become infeasible), or (2) by substantially changing how our economic system is organized to prevent such collapse. Either is likely to be profoundly disruptive.

The first step in resolving this challenge is to avoid treating the relationship between capitalism and the environment as a natural and unchanging given. Both environmentalist critics and supporters of capitalism see the relationship as a simple either/or. Dichotomous choices between the environment and wealth are partially false, however. It is not simply that we have a choice between a wealthy but environmentally destructive system, and one more ecologically sustainable but poorer. There may be some trade-offs, but there are also a myriad of alternatives. The choice is not between wealth and penury, but how to generate that wealth. It is important to recognize that, while there is an obvious relationship between use of resources and wealth, it is not perfectly linear.[1]

As with other aspects of global capitalism discussed in this book, we need to place the relationship between capitalism and the environment in its proper historical, political, and geographical context. The geography of the interaction reveals many of the same divisions discussed in the previous chapter and represents a similar challenge to the ongoing expansion of the economic order. The historical context demonstrates that this is not the first time that environment and economics have confronted each other, and that the lessons of the past are sobering. Moreover, a historical perspective reveals how the current relationship was built and how it can be reworked. Finally, the relationship is bounded by political choices and structures. There is little absolutely functionally determined about the challenge of the environment to the economy; it is a question of decisions and costs and these involve acts of power.

From Wood to Oil

Our current environmental dilemmas are not new. Previous societies have also faced their own environmental limits, whether these
involve the decline in soil fertility, depletion of water, or climatic
changes. The evidence would indicate that human societies are
not particularly adept at dealing with such crises and that these
moments often end up in societal collapse (Tainter 1988). The
very complexity and mutual interdependence that characterizes
advanced societies and which global capitalism has taken to the
greatest historical extreme, make these same systems fragile and
susceptible to disruptions.

To this scenario we need to add the critical element of the
energy dependence of contemporary society. This is not solely a
question of location and transportation of resources. Rather, it is
important to appreciate that, for the first time in history, humanity now runs on energy produced outside our bodies. In the words
of environmental historian J. R. McNeil: "After 1820 the world's
economy became increasingly based on work done by non-
muscular energy. By 1950 any society that did not deploy copious
energy was doomed to poverty" (2000: 298). The key to economic
success therefore became assuring oneself of adequate energy supplies. How can capitalism continue this dependence on energy in
light of the associated costs?

The contemporary global economy has already dealt with one
resource crisis. For millennia, wood represented the sole source of
stored energy available to complement human and animal labor.
Even after the use of water for milling and so forth, the world ran
on wood. The consequences should serve to remind us of dangers
ahead. The Middle East was deforested and trees disappeared in
many parts throughout the Mediterranean and north to Britain, as
well as in China. The need for wood as the basic building block
and for charcoal led to the deforestation of huge parts of land, and
pressures to clear land for commodity production compounded
these strains. The result is that one can trace the history of development prior to 1800 by the absence of a forest cover. Most of
Eurasia's forests were cleared long ago: what we see in China and

Europe are the younger and much less dense descendants of these primeval forests. It is no accident that those areas without experience of a dramatic economic revolution in the past 1,500 years (such as the Amazon, large parts of sub-Saharan Africa) are the ones that still have old growth wood left.

The global economy was essentially saved by the development of a new source of energy: coal. Just as having wood had previously meant power, so having coal close to places where it could be used became crucial for the next phase of development. The correlation between possessing vast amounts of coal ready for exploitation and industrial development in the nineteenth century is quite high (Pomerantz 2000). Coal came to represent 90 percent of the world's energy resources until early in the twentieth century, and allowed for an unprecedented economic growth that simply could not have been fueled by wood (Ponting 1991).

Coal, of course, has its downsides. First, it is relatively expensive to transport; second, it is extremely dirty; and, third, the ratio of energy delivered to weight and volume is low compared to oil and gas. Beginning in the twentieth century in the US and then after World War II in the rest of the world, oil and gas came to supplant coal and now account for over half of the sources of energy used in the world. This has meant yet another shift in power, as societies that were economically marginal even fifty years ago now not only provide their citizens with the highest living standards in the world, but also play significant roles in the global economy. But note that simply having oil and gas is not a guarantee of success: the "resource curse" often perversely condemns societies that posses these riches to perpetual war and poverty (Ross 1999).

The world now literally runs on oil and gas: not only to transport us from place to place, but also to produce electricity (although coal and other sources such as nuclear power play an important role here), and, most critically, to maintain the complex web of transactions described in chapter 2. According to many, the boom of the 1990s had little to do with the various structural factors often cited (collapse of communism, rise of computers, freer trade regimes) and was simply the result of the price of oil. The correlation between the price of oil and a variety of economic indicators is quite high. This is because the efficiency of the global economy and its high level of specialization depend on being able to ship materials and manufacturers relatively cheaply. No cheap oil, no high growth. Worse: no oil, no global economy.

The dependence of the global economy on primary resources is not limited to oil. The vast quantities consumed by the typical person in the rich world involve a surprising range of commodities, many of which are non-renewable, from zinc and nickel to indium and platinum. Even conservative estimates indicate that the amount available of many of these materials may be inadequate even in the medium term. Moreover, although fewer people have been needed to grow our food, our intake capacity has exploded. The creation of the global food chain and the Westernization of diets have also meant a massive increase in the consumption of land and water through the expansion of animal production: from 1960 to 2000, global consumption of wood and grains roughly doubled, while meat consumption increased fivefold (FAO 2004).

Humanity needs to find, extract, and process an enormous amount of resources, even while much of the world lives in destitution. If global capitalism is indeed setting us on a track to make everyone materially richer – be it the poor or already rich – these very large consumption figures can be expected to grow. The strains that such consumption places on the environment are not restricted to what is physically consumed by individuals, but also lead to damage incurred by processing and transporting these products. Taken together, the resulting depletion of resources means this increasingly bountiful economy presents a wide range of new or exacerbated challenges.

One central characteristic of the environmental phenomenon that is especially relevant here is its geographical distribution. Not all parts of the world consume in the same way or with the same abandon. There is no question that the global rich get much larger slices of the resource pie. The World Bank estimates that the high-income countries consume at roughly fifty times the rate of the poorest, and at roughly five times the rate of even the middle-income societies. A recent study estimated the top 700 million richest people (most of whom are in the OECD) are responsible for half of the world's emissions (Chakravarty 2009). But the environmental challenge facing us is not so much about the fairness of this distribution, but rather the fact that ever large parts of the world are claiming an equally large slice. Assuming a constant size of the pastry metaphorically in question, this means one of two things: either the "old" rich begin to consume less, or we will have no cake left.

How Much is Left?

Even considering the massive amounts that we currently consume, the future of capitalism as we know it will require many times more. Over the next fifty years, global economic activity is expected to increase fivefold and energy and other material demands to increase threefold (Matthews 2000: v). Will we have enough to go around? Audits of resource availability are obviously fraught with political biases. If the global accounting comes up with a significant surplus, then there is no need to concern ourselves with environmental limits. If, on the other hand, we are running a deficit, then simple fiduciary responsibility requires that we pay attention.

Given the centrality of energy to the fate of global capitalism, we focus on this sector.[2] Beginning with oil, we need to first understand that the quality of the data regarding how much is produced and how much is in the ground is quite low. For reasons of corporate and national security, the institutions responsible for measuring the amount in reserves have not been very forthcoming. Some estimates may be overly optimistic in order to maintain stock prices (at one point, Shell Oil appears to have been inflating its reserves by 20–25 percent), or in order to appear more significant in a global market, or to assuage investors' fear of an empty national tank (Mexico has routinely exaggerated its oil reserves and will probably become a net importer before the end of the decade). Because of quotas, corruption, and simple manipulation, production figures are less than precise or absolute.

Aggregate oil consumption (the level where we can come closest to reality) is roughly 85 million barrels per day (mbpd), of which

55 mbpd was exported. The simple math of multiplying by price gives an indication of the sheer enormity of the global oil business: at a relatively low $50 per barrel, nearly $3 billion is transferred globally on a *daily* basis or over trillion dollars per year. Consider what these amounts tell us about the centrality of oil, not merely as a fuel, but as a key part of the trade and finance flows of the world. The energy system is not merely about the physical product changing hands, but also about how the exchange in and of itself drives much of the economy.

The question of how much is in the ground depends on one's level of optimism: proven oil reserves (in itself a problematic concept as per above) would last about forty years. Shale deposits might add another fifty. But, even assuming we have a century of oil left at current levels of consumption, we should not assume all will be well. First, the price of oil will skyrocket as production begins to go down (the peak of production is expected to come in the next decade) and, even if it is available, will be so expensive as to make the fueling of globalization difficult if not impossible. Second, the last twenty years have seen new entrants into the global economy and their growth (and of those behind them) will only increase the tapping of this resource. China consumed 217,000 barrels of oil per day in 1965. By 1990, the figure was 2.3 million, and by 2006, 7.5 billion. For all of Asia, consumption practically doubled in the last fifteen years.

Often found in the same places as oil, natural gas is a second leg in the energy production and consumption of the world, accounting for roughly a fourth of the global total. The annual trade in gas adds another half trillion dollars per year in energy transactions. Gas has a significant advantage over oil in that it releases roughly a quarter less global warming gases than oil and 50 percent less than coal. Its end uses are closer to those of coal as it is concentrated in industry, power generation, and home heating. A major disadvantage of gas is that it is expensive to transport across areas not linked by pipelines (technically challenging under water, for example). This means that the supply of gas is very geographically sensitive. This is important because even more than in the case of oil, gas is concentrated in a relatively few countries, and few of the consuming societies can rely on even medium-term reserves. The geographical sensitivity of natural gas is even more critical as 70 percent of the reserves are in Russia, Central Asia, and the Middle East – the most geopolitically unstable zone in the world. Politics is therefore very much a part of the global energy market.

Consumption of gas has been increasing in all regions of the world but, again, particularly in China and India. Current consumption is around 100 trillion cubic feet. This is expected to increase by 60 percent in the next two decades. While one should have even less confidence in gas reserves than in their oil equivalents, estimates of the amount available range from 60 to 100 years. Within a newborn's lifetime, therefore, gas will be at a significant premium, in the hands of a virtual geographical monopoly, and politically difficult to transport.

One fourth of global capitalism still runs on coal. Coal remains dominant in certain sectors: it is the main fuel for generating electricity and it remains the foremost energy source in China and India. In many ways, coal is the perfect energy source. First, there is a lot of it: estimates range from 150 to 300 years of coal available at projected rates of usage. Second, coal deposits are spread much more evenly than other fossil fuels and each major region has significant sources. Thus, coal could and has been exploited without transglobal transport systems.

Unfortunately, coal is dirty and not particularly efficient. It is responsible not only for the most visible forms of pollution but also for the greatest production of greenhouse gases. It only generates a fraction of its stored energy. Of all the fossil fuels, however, coal has perhaps the greatest potential for a technological fix in that efforts to mass gasify or liquefy it *might* produce a cleaner and more effective energy source (although this is a controversial area and many believe that "clean coal" is an oxymoron).

Roughly one sixth of current global energy comes from non-fossil fuels: hydro, nuclear, thermal, solar, and wind. The advantage of these (with the exception of nuclear) is that they are by definition renewable and in several cases have the potential to resolve the economic and political issues having to do with transport. Hydroelectric power represents a potentially perfect combination of relatively low environmental impact and steady and predictable flows of energy. It is an important source of electricity in many countries. However, the production and distribution of this form of energy will require a significant lead-time and very large investment. Similar concerns possibly limit the use of geothermal and solar energy as well as wind power, although estimates indicate that there would be enough of this to supply the planet with energy well into the future. The development of these resources represents a critical challenge for global capitalism and will require the appropriate institutional incentives. The problem here for capitalism is the reliance on individual or even conglomerated investors to make such massive and very long-term commitments. Can we realistically expect a private enterprise to invest today's billions for a return that may be fifty years in the future?

Nuclear energy already accounts for a significant part of power supply in several countries and accounts for roughly the same amount of electricity generated as hydropower. France is arguably the most important user of nuclear power as it accounts for three-quarters of its electricity needs. The rest of Europe, as well as Japan, South Korea, and Taiwan, are also highly dependent on nuclear power. Some of the problems associated with nuclear power are similar to those discussed for renewable energy sources: very significant capital investment and lead-time prior to production of energy. There are currently over 400 reactors worldwide, yet only an estimated 100 are either being built or are immediately planed. The cost of each one is astronomical (perhaps \$10 billion) and the lead-time necessary quite long (ten to fifteen years). The speed at which these would have to be built in order to wean us significantly off coal makes it an unlikely short- to medium-term solution.

The other obvious problems with nuclear energy have to deal with safety. There is, of course, the question of terrorism or use for weapons, as well as the potential for disastrous accidents. (The Chernobyl region still has a 19-mile zone of exclusion which will be uninhabitable for hundreds of years. The contaminated zone with lower levels of radioactivity is much larger.) Of less apocalyptic concern is what to do with the radioactive waste generated by plants, an issue to be addressed below.

If we face a 50- to 100-year window in terms of our fuel use and the beginning of transformation to alternatives, the leeway in terms of other resources may not be as wide. Many metals critical to industrial production (and several critical to the new technologies on which we may be counting for our environmental salvation) are in relatively short supply (Gordon et al. 2006). Estimates indicate that many of these resources have far less than a century of stocks available and much less time if the rest of the world approaches US levels of consumption. While the global system could deal with precious woods as a luxury commodity and might even find replacements for some metals, the expected depletion of such critical elements as copper, zinc, and platinum would represent a much more difficult challenge.

A similar situation may be arising in the supposedly renewable agricultural commodities. The latest price hike in commodity process was not a purely short-term reaction (composite index prices practically doubled over a three-year span, but began declining in the summer of 2008), and there are many who argue that the increasing consumption of rice, corn, soybeans, and coffee throughout the world may lead to a permanent price rise.

The UN expects that world food production will need to double to meet new demands by 2050. It may be physically impossible to do so with our current technology. The reason for this is again a combination of the increased demand, as discussed in previous chapters, but also possible constraints on the basis of the supply. Simply, we may also be running out of agricultural land (the *Guardian*, December 6, 2005). A report from a research group at the University of Wisconsin noted that since 1700, the use of land for agriculture has increased from 7 percent of that available to 40 percent. While some areas had long been "farmed out," the expansion of soybean and beef in South America has been perhaps the most spectacular.

The increasing intensity of farming (meaning each acre produces much more food) is one of the miracles of the modern age and is responsible for bumper crops (see chapter 2 for other concerns), but is also leading to serious land degradation in some countries. The simple process of farming and irrigating land produces 15 million tons of erosion in the US alone. To this we may add the loss of nutrients through continued cropping of "thirsty" plants. This is particularly a problem in sub-Saharan Africa. Another important resource that may be in danger as a result of the increase in cropland is the forest cover of the planet.

Similarly, we may be running out of water. The intensification of agriculture, the non-renewable uses in industry and simple domestic consumption have all contributed. While in some places water is available in plenty, others, such as China, have seen dramatic reductions in deposits. The Chinese water table may actually be the most significant constraint on that country achieving global superpower status. Moreover, increased use has also led to a lowering of the quality of the water available, making significant portions of it unusable. By 2025, perhaps a quarter of the planet will be living in conditions of absolute water scarcity (where there are health effects) and two thirds of the population will be living under conditions of "water stress" (when demand exceeds supply) (UNEP 2007).

In sum, there is increasing agreement that our use of natural resources, from oil to water, is not sustainable in the medium term. This is not the opinion only of those long associated with such alarms (Ehrlich and Goulder 2007; Meadows et al. 2004) but also of the supposedly more "hard-headed" *Wall Street Journal* (March 24, 2008, A1) which, while attempting to disarm some fears, admitted the need for "analysis and tough action" on the environmental front. Timothy Bond, a senior executive at Barclays' Capital in London (not the usual "green" outfit) had this to say in the *Financial Times* of March 5, 2008: "The broad story is of depletion. Most of the easily obtainable resource deposits have already been exploited and most usable agricultural land is already in production."

And How Much Can We Get Rid Of?

Even assuming that there is plenty left to use, we still have a problem of getting rid of what we don't use or what we simply discard. It is important to understand that this is not simply an issue of "being green" for its own sake. As in the case of depleted resources, burdening the environment with too much waste will severely limit the potential for capitalism to develop or even maintain itself over the next century.

To understand the nature of the challenge, the concept of a resource flow is important. These are studies that analyze not only the value of the economic activity, but also the sheer physical material being exploited. These include the "hidden flows" involved in the production, including erosion, mining waste, and construction materiel. Estimates of the amount of resources, from oil for our cars to rock for our roads, is anywhere between 45 to 80 metric tons per person, per year (Matthews et al. 2000: vi). For the US economy, the total material flow is around 23 billion metric tons per year.

The optimistic reading of these flows over the past quarter-century reveals that the wealthy economies have reduced the per capita amount needed to produce our output and made significant inroads into decoupling our economic growth from sheer material usage. This is partly due to the rise of the service economy and to improvements in technology. This trend, however, does not apply to developing economies still building their infrastructure or those still largely involved in making something material. Nor does it mean that the absolute amount of garbage, mining overburden, and the like has decreased even in the rich world, but just the opposite.

We've discussed the difficulties in simply producing this much material. But it is also critical to understand that the vast majority of it is discarded in the process of production and consumption. Where does it go? Moreover, in the process of being used and transformed, the raw material becomes hazardous to our health (e.g., from carbon to carbon dioxide). In order to better understand these "outflows" we can divide them into four different categories: hazardous materials, and those that do longer-term damage to the air, water, and soil, respectively.

Hazardous waste

A significant amount of consumption/production by-products are immediately hazardous to humans. These include chemicals such as chlorine, lead, cadmium, mercury, or arsenic, through to radio-active waste. The problem of hazardous waste is not new, as early industrial processes generated some dangerous substances and we already have a legacy of perhaps as many as 2 million storage sites, only a few of which are appropriately guarded. As the economy has become more technologically sophisticated, our production of potentially hazardous waste has increased: between 25 percent to 100 percent (depending on the material) in the US between 1975 and 1996 (Matthews et al. 2000: xi).

One of the most important issues dealing with such hazards concerns what limits they represent for new technologies. The obvious case is the possible expansion of the nuclear power industry. Today, the nuclear power plants in the US produce about 2,000 metric tons of radioactive waste. To place this number into perspective, note that the still inactive and politically sensitive storage at Yucca Mountain would barely be able to handle any addition to the considerable backlog of years of inadequate storage. Even another site with the same capacity as Yucca would take only thirty-five years to fill up at such a rate.

More plebian forms of hazardous waste may be less frightening, but the sheer amounts of it threaten to overwhelm the system. Non-radioactive hazardous waste in the US totaled 45 million tons in 2008.[3] How to regulate this storage and how to create the appropriate institutions within which to create a market is made especially difficult by the fact that some of these materials (but especially highly radioactive ones) will be dangerous for 1 million years.

Is capitalism organizationally or systemically capable of dealing with such a challenge? How is one to write a contract involving such a half-life? Could markets deal with such challenges? Can the governance structures of capitalism handle such long-term commitments? The evidence of our experience with the residue produced by mining and using coal does not give much room for optimism. Over the past 100 years, millions of acres have been destroyed due to mining or the inappropriate storage of coal sludge. Time and again, it has been shown that without very rigorous oversight, entities will seek to avoid paying for the "externality"[4] of post-production costs.

Dirty air

The atmosphere is the most significant dumping ground of our material output; it is literally choking on the carbon dioxide produced by our industrial economy. Pollution is not a new phenomenon; even the earliest cities had to deal with the problem of concentrated generation of human waste and its healthy disposal. The early Industrial Revolution saw the creation of smog in new quantities. As regions industrialized, surrounding areas became literal wastelands and the rivers poisonous. In more than one contemporary city, newspaper accounts describe schoolchildren who color the sky brown or grey. But these are just the most visible signs of the pollution. There is no question that we have witnessed a dramatic increase of global emissions of products that will impair the future of the planet. Combined with the spread of insecticides and the inadequate disposal of toxic waste, this is simply killing the nature on which we rely to survive. The concentration of carbon dioxide in our atmosphere has increased by 25 percent since the pre-industrial era. This in itself might not appear to be very much, but we essentially have no idea how much it is possible to put into the air and we do have very strong suspicions that close to 400 parts per million (our present state) is already far too much.

This is particularly worrisome as, where previously the world had to worry about only one major economy as the main polluter, we now have two. In 1990, the US emitted five times as much CO^2 as Japan and was by far the worst polluter. By 2015, it will be overtaken by China. Since 1990, the combined amount of CO^2 thrown into the atmosphere by these two economies will have doubled. The issue to reflect on here is not the blame or responsibility that needs to be assigned for costs (although that is relevant). Rather, it is important to consider that a large part of atmospheric damage is being done by two driving forces of the global economy (US consumption and Chinese production). Thus, simple solutions involving the lowering of these amounts cannot happen without significant adjustments in the structure of the global economy. The rise of the Chinese pollution contribution has also clouded the policy waters in the US, as it has allowed some to shift the question to what the Chinese are going to do about it without appropriate attention paid to the continuing rise in American emissions.

Perhaps the most frightening aspect of the various forms of pollution is that several pollutants remain in the atmosphere for years, and in some cases centuries. The deposits we are making today will linger and perhaps cause serious damage after we are long gone. The danger of global warming aside (popularized enough not to require emphasis here), air pollution is directly responsible for the deaths of hundreds of thousands per year and adversely affects the health of millions more. The economic costs of these health losses are too large to be dismissed.

Bad water

Perhaps even more than the atmosphere, the planet's water system has taken the brunt of the carbon dumping and the subsequent warming effect. There has been a clear warming trend in the world's oceans since the 1960s. This has led to increasing pressure on populations in low-lying regions. The viability of whole countries such as Bangladesh (not to speak of the Pacific and Caribbean micro states) may be in question over the next century.

The increases in temperature and levels of pollution have also been associated with the creation of zones where marine life is practically non-existent. The Mediterranean is in danger of becoming a dead sea. In broader areas, stocks of popular fish have been driven to unsustainable levels and the overexploitation of some species (tuna, for example) has led to their virtual replacement in ocean zones by less desirable fish.

The environmental changes of the past 100 years have also increased the variability of precipitation. This has meant more erratic distributions of drought and flooding play havoc with any form of agricultural planning.

The development associated with global capitalism has also had paradoxical effects on water quality. On the one hand, wealth and technology have vastly increased the availability of safe water. On the other hand, the intrusion of industrial and consumer wastes into the water sources have created new problems in purification. In several developed countries, the contamination of watersheds has become critical. In less developed zones, the capacity of existing systems to absorb increases in use has broken down and led to periodic explosions of diseases such as cholera.

One possible benefit of the changes in the water surface of the planet is the creation of a true North–West passage across the Arctic Ocean. This might lead to dramatic reductions in transport times to and from Eurasia and North America, as well as access to the abundant resources no longer locked in the ice. But such drastic melting and subsequent changes in water temperature and salinity might adversely affect the basic circulation of water and air streams. These effects could lead to disastrous changes in temperatures in precisely those countries that are at the heart of global capitalism: the North Atlantic economies.

Filling up the land

Significant parts of the "hidden flows" behind the economy end up on the land. One critical problem is the massive amounts of "consumer" waste that now spill out of the rich world's households and which are pouring out of an increasing number of homes in the developing world. Each American, for example, throws away over 1,500 pounds of waste a year into municipal systems. Since per capita and absolute amount of waste have practically doubled in 1960, they are rapidly overwhelming the municipal waste system in the US.

Much of this goes to pollute our air and water, but the largest amount (50–65 percent, depending on the site) goes into landfills. Since, in order to be practical, these landfills cannot be too distant from centers of population, this is leading to the exhaustion of available capacity and serious difficulties in creating new sites. To this shortage we can add concerns with the leakage of poisonous materials into the soil and water supply precisely where it might be most precarious.

A global issue

How are these environmental concerns "global"? The disposal of waste has become a massive international industry. Much of the hidden flows in the economies of individual countries (and often the majority of the hazardous waste) end up in someone else's backyard. Between 1993 and 1999, the number of international waste shipments increased sevenfold and totaled 12 million metric tons. Much of this involved exchanges of particular materials between the developed countries: Germany, for example, was a leading exporter *and* importer of waste. Inside the EU, over 3.5 million tons were transferred from one country to another. These included tons of lead, zinc, oil/water mixtures, acids, and industrial solvents. The potential for an environmental disaster involving several countries other than shippers and receivers is quite high.

This transfer is officially regulated through the Basel Convention. Much less well policed are transfers of often-dangerous garbage from the rich to the poor. This trade is partly driven by the fact that the rich produce much more waste than the poor. Monaco, for example, generated 1,176 kilos of municipal waste per person in 2002, but Burkina Faso only 10 (<www.worldmapper.org>). The incentives for this flow are clear: lower costs (even taking into account transportation) because of lower regulatory demands and oversight. One recently infamous case involved a ship-ment of petrochemical waste on a Greek-owned tanker, flying a Panamanian flag, leased by a London branch of a Swiss company with headquarters in the Netherlands. The shipment was dumped in the suburbs of Abidjan, with no safety measures, and led to the death of at least eight people and hospitalization of many more. This form of trade has become routinized for the process of ship dismantling, which is now a practical monopoly of South Asian nations and which regularly results in not only long-term environmental damage, but several workers' deaths per year.

The environment is a potentially perfect global "tragedy of the commons" (Hardin 1968). This term refers to situations where consumption and consequences thereof are decoupled enough so as to create perverse incentives. The original example is the common land available for all members of the community for grazing. For any single member, there exists a strong incentive to allow as many of his or her livestock as possible on the land: the individual will receive the benefit of more meat, milk, or wool, while not bearing any of the costs of feeding the extra animals. If all members of the community behave in the same way, however, the common land will be overgrazed and will soon be unavailable for anyone. Similar problems haunted communist systems in which the use of public resources for private gain was an accepted part of life, resulting in poor and decaying common services and areas. In the contemporary global system, the decimation of fisheries may be the best example: for any individual ship it makes sense to exploit the waters as much as possible, especially if owned by nationals of different countries than the ones on whose shores the relevant seas may lie.

A Different Capitalist Model?

How are these challenges related to capitalism? How can we go about determining the amount of this process that is connected with capitalism? Certainly, the record of environmental stewardship of the Soviet bloc or the other communist regimes would indicate that environmental catastrophe is not a purely capitalist phenomenon (Feshbach and Friendly 1993). Disasters from the Aral Sea, to Chernobyl, to Norilsk, make the worst outcomes of capitalist development appear benign. There is no doubt that, more than capitalism, it is the now globalized model of industrial development that is responsible for the environmental challenges we face.

But how can that model of development be separated from capitalism per se? The earlier stages of industrialization were clearly capitalist and, as of 1989, the further degradation of the planet has very much reflected a capitalist coloration. Certainly, the emphasis on growth of profits and consumption which fuels capitalism is at least partly responsible for the dirty skies, mountains

191

of trash, and holes in the ground all around us. Capitalism has yet to design a system through which the price of these "externalities" is reflected in either the cost of the product or the profits from the sale. Capitalism is responsible in that there exist few short- to medium-term incentives to protect the environment. This was not a systemic problem when there was "enough" environment to despoil but, as we reach ecological constraints, these incentive structures may be self-destructive.

At the very heart of capitalism is the idea that all can participate in the ever expanding binge of production and consumption. Both mainstream economists and their critics recognize the central importance of growth to capitalism. By its very nature, this is not a system that can sit still at some perfect equilibrium point (even if that were definable), but one that must keep moving to even stay in the same place.

For two centuries, the perpetual growth has not been challenged by any physical limits. Even the generation of externalities (unfortunate and unattractive as these were) did not represent a danger to the enterprise itself. But the environmental limits do represent a danger to business as usual, a threat to the very viability of the capitalism model as it stands. For example, capitalism accepts present-day inequality by promising longer-term returns. But what if the products being consumed today will limit my ability to consume tomorrow? This is perhaps the thorniest issue for global capitalism, as it can no longer necessarily rely on a perpetually larger pie for everyone to share. If there are limits (and the evidence is pretty overwhelming that there are), then the size of respective shares becomes very much a legitimate topic. It is vital to recognize how much this new constraint transforms the basic underpinning of capitalism and its legitimacy, for it invariably links current property rights to potential future ones.

The debate on who will pay for environmental consequences has already created tensions in the global system, as shown by the failure to resolve the long-running divide concerning environmental policies between the already developed countries and those in the midst of the process. The already rich ask those who are beginning to consume to be ecologically sound and earth-friendly for the sake of the planet. The still poor wonder why they have to pay for the binges of Europe and North America. The same dynamic may soon come into play domestically between different classes and generations. In all of these cases the conflict is the same: why should one party be allowed to consume (borrow, pollute) so much as to endanger the prosperity of another? Again, note that this calls into question the fundamental autonomy of the property relationship: if consuming yours leaves less for me, should you be free to do so?

What of a technological *deus ex machina*? It is well known that, as the prices of commodities increase, the technology not only improves means with which to produce it but also develops alternatives to them. We have seen this in the case of oil. But note the "Jevons paradox" where improvements in the technological efficiency of a resource often lead to increased demand for it, not less (Clark and York 2005). In any case, such technological "fixes" (if there are any) would take a great deal of time to develop and implement on a broad basis. But what of a disaster of such speed and extent as to make Katrina seem prosaic? What of an explosion forcing France off some of its nuclear power grid? What of war or a terrorist strike shutting the Straits of Hormuz, the gate though which one fifth of the world's oil flows?

Any one of these disruptions in and of themselves is arguably survivable. But recall that the environment is a complex system and the relationship of the economy with it even more so. These apparently limited (if serious) disruptions could produce unimaginable side effects. As in the case of the credit crisis, a responsible global capitalism cannot simply wish these potentials away. Just as we may now wish we had listened to the Cassandras preaching about the housing bubble, we may now want to listen to those warning of an "environmental" bubble.

Does this mean that we need to give up on the benefits we have attained as a result of the developments of the last 200 years? In many ways, the success of capitalism has created the environmental danger. If we hold capitalism responsible for the environmental mess, than we at least also need to give it significant credit for the underlying reasons behind it: longer lifetimes, greater choices in consumption, richer material lives, and vast improvements in basic living standards. Pointing fingers and assigning blame would only appear to create endless political tussles, while neglecting the basic fact that the vast majority enjoy or would like to be able to enjoy the fruits that global capitalism has wrought. In any case, the chances are not very good in terms of convincing a part of the global population to go without products that have come to be seen as necessities. Convincing the majority that it should simply accept a diminished future because of the profligacy of the rich seems even less likely.

Yet we may have no choice but to give up on at least some of the more egregious forms of consumption. This is not about a moral or ethical decision, but one similar to choices faced by anyone with an inheritance. The spendthrift may enjoy a few days to years of delight by spending the principal, but some reckoning will come. A large part of any adjustments to be made will be connected with the model of industrial development we have adopted since the late eighteenth century. The more relevant question for this book is: how can shifts in capitalist institutions be changed to address these environmental challenges? We suggest three critical ones for discussion.

The first transformation needs to involve some form of pricing and cost management for so-called externalities, or the costs borne by others than those involved in the immediate transaction. Perhaps the most obvious cases involve acid rain falling on a country other than the polluter's, or upstream depletion of a water resource. Pollution and other environmental consequences must be priced and charged to the relevant industries and individuals. One form of this, for example, is a system of "congestion pricing" where driving at particular moments or in specific zones costs an extra premium. Another might be taxes on consumption of resources that are partly determined, not by their current rarity (already reflected in the market price), but by the expected depletion.

As it stands, all of these costs tend to be charged by the state and involve non-market policing. But even the most environmentally progressive countries of the OECD – the environmental equivalents of the Scandinavian welfare states – still have not seriously impaired the degrading effects of their production and consumption. These states have been unable to fight the inherent logic of capitalist accumulation and have failed to legislate serious change, much less aggressive policing (Seis 2001). We will need to create institutions that use market mechanisms to charge the appropriate premiums for environmental externalities. The sale of air rights and the use of carbon emission credits are promising possibilities, but global capitalism will need to create many such avenues.

The second adaptation that capitalism must make is in a sense a continuation of the principle of pricing externalities. In this case, we need to begin accounting for externalities defined by time horizons and to promote longer-term sights in planning and incentives. As currently structured, there are few, if any, incentives for either institutions or people within them to take into account the medium- to long-term consequences of the environment. Much as in the credit crisis or previous bubbles, those making decisions can expect that they will not bear the costs associated with them. So bad loans made early in a career need not hamper the rise of an executive, nor will excessive use of a resource hamper the payout at retirement. The stockholders of companies abusing an environment will certainly not pay for the environmental consequences arising years after they sold their stock. As currently structured, capitalist incentives are perversely present-oriented. There is no positive inducement to invest responsibly and every possible reason to inflate today's returns at tomorrow's costs. Changes in accounting rules and in the taxation of capital gains might allow for a significant transformation in such behaviors.

The expectation that capitalist institutions can create new governance structures may seem overly optimistic, but it is difficult to imagine how the system can survive without such a reform. We do possess examples of economies of the common being properly exploited (Dolsak and Ostrom 2003). It *is* possible to come up with more sustainable strategies. It is also necessary.

The third and most difficult transformation for capitalism is to shift from the assumption of non-zero-sum games to ones where enjoyment of a good or a service by one person might involve the loss of that possibility by another. The very fundamental assumption of capitalism is that we can all grow rich simultaneously, that capitalist growth is a "win-win" phenomenon. The environmental limits discussed in this chapter would indicate that this is not the case. An acceptance of limits would mean some radical shifts in people's behavior and we cannot predict with any level of certainty how that may happen. But the first thing we need to realize is that it is unsustainable to have 6½ billion people enjoying the material lives of the richest 1 billion, not to speak of emulating North American lifestyles (Daly 1996). It is unsustainable to have even the 300 million Americans living the way they currently do.

Environmental Bankruptcy

In order to provide a useful scenario of the environmental challenges facing capitalism, we can look to the more recent credit debacle. How is credit like the environment? First, and most obviously, both can be seen as limitless resources. Until relatively recently, few mainstream economists spoke or wrote about the importance of having a limited amount of "nature" around. Similarly, while many began cautioning about the huge debt overhang that characterized the global economy, but particularly the US, few actually predicted the depth and extent of the credit crisis of 2008.

Just as it has traditionally appeared that there would be enough material for all to get richer simultaneously, borrowing and lending seemed a perpetual generator of consumption. As long as one manipulated the right reserve requirements, and as long as everyone had faith in the system, we could borrow forever. In a perverse twist, many lenders no longer expected or even hoped to be paid back. Instead, loans and credit card balances could be maintained as ever growing assets fueled by high interest rates, which could magically be listed as income. Only minimal cash ever need to flow back from customers, who, armed with new credit devices and the ability to rollover debt, could borrow ever more.

Much as the situation with early wildcatters burning off the gas in oil wells, there seemed no need to protect a patrimony or prepare a system for change.

The events of 2007 and 2008 have shown us that apparently small disturbances in the system can have disastrous consequences. The overbuilding in "hot markets" and the provision of credit to those who had no capacity to pay back, combined with the interest of financial executives to use questionable accounting to increase their bonuses, all combined to produce a "perfect storm." The almost certain environmental constraints that the global economy will hit very soon in the twenty-first century closely resemble the credit crisis of 2007–8. Any one of a series of products or environmental consequences could pay the role of the housing bubble. It is possible that, as in the credit crisis, what begins it all has more to do with expectations than with any reality. An unseasonably warm January, flooding in Eastern Europe, disastrous typhoons and hurricanes, any of these could produce that crisis of confidence that would send the prices of materials to such heights as to make the operation of the global system impossible. While nineteenth-century thinkers may have spoken of conquering nature, perhaps we need to realize that we have simply become even more dependent on it.

Conclusion

This book has had two central goals: explaining how global capitalism developed into its present condition, including the events of 2008, and providing a guide for determining where it will go. For both tasks we have applied the two central principles of our analysis: that global capitalism is a historical creation whose rise and development can tell us much about its current structure, and that these developments have created a complex system whose properties and outcomes may not be fully predictable or controllable. In our conclusions we summarize our central findings and suggest the contours of future policies with which to manage our global economic reality.

How We Got Here

In tracing the history of global capitalism there are four critical turning points that can help us understand its current structure. The first of these is 1500. The specific date is not important except as a marker of the beginning of the European domination of the globe. Beginning in the previous century and continuing for 400 years, global history can be at least partly understood as a saga of conquest and domination. The genocide of the Americas, the organization of the Atlantic Slave Trade, the imposition of control over East Asia and later India, and the subjugation of China, all helped shape the current structure of the global economy. There have been and will be endless debates concerning the extent to which this European onslaught was responsible for the rise of the Atlantic economies or the concurrent relative decline of potential competitors. We suggest that the correlation between this process and the underlying development of global capitalism is too strong to ignore and has to be understood as an integral part of its history. In any case, regardless of the historical veracity of the association, in many parts of the world capitalism and Western domination are considered synonymous. This presents a perpetual problem of legitimacy for the global economic system whose challenge cannot be ignored.

The next critical date is 1800. This represents a turning point in three ways. First, during this period a series of technical and organizational barriers were removed that allowed production and consumption to explode and thus created the circulation system on which global capitalism is based. The most important of these barriers was the agricultural ceiling, which limited urbanization, specialization of labor, and subsequent industrial production. The concurrent application of non-human energy to manufacturing allowed the revolution in productivity that has characterized the last 200 years. The second turning point is related to our first date above. The divergence we have noted throughout the book between the production and consumption of the "West and the rest" begins roughly in the early nineteenth century. Many have argued that the continuing inequalities of the world all stem from where a society was at this period and that this legacy has been extremely difficult to escape. Third, this era saw the consolidation of private property and market exchange as the central institutions of European societies and the final eradication of feudalism. This shift allowed the particular practices and assumptions associated with capitalism to dominate first a small number of societies and then the world.

For the subsequent two centuries, global capitalism experienced spectacular rises and falls. Throughout the nineteenth century not only did production increase, but so also did the range of countries involved in it, the breadth of markets consuming it, and the intricacy of trade linking these expanded. By 1914, the world already had a well-developed global economy. Over the next three decades this was almost destroyed by competition within the capitalist world and from without by ideological opponents. The contagion effect that characterized the onslaught of the Great Depression also demonstrated some of the characteristics of a complex system. Our third date, 1945, marks the rebirth of the global capitalist economy led by the United States and its allied institutions. This period saw the creation of a new form of capitalism with greater regulation and more welfare provisions. The resulting "Glorious Thirty" saw a second expansion of capitalism, but it was slowed by the crisis of the 1970s and 1980s.

The fall of the Berlin Wall in 1989 marks our last great turning point. Three trends converged in the following decade. The first was the ideological victory of capitalism as it not only expanded its reach to all parts of the world, but also deepened its penetration of societies with new logics and mores. The second was the entry of the Pacific economies into what had previously been a largely North Atlantic system. This allowed for new sources of production and innovation as well as adding hundreds of millions of new consumers. A technological revolution equal in impact to that of the eighteenth and nineteenth centuries was the third trend. This made the interactions between the various parts of the global system possible. However, the confluence of these trends resulted in not only twenty years of unprecedented growth, but also new complexities and tighter coupling in the system, which made it much more fragile.

Throughout the text, and for each of these turning points, we have highlighted the interaction between states and markets and between political and economic rationales. This is particularly obvious for our first historical turning point, as the creation of the European empires would have been impossible without considerable state support. That the outlines of the global economic system still follow those of empires is clear from any analysis of its networks and hierarchies. The nineteenth century is often treated as the zenith of laissez-faire, yet we must recognize how much protectionist policies (again inseparable from state rule) served as the basis of the industrialization of many societies. Moreover, the infrastructure and policing needed to function in ever growing markets was a function of state capacity. The role of politics in the creation of the Cold War world is even more obvious. It would be impossible to understand the post-war economic order without reference to geopolitical competition. Moreover, there is little doubt of the importance played by a set of global institutions providing basic governance for international transactions and supported by the hegemonic state power. The last twenty years witnessed an attempt to move markets away from states. To a certain extent this was always more rhetoric than reality, but the impact of market fundamentalism in shaping the twenty-first-century economic system should not be underestimated. The crisis of 2008 was a product of such an ideology, which ignored the social and political basis of global capitalism.

The very institutions of the market on which we have focused, property and markets, are impossible without some form of political governance. Unless we wish to rely on individualized vigilante enforcement, governance structures are necessary to establish and protect property rights. Negotiations between property holders wishing to engage in some exchange are made immeasurably easier by the existence of contract enforcement mechanisms. States are not the enemies of markets, but their partners.

History is also behind the hierarchies we observe in our global system. A central message of this book has been the limits of the term "global." The world is not flat. For large parts of humanity (if not the majority) economic globalization has been much more of a whimper than a bang. The kinds of transactions that we associate with the global economy – eating at a McDonald's, logging onto the Web, and flying to a different country – are not universally available. Even for those who do participate in the global economic system, the majority do so on a relatively limited basis.

Why does this hierarchy appear and to what extent is global capitalism responsible? Much of the global income gap pre-dates the creation of the contemporary global economic order. One could argue, for example, that pre-capitalist destruction had more to do with African or South American underdevelopment than the actions of contemporary transnational corporations. The history with which societies enter into the global capitalist system has inertial qualities. One of the most astounding aspects of the Pacific boom of the past thirty years has been the region's apparent escape for a historical legacy. But we should appreciate the particularities of that history, as well as the domestic and political context in which it occurred, and not expect that this particular path is open to all. We argue that global capitalism can make societies richer, but first they need to be integrated into the system, and this needs to be done in ways conducive to development. Neither autarchy nor simple exploitation will work.

Where We Are

We have often referred to the underlying complexity of the global economic system. The events of 2007 and 2008 and their consequences perfectly demonstrate the nature of this complexity and the dangers associated with it. The global economic system involves the interactions of billions of transactions. Moreover, many of these are conditioned by the outcomes of others; the system is internally reflexive in that its actions are in part dictated by observations of itself. Computer technology has made it possible to link these transactions in an ever tightening and quickening web. There is very little slack in the system and even less time to make adjustments. Errors are multiplied and extremely contagious.

Consider the linking of the three structures we have highlighted: the flows of merchandize, money, and marketing. We can begin with the explosion in consumer demand which characterized the rise of global capitalism for 200 years, but which became more global and more powerful over the past two decades. This created opportunities in the two other structures: demand fueled trade, and the credit that was needed to pay for the demand led to an expansion of capital markets. The growth of finance in turn made the transactions of international trade possible, as without international credit many of these exchanges would have been impossible. The need for constant growth in the financial industry led to a search for ever more customers whose borrowing limits were stretched ever forward. The global system of trade, in turn, made the revolution of consumption possible by drastically lowering the prices of many goods thanks to the scale and level of specialization and completion it permitted. Money followed goods as previously closed national capital markets had to open up in order to compete for investments.

These same reinforcing relationships allowed a crisis in one sector to immediately infect the others. In order to maintain some accounting control over the spiraling mortgage markets, banks were forced to finally accept the fact that many of the loans they had made were now non-performing. Given the abuse of leverage and the spread of risk through securitization, this led to a freezing of the financial sector. Since a significant percentage of consumption was being done on credit, this tightening led to immediate reductions in purchases of everything, from houses to furniture to automobiles. This led to the overstocked warehouses and parking lots around the globe. The reduction in sales and trade, of course, made it ever more difficult to pay other debts, further straining the credit markets, and so on. This process occurred from the enterprise level to that of national treasuries. The link between US over-consumption and Chinese "over-saving" was a concrete example of how the various sectors of global capitalism were integrated. The fall in Chinese exports and the apparent weakness of the dollar led the PRC government to begin reconsidering its commitment to US Treasury Bills. This caused jitters throughout the world, further weakening stock markets and thus the ability of consumers to purchase Chinese goods. The speed at which these forms of interactions took place made it practically impossible to predict the direction or scope of change, much less to do something about it.

This complexity also haunts the challenges we have identified for global capitalism. We have made clear that the economic system needs a much stronger and more explicit system of governance and that the successes of periods such as the "Glorious Thirty" were partly based on state intervention that not only increased consumption through welfare, but also allowed the creation of a stable and predictable international trading regime. Yet the very complexity that would appear to require some governance may also make it impossible. By their very nature, complex systems frustrate control; when confronted by a crisis, one can never be sure where it originated and how different attempted cures will affect the system.

Trying to make the global system more equal involves contradictory forces that have been clear by the spread of globalization: the opportunities it has brought for some have often come at the expense of others. While the aggregate benefits from globalization are fairly clear, this does not mean that every individual has done better. The loss of unionized manufacturing jobs in the US is a good example. The move of production overseas has created new jobs at usually higher pay for many and the accompanying competitive dynamics have brought down the relative cost of products and increased their quality. This shift of jobs has led to a decline in between-country inequality. But, for the displaced workers, this has meant the disappearance of an economic way of life. Combined with the greater profits some of these moves have produced (which largely accrue to the very different social class that owns capital), this has led to increased inequality within the US. It has also increased inequality in the countries receiving the new jobs, as the distance between workers in new industries and their co-nationals left outside of the globalized economy has also grown. Such distributions shifts involve political choices and these may often contradict immediate economic logic. Global capitalism cannot ignore political pressures and attempt to exist in a world in which the social consequences of its actions do not matter, nor cannot it be a simple tool of politics. Defining a middle ground will be one of the major tasks for the next stage of global capitalism.

All these challenges pale in light of the environmental limits we are facing. There is a spectrum of models and analyses providing different timelines and risks, but all agree that we cannot act as if the current resource availability were eternal. The environmental sustainability of capitalism has to be a part of any policy decision made. The problem is that no single entity owns or runs global capitalism. Rather, it is a collective enterprise where all incentives push participants to let others pay the environmental bill. Moreover, the choices that need to be made will also involve distributional issues of who gets what and how much. The very inequality discussed earlier makes transnational cooperation difficult: when, for example, should we start the environmental meter? In 1800 or 2010? The debate on this will not be only between countries, but also within them, as some groups must pay more for what they have taken for granted. This will again involve political choices and pressures that may contradict ones stemming from the needs to resolve the governance and inequality dilemmas.

Finally, each of the challenges is inherently linked to the various structures we have described. The construction of global finance helps shape (but does not necessarily determine) levels of inequality. This sector may also be the most difficult, but also the most necessary, to control. Trade makes us so interdependent that we need to consider rules for assuring both stability and some form of equity. Our focus on consumption, of course, is perhaps the biggest threat to the environment and we will either need to accept new standards or new policing. In other words, the very things that threaten capitalism may also be the ones responsible for its dynamism. Efforts to address problems may produce greater ones. Much as in complex engineering systems, solutions may create worse dilemmas.

Paradoxes of Global Capitalism

Future generations will see 2008 as the concluding scene of another chapter in capitalism's history. It is hard not to expect that this year will be spoken in the same breath as 1929 or 1973. So what occurs in the new chapter that we are now starting? A cynical – yet empirically justifiable – view is that we are probably sowing the roots of the next great crisis. A hopeful – yet reasonable – view is that we are also being presented with an opportunity to make significant societal advances before this next great crisis comes. There is no doubt, however, that we sit at a critical moment, in which old institutions are frail, and what we do over the next few years will lay the groundwork for the next generation's institutionalized "rules of capitalism."

If we reflect on what happened in the last chapter of capitalism's saga, we see a story of dramatic gains and equally dramatic collective failures to meet serious concerns. The task at hand is to seek useful lessons that might help us build a better economic-organizational machine. What to keep and what to jettison? No social science can provide an absolute answer to this question as it involves not just institutional means, but also ethical ends. What we can do is to provide the analysis and information about the past and present that is required so that the future means match the ends we most value.

Over the past two decades, capitalism became more globally integrated and specialized, more privately owned and administered, less regulated, more commodified and commercialized, and more unified in a system of common political and legal rules and norms. These changes stem from the investment of authority in, diffusion of and entrenchment of, two basic economic-organizational precepts: private property and market exchange. The results were mixed. People were enriched, though unequally so. We invested in economic expansion aggressively, but pushed our luck with financial stability and the natural environment in the process. In many respects, we forewent tradition and a more locally rooted material life and progressively embraced a more globally oriented, and possibly consumption-addicted, lifestyle and culture. We overcame the great stresses of stagflation, but unleashed new stresses in the process.

The calamity in which we are now immersed may be an unavoidable facet of human economic organization. Joseph Schumpeter may have seen such moments as a desirable process of ruin and renewal that is capitalism's "creative destruction." Such destruction *is* creative, in the sense that much of today's capitalism was built on the ruins of former economic, political, and social systems; old institutions were destroyed to make room for the modern economy's creation. Whether or not this creativity is always wholly desirable is an entirely different matter.

If global capitalism is in fact responsible for all the new wealth, the rich opportunities for cross-cultural contact, the new personal liberties, the novel consumer and investment opportunities, or the relative geopolitical harmony among the world's core powers, then we should be concerned that we may lose these benefits. However, if inequality, continual economic pressure, environmental degradation, casino-like financial systems, or the subversion of cherished traditional cultural values are not being addressed well under global capitalism (or even caused by it), then we might well reconsider some of its principles.

First, expecting global capitalism to manage itself is not only wishful thinking, but also a folly we cannot afford to repeat. Global capitalism has produced historically unimagined prosperity, but it requires some form of governance to prevent the distortions that individual incentives can cause. Global capitalism is a product of historical turns, political choices, and social expectations, and these have to be taken into account whenever contemplating its costs and benefits.

Second, global capitalism cannot ignore the constraints of the environment or simply hope to resolve them through either technology or price mechanisms. Such expectations leave our entire world open to unacceptable risk. The premium gained by letting things go on as they are does not and cannot come close to balancing the potential catastrophe that awaits us. Given that our inability to predict at which point our actions might condemn us to a post-apocalyptic horror, it is not unreasonable to behave as conservative investors and begin accepting lower rates of return from our economy. This will necessarily involve both institutional shifts in how we measure costs and cultural changes in how much consumption we can reasonably expect.

Third, these decisions will run into the same distributional asymmetries we have written about throughout the book. The choices regarding what to do about these are arguably the most vexing for global capitalism. The lessons of history are less clear here. On the one hand, societies have survived with massive inequities for centuries. On the other hand, the very complexity and integrative properties of global capitalism may make long-term inequities untenable. Global capitalism has created an open world and this has, in turn, enriched our lives. It has also made us much more dependent on each other. With dependence comes a responsibility to ensure that the system takes care of all, not just the privileged few. Whether global capitalism can deliver on that promise will help determine its fate.

Notes

Introduction

1 *Washington Post*, January 11, 2009, p. 5.
2 Listing bibliographic references for each author cited here would be cumbersome. Interested readers can obtain an introduction as well as a full list of works in Smelser and Swedberg (2005).

Chapter 1 Global Capitalism

1 Unless specified, the figures in this chapter are for 2007; the details of 2008 are dealt with at the end of the chapter. Data for this section is from the World Bank and the UNDP.
2 Our division of the world is geographical. Some would argue for a more class-centered categorization but, as we show in chapter 6, global inequality begins with the society in which one lives.
3 For a start, see Pomeranz 2000, and Pomeranz and Topik 2005.
4 *Les trente glorieuses* is the French term for the period from the Liberation of Paris in 1944 to the oil crisis of 1973 when French and Western European economic and social life was transformed.
5 Given the "literary" flavor of socialist statistics, the gap was no doubt even wider. Data from: <http://www.conference-board.org/economics/database. cfm>.
6 Import-substituting industrialization (ISI) was a policy designed to replace relatively expensive inputs from abroad with domestic equivalents.
7 IMF *World Economic Outlook (WEO) Crisis and Recovery*, April 2009. Available at: <http://www.imf.org/external/pubs/ft/weo/2009/01/index.htm>.

Chapter 2 Trade

1 Within these, the leading sector is "Office and Telecommunications" equipment which has increased almost twenty-fold since 1980 and now accounts for 12.3 percent of merchandise trade. Another dynamic sector is clothing which has grown eightfold and accounts for 2.6 percent of all trade. Other leading manufacturing sectors (and their share of world trade) are chemicals (10.6 percent) and automotives (8.6 percent).

2 In autos, as late as 1961, the United States accounted for 48 percent of passenger car production in the world. By 1971, the number was 32 percent, by 1981, 23 percent, by 1991, 15 percent, and by 2006, 9 percent. Japan and Germany were obviously the major factors in this decline as their share rose from 18 percent in 1961 (overwhelmingly from Germany) to 33 percent in 2006 (with Japan producing roughly twice that of Germany). New major entrants include Brazil, South Korea, Spain, and, beginning in the twenty-first century, China, which now accounts for over 8 percent of passenger car manufacturing (Bureau of Transportation Statistics).

3 Because of this geographic division, it is important to treat with caution statistics speaking of an aggregate transformation in the relationship of "developing countries" with the global market. The key is whether or not this category includes China.

4 For some more detail on networks and suggesting what the trade network looks like, see: <http://qed.princeton.edu/main/MG/Data_and_Analysis>.

5 Also known as the "paradox of plenty," this is the observed relationship between possessing valuable natural resources (oil, diamonds, etc.) and having both authoritarian regimes and low growth.

6 Another possible comparison is with Spain and the EU. From 1986 to 1996, the ratio of Spain and Portugal's GDP to the rest of Western Europe improved significantly, while from 1994 to 2004, Mexico actually lost ground against the United States.

7 Growing food industry concentration is an important issue. In the US, for example, a few companies control the production of meats. One company, Cargill, is not only a top packer of meat, but also handles a large part of grain production. A few companies largely control the global market for fertilizers and for seeds (FAO: <http://www.fao.org/docrep/005/y4671e/y4671e0e.htm>).

8 See the World Bank report: <http://www.worldbank.org/foodprices/>.

Chapter 3 Finance and Wealth

1 This means that it is dedicated to being held in a particular currency.

2 For detailed data, see: <http://www.treas.gov/tic/mfh.txt>.

Chapter 4 Marketing and Consumption

1 All in 2005 US dollars (Economist Intelligence Unit 2006).

2 The average person in the "First World" consumes roughly double that of the typical Eastern European, roughly four times the typical Middle Easterner or Latin American, or fifteen times the typical sub-Saharan African.

3 The net effect of these new forms of retail is a matter of dispute. In the US, counties appear to experience more poverty when Wal-Marts are present (Goetz and Swaminathan 2006), perhaps with more jobs, but poorer prevailing wages (Neumark, Zhang, and Ciccarella 2007). In many of the world's cities, the disappearance of small stores meant whole sectors of the relatively new urban classes (the petty bourgeoisie) practically disappeared.

Chapter 5 Governance

1 Obviously, the Soviet-led version took coercion to very different levels.

2 Consider the improbability of sociologists, anthropologists, and psychologists playing a powerful intellectual in the definition of a national political economy. The phenomenal exception of Brazil's Fernando Henrique Cardoso may actually prove the rule: he was most celebrated for using his political charisma and skills in selling a fairly orthodox model.

3 See Gwartney and Lawson (2007) for detailed information on these indices.

4 The following observations are rooted in changes to liberalization indexes in Gwartney and Lawson's (2007) data.

5 Governments are generally held to be larger in bigger economies (called "Wagner's Law") (see Peacock and Scott 2000). Likewise, democracies may face stronger pressures to redistribute and protect laborers.

6 For data, see: <http://info.worldbank.org/governance/wgi/index.asp>.

Chapter 6 Inequality

1 One estimate is that North America accounts for 34 percent of the world's wealth, Europe 30 percent, the Asia Pacific region 24 percent, and the rest of the world 12 percent. The top five countries (US, Japan, Germany, Italy, and the UK) account for two thirds of the world's wealthiest individuals (Davies et al. 2006).

2 See the Inequality Project at the University of Texas, run by James Galbraith: <www.utip.gov.utexas.edu/data.html>, or the UNDP Human Development Report: <http://hdr.undp.org/en/reports/global/hdr2006/>. See also <www.gapminder.org>.

3 Based on the Lorenz curve, the Gini coefficient is a statistical measure of income or wealth distribution. It is essentially a ratio with values between 0 and 1. The value 0 means a perfect equality where everyone has the same and 1 is perfect inequality (where one person has all the income). Usually

expressed as a Gini index (Gini coefficient multiplied by 100) with values of 0 to 100.

4 Simon Kuznets (1955) posited that, as national income rose, inequality would first increase and then decline.

5 Human Development Index (HDI) is a relative measure of well-being that takes into account wealth, education, and health.

6 Two excellent summaries may be found in the IMF's *World Economic Outlook* for 2007 (chapter 4), and Firebaugh 2000.

7 Derived from data from the Conference Board: <www.ggdc.net/databases/ted. htm>.

8 This is a term the financial industry uses for those with investible assets of over $1 million (before the summer of 2008).

Chapter 7 Living with Limits

1 Within the same rough income categories, Japan consumes half the energy per capita as the United States, Spain one third that of Canada, and Brazil one third that of Russia.

2 See US Energy Information Administration at: <http://www.eia.doe.gov/>; the UN Environmental Program at <http://www.unep.org/>; the American Petroleum Institute at: <http://www.api.org/>; and OPEC at: <http://www. opec.org/home/>. More details are available through the British Petroleum kuy78yijStatistical annuals: <http://www.bp.com/productlanding.do?categor yId=6929&contentId=7044622>.

3 For data on these issues, see: <http://www.epa.gov/cleanenergy/energy-and-you/affect/nuclear.html> and: <http://www.enotes.com/science-fact-finder/environment/how-much-solid-waste-generated-annually-united>.

4 Externalities are costs from the transaction that are not directly borne by those doing the buying and selling.

References

Abaza, Mona. 2001. "Shopping Malls, Consumer Culture and the Reshaping of Public Space in Egypt." *Theory, Culture and Society* 18: 97–122.

Abu-Lughod, J. L. 1989. *Before European Hegemony: The World System A.D. 1250–1350*. New York: Oxford University Press.

Acemoglu, Daron. 2005. "Politics and Economics in Weak and Strong States." *Journal of Monetary Economics* 52: 1199–1226.

Alesina, Alberto, Sule Ozler, Nouriel Roubini, and Phillip Swagel. 1996. "Political Instability and Economic Growth." *Journal of Economic Growth* 1: 189–211.

Alvarez, R. Michael, Geoffrey Garrett, and Peter Lange. 1991. "Government Partisanship, Labor Organization, and Macroeconomic Performance." *American Political Science Review* 85: 539–56.

American Association for the Advancement of Science. 2000. *Atlas of Population and the Environment*. Berkeley, CA: University of California Press.

Anand, Sudhur, and Paul Segal. 2008. "What Do We Know about Global Income Inequality?" *Journal of Economic Literature* 46/1: 57–94.

Andrews, David M. 1994. "Capital Mobility and State Autonomy: Toward a Structural Theory of International Monetary Relations." *International Studies Quarterly* 38: 193–218.

Appelbaum, Richard P., and Nelson Lichtenstein. 2006. "Supply-Chains, Workers' Chains and the New World of Retail Supremacy." Forthcoming in *International Labor and Working Class History*.

Armijo, Leslie Elliott, and Philippe Faucher. 2002. "'We Have a Consensus': Explaining Political Support for Market Reforms in Latin America." *Latin American Politics and Society* 44: 1–40.

Arrighi, G. 1994. *The Long Twentieth Century: Money, Power, and the Origins of Our Times*. London; New York: Verso.

Aslund, Anders. 1995. *How Russia Became a Market Economy*. Washington, DC: Brookings Institution Press.

References

Attewell, Paul, and S. Madheswaran. Forthcoming. "The Price of Globalization: Wage Penalties and Caste Inequality in 'Liberal' India." In Centeno and Newman, forthcoming.

Bank for International Settlements. 2005. "Triennial Central Bank Survey: Foreign Exchange and Derivatives Market Activity in 2004." Basel: Bank for International Settlements.

Bartels, Larry M. 2008. *Unequal Democracy: The Political Economy of the New Gilded Age*. New York/Princeton, NJ: Russell Sage Foundation/Princeton University Press.

Bartels, Robert. 1976. *The History of Marketing Thought*. Columbus, OH: Grid Publishers.

Baumol, William J., Robert Litan, and Carl Schramm. 2007. *Good Capitalism, Bad Capitalism*. New Haven, CT: Yale University Press.

Bayly, C. A. *The Birth of the Modern World, 1780–1914*. 2004. Oxford: Blackwell.

Bebchuk, Lucia Ayre, and Lars Stole. 1994. "Do Short-Term Managerial Objectives Lead to Under- or Over-Investment in Long-Term Projects?" In *NBER Working Paper No. T0098*. Cambridge, MA: National Bureau of Economic Research.

Bell, D. 1973. *The Coming of Post-Industrial Society; A Venture in Social Forecasting*. New York: Basic Books.

Bertaut, Carol, and Martha Starr-McCluer. 2000. "Household Portfolios in the United States." In *Federal Reserve Board Finance and Economics Discussion Series Paper, 2000–26*. Washington, DC: Federal Reserve Board.

Bhagwati, Jagdish. 2004. *In Defense of Globalization*. New York: Oxford University Press.

Bikhchandani, Sushil, David Hirshleifer, and Ivo Welch. 1992. "A Theory of Fads, Fashion, Custom, and Cultural Change as Informational Cascades." *Journal of Political Economy* 100: 992–1026.

Birdsall, Nancy. 2005. "The World is Not Flat: Inequality and Injustice in our Global Economy." Helsinki: WIDER Annual Lecture.

Black, Donald. 1976. *The Behavior of Law*. New York: Academic Press.

Black, Sandra E., and Elizabeth Brainerd. 2004. "Importing Equality? The Impact of Globalization on Gender Discrimination." *Industrial and Labor Relations Review* 57/4: 540–59.

Block, Fred L. 1977. *The Origins of International Economic Disorder: A Study of United States International Monetary Policy from World War II to the Present*. Berkeley, CA: University of California Press.

Block, Fred. 1994. "The Roles of the State in the Economy." In Neil J. Smelser and Richard Swedberg, *The Handbook of Economic Sociology*. Princeton, NJ: Princeton University Press/Russel Sage Foundation, pp. 691–710.

Bookstaber, Richard. 2007. *A Demon of Our Own Design*. Hoboken, NJ: John Wiley & Sons.

References

Bordo, Michael D. 1993. "The Bretton Woods International Monetary System: A Historical Overview." In Michael D. Bordo and Barry Eichengreen, eds, *A Retrospective on the Bretton Woods System: Lessons for International Monetary Reform*. Chicago, IL: University of Chicago Press, pp. 3–98.

Bourdieu, Pierre. 1984. *Distinction: A Social Critique of the Judgement of Taste*. Cambridge, MA: Harvard University Press.

Bover, Olympia. 2008. "Wealth Inequality and Household Structure: US and Spain." In *Documetos de Trabajo 0804*. Madrid: Banco de España.

Braudel, F. 1982. *Civilization and Capitalism, 15th–18th Century*. New York: Harper & Row.

British Petroleum. 2009. *Statistical Review of World Energy 2009*. Available at: <http://www.bp.com/productlanding.do?categoryId=6929&contentId=70446 22>.

Brooks, Sarah M. 2005. "Interdependent and Domestic Foundations of Policy Change: The Diffusion of Pension Privatization Around the World." *International Studies Quarterly* 49: 273–94.

Bruton, Henry J. 1998. "A Reconsideration of Import Substitution." *Journal of Economic Literature* 36: 903–36.

Bulmer-Thomas, Victor. 1995. *The Economic History of Latin America since Independence*. New York: Cambridge University Press.

Burkett, Paul. 1999. *Marx and Nature*. New York: St Martin's Press.

Bussiere, Dave. 2000. "Evidence of a Marketing Periodic Literature within the American Economic Association, 1895–1936." *Journal of Macromarketing* 20: 137–43.

Calavita, K., R. Tillman, and H. N. Pontell. 1997. "The Savings and Loan Debacle, Financial Crime and the State." *Annual Review of Sociology* 23: 19–38.

Calder, Lendol Glen. 1999. *Financing the American Dream: A Cultural History of Consumer Credit*. Princeton, NJ: Princeton University Press.

Cameron, Pondo, and Larry Neal. 2004. *A Concise Economic History of the World*, 4th edn. Oxford: Oxford University Press.

Campbell, Colin. 1987. *The Romantic Ethic and the Spirit of Modern Consumerism*. Oxford/New York: Blackwell.

Campinale, Claudio. 2005. "Increasing Returns to Savings and Wealth Inequality." In *Instituto Valenciano de Investigaciones Economicas, S.A.*, WP-AD 2005–20. Valencia: Instituto Valenciano.

Cardoso, F. E., and Enzo Faletto. 1979. *Dependency and Development in Latin America*. Berkeley, CA: University of California Press.

Castells, M. 1996. *The Rise of the Network Society*. Malden, MA: Blackwell.

Centeno, Miguel. 1994. *Democracy within Reason*. University Park, PA: Penn State University Press.

Centeno, Miguel, and Katherine Newman, eds. Forthcoming. *Discrimination in a Globalized World*. Oxford: Oxford University Press.

References

Chakravarty, Shoibal, et al. 2009. "Sharing Global CO2 Emissions Among 1 Billion High Emitters." *Proceedings of the National Academy of Sciences*, July 7.

Chandler, Alfred. 1999. *Scale and Scope: The Dynamics of Industrial Capitalism.* Cambridge, MA: Harvard University Press.

Chang, Ha-Joon. 2002. *Kicking away the Ladder.* London: Anthem Press.

Chappell, H. W., and L. G. Viega. 2000. "Economics and Elections in Western Europe, 1960–1997." *Electoral Studies* 19: 183–97.

Chen, Shaohua, and Martin Ravallion. 2007. "Absolute Poverty Measures for the Developing World, 1981–2004." *Proceedings of the National Academy of Sciences of the United States of America* 104: 16575–762.

Chotikapanich, Dunagkamon, and D. S. Prasado Rao, William E. Griffiths, and Vicar Valencia. 2007. "Global Inequality: Recent Evidence and Trends." *UNU-WIDER, Research Paper No. 2007/01.* Helsinki: UNU-WIDER.

Clark, Brett, and Richard York. 2005. "Carbon Metabolism: Global Capitalism, Climate Change, and the Biospheric Rift." *Theory and Society* 34: 391–428.

Cohen, Joseph Nathan, and Miguel Angel Centeno. 2006. "Neoliberalism and Patterns of Economic Performance, 1980–2000." *Annals of the American Academy of Political and Social Science* 606: 32–67.

Cohen, Lizabeth. 1996. "From Town Center to Shopping Center: The Reconfiguration of Community Marketplaces in Postwar America." *American Historical Review* 101: 1050–81.

Cohen, Lizabeth. 2003. *A Consumers' Republic: The Politics of Mass Consumption in Postwar America.* New York: Knopf; distributed by Random House.

Collier, Paul. 2007. *The Bottom Billion.* New York: Oxford University Press.

Connor, John M. 2001. *Global Price Fixing.* New York: Springer.

Cooke, Abigail, Sara Curran, April Linton, and Andrew Schrank, eds. 2008. "Trading Morsels." Special issue of *Globalizations* 5/2.

Cornia, Giovanni Andrea. 2003. "Impact of Liberalisation and Globalisation on Within-country Income Inequality." *CESifo Economic Studies* 49: 581–616.

Cornia, Giovanni Andrea, and Sampsa Kiiski. 2004. "Trends in Income Distribution." In G. Cornia, ed., *Inequality, Growth and Poverty in an Era of Liberalization and Globalization.* Oxford: Oxford University Press, pp. 26–55.

Cukierman, Alex, Steven B. Web, and Bilin Neyapti. 1992. "Measuring the Independence of Central Banks and Its Effect on Policy Outcomes." *World Bank Economic Review* 6: 353–98.

Cybriwsky, Roman. 1999. "Changing Patterns of Urban Public Space: Observations and Assessments from the Tokyo and New York Metropolitan Areas." *Cities* 16: 223–31.

Daly, Herman. *Beyond Growth.* 1996. New York: Beacon.

Davies, James, Susanna Sandström, Anthony Shorrocks, and Edward Wolff. 2006. *World Distribution of Human Wealth.* Helsinki: UNU-WIDER.

References

Deaton, Angus. 2006. "Global Patterns of Income and Health: Facts, Interpretations, and Policies." Helsinki: WIDER Annual Lecture.

de Ferranti, David, Guillermo Perry, Francisco H. G. Ferreira, and Michael Walton. 2003. *Inequality in Latin America and the Caribbean: Breaking with History?* Washington, DC: World Bank.

DeLong, J. Bradford. 1993. "Growth in the World Economy, ca. 1870–1990." In Horst Siebert, ed., *Economic Growth in the World Economy*. Tübingen: J. C. B. Mohr.

Dewan, Sanjeev, and Kenneth L. Kraemer. 2000. "Information Technology and Productivity: Evidence from Country-Level Data." *Management Science* 46: 548–62.

Dicken, Peter. 2003. *Global Shift*. London: Sage.

Dikhanov, Yuri. 2005. "Trends in Global Income Distribution, 1970–2000, and Scenarios for 2015." Presented at Third Forum on Human Development, January. Paris: UNDP.

DiMaggio, Paul J., and Walter W. Powell 1983 "The Iron Cage Revisited: Institutional Isomorphism and Collective Rationality in Organizational Fields." *American Sociological Review* 48: 147–60.

DiMaggio, Paul J., and Walter W. Powell. 1991. "Bringing Society Back In: Symbols, Practices, and Institutional Contraditions." In Walter W. Powell and Paul J. DiMaggio, eds, *The New Institutionalism in Organizational Analysis*. Chicago, IL: University of Chicago Press, pp. 1–38.

Dobbin, Frank R. 1993. "The Social Construction of the Great Depression: Industrial Policy During the 1930s in the United States, Britain and France." *Theory and Society* 22: 1–56.

Dollar, David. 2005. "Globalization, Poverty and Inequality." *World Bank Research Observer* 20: 145–75.

Dollar, David. 2007. "Poverty, Inequality, and Social Disparities during China's Economic Reform." *World Bank Working Paper, WPS4253*, June. Washington, DC: World Bank.

Dolsak, Nives, and Elinor Ostrom, eds. 2003. *The Commons in the New Millennium*. Cambridge, MA: MIT Press.

Dooley, Michael P., David Folkerts-Landau, and Peter Garber. 2003. "An Essay on the Revived Bretton Woods System." In *NBER Working Paper No. 9971*. Cambridge, MA: National Bureau of Economic Research.

Dooley, Michael P., David Folkerts-Landau, and Peter Garber. 2004. "The Revived Bretton Woods System: The Effects of Periphery Intervention and Reserve Management on Interest Rates and Exchange Rates in Center Countries." In *NBER Working Paper No. 10332*. Cambridge, MA: National Bureau of Economic Research.

Dornbusch, Rudiger. 1998. "Capital Controls: An Idea Whose Time Has Passed." In Stanley Fischer, Richard N. Cooper, Rudiger Dornbusch, Peter M. Garber, Carlos Massad, Jacques J. Polak, Dani Rodrik, and Savak S.

References

Tarapore, eds, *Should the IMF Pursue Capital-Account Convertibility? Essays in International Finance No. 207*. Princeton, NJ: Princeton University Press.

Dorussen, Hans, and Harvey D. Palmer. 2002. "The Context of Economic Voting: An Introduction." In H. Dorussen and M. Taylor, eds, *Economic Voting*. New York: Routledge, pp. 1–14.

Dreher, Axel. 2008. "IMF Conditionality: Theory and Evidence." in *KOF Working Papers No. 188*. Zurich: Swiss Federal Institute of Technology.

Druckman, James, and Paul Warwick. 2005. "The Missing Piece: Measuring Portfolio Salience in Western European Parliamentary Democracies." *European Journal of Political Research* 44: 17–42.

Drummond, Helga. 2002. "Living in a Fool's Paradise: The Collapse of Barings' Bank." *Management Decision* 40: 232–8.

The Economist. 2008. "Foreign Reserves." *The Economist*. Economist.com Economic & Financial Indicators. Available at: <http://www.economist.com/markets/indicators/displaystory.cfm?story_id=14288967>.

Economist Intelligence Unit. 2006. "EIU Country Data." Bureau Van Dijk Electronic Publishing, London: Economist Intelligence Unit.

Economist Intelligence Unit. 2008. "EIU Country Data." Bureau Van Dijk Electronic Publishing, London: Economist Intelligence Unit.

Edwards, Sebastian. 1995. *Crisis and Reform in Latin America: From Despair to Hope*. New York: Published for the World Bank [by] Oxford University Press.

Ehrlich, Paul R., and Lawrence Goulder. 2007. "Is Current Consumption Excessive?" *Conservation Biology* 21/5: 145–1154.

Eichengreen, Barry. 1999. "Hegemonic Stability Theories of the International Monetary System." In Jeffry A. Frieden and David A. Lake, eds, *International Political Economy*. New York: Routledge, pp. 220–45.

Eichengreen, Barry. 2007. *The European Economy since 1945*. Princeton, NJ: Princeton University Press.

Eichengreen, Barry, and Carlos Arteta. 2002. "Banking Crises in Emerging Markets." In Mario I. Blejer and Marko Skreb, eds, *Financial Policies in Emerging Markets*. Cambridge, MA: MIT Press, pp. 47–94.

Evans, Peter. 1995. *Embedded Autonomy*. Princeton, NJ: Princeton University Press.

Evans, Peter, and James Rauch. 1999. "Bureaucracy and Growth: A Cross-national Analysis of the Effects of 'Weberian' State Structures." *American Sociological Review* 64: 748–65.

Ewen, Stuart. 1976. *Captains of Consciousness: Advertising and the Social Roots of the Consumer Culture*. New York: McGraw-Hill.

Federico, Giovanni. 1996. "An Econometric Model of World Silk Production, 1870–1914." *Explorations in Economic History* 33: 250–74.

Feinstein, Charles H. 1998. "Pessimism Perpetuated: Real Wages and the Standard of Living in Britain During and after the Industrial Revolution." *Journal of Economic History* 58: 625–58.

References

Feldstein, Martin. 1999. "Self-Protection for Emerging Market Economies." In *NBER Working Paper No. 6907*. Cambridge, MA: National Bureau of Economic Research.

Ferraro, Vincent, and Melissa Rosser. 1994. "Global Debt and Third World Development." In Michael Klare and Daniel Thomas, eds, *World Security: Challenges for a New Century*. New York: St Martin's Press, pp. 332–55.

Ferreira, Francisco H. G., and Martin Ravallion. 2008. "Global Poverty and Inequality: A Review of the Evidence." In *World Bank Policy Research Working Paper No. 4623*. Washington, DC: World Bank.

Feshbach, Murray, and Alfred Friendly Jr. *Ecocide*. 1993. New York: Basic Books.

Findlay, Ronald, and Kevin O'Rourke. 2007. *Power and Plenty: Trade, War, and the World Economy in the Second Millennium*. Princeton, NJ: Princeton University Press.

Finley, Moses I. 1999 [1973]. *The Ancient Economy*. Berkeley, CA: University of California Press.

Firebaugh, Glenn. 1999. "Empirics of World Income Inequality," *American Journal of Sociology* 104: 1597–1630

Firebaugh, Glenn. 2000. "The Trend in Between-Nation Income Inequality". *Annual Review of Sociology* 26: 323–39.

Firebaugh, Glenn. 2003. *The New Geography of Global Income Inequality*. Cambridge, MA: Harvard University Press.

Fischer, Stanley, Ratna Sahay, and Carlos A. Végh. 2002. "Modern Hyper- and High Inflations." *Journal of Economic Literature* 40: 837–80.

Fligstein, Neil. 1990. *The Transformation of Corporate Control*. Cambridge, MA: Harvard University Press.

Flood, Robert, and Nancy Marion. 1999. "Perspectives on Recent Currency Crisis Literature." *International Journal of Finance and Economics* 4: 1–26.

Food and Agriculture Organization. 2004. *The State of Food Insecurity in the World*. Geneva: ILO. Available at: <http://www.fao.org/docrep/007/y5650e/y5650e00.HTM>.

Fortune Magazine. 2008. "Global 500: Our Annual Ranking of the World's Largest Corporations." *Fortune Magazine*. Available at: <http://money.com/magazines/fortune/global 500/2008/full_list/>.

Foster, James Bellamy. 2000. *Marx's Ecology*. New York.

Fratzscher, Marcel. 2003. "On Currency Crises and Contagion." *International Journal of Finance and Economics* 8: 109–29.

Frieden, J. A. 2006. *Global Capitalism: Its Fall and Rise in the Twentieth Century*. New York: W.W. Norton.

Friedland, Roberg, and Robert R. Alford. 1991. "Bringing Society Back In: Symbols, Practices, and Institutional Contradictions." In Walter W. Powell and Paul J. DiMaggio, eds, *The New Institutionalism in Organizational Analysis*. Chicago, IL: University of Chicago Press, pp. 232–66.

References

Friedman, M. 2002 [1962]. *Capitalism and Freedom*. Chicago, IL, University of Chicago Press.

Friedman, T. L. 2005. *The World Is Flat: A Brief History of the Twenty-First Century*. New York: Farrar, Straus, and Giroux.

Fukuyama, Francis. 1992. *The End of History and the Last Man*. New York: Free Press.

Garber, Peter. 1994. "Famous First Bubbles." In Robert Flood and Peter Garber, eds, *Speculative Bubbles, Speculative Attacks, and Policy Switching*. Cambridge, MA: MIT Press, p. 31.

Garibaldi, Ida. 2008. "NATO and European Energy Security." *AEI European Outlook*, March,1. Available at: <www.aei.org/outlook/27719>.

Gereffi, Gary. 2005. "The Global Economy." In Neil Smelser and Richard Swedberg, eds, *The Handbook of Economic Sociology*. Princeton, NJ: Princeton University Press.

Gereffi, Gary. 2006. "New Development Regimes: Insights from China and Mexico". Paper presented at Observing Trade Conference. Princeton, NJ: Observing Trade Conference.

Gereffi, Gary, and Miguel Korzeniewicz, eds. 1994. *Commodity Chains and Global Capitalism*. Prager Press.

Giersch, Herbert, Karl-Heinz Paqué, and Holger Schmieding. 1992. *The Fading Miracle: Four Decades of Market Economy in Germany*. New York: Cambridge University Press.

Goetz, Stephan J., and Hema Swaminathan. 2006. "Wal-Mart and County-Wide Poverty." *Social Sciences* Quarterly 87: 211–26.

Goldberg, Pinelopi, and Michael M. Knetter. 1996. "Goods Prices and Exchange Rates: What Have We Learned?" In *NBER Working Paper No. W5862*. Cambridge, MA: National Bureau of Economic Research.

Gordon, R.B., M. Bertram, and T.E. Graedel. 2006. "Metal Stocks and Sustainability." *Proceedings of the National Academy of Sciences* 103/5: 1209–14.

Gramsci, Antonio. 1992 [1927]. *Prison Notebooks*. New York: Columbia University Press.

Gray, Mark, et al. 2006. "Women and Globalization: A Study of 180 Countries, 1975–2000." *International Organization* 60/2: 293–333.

Gunder Frank, Andre. 1966. *The Development of Underdevelopment*. New York: Monthly Review Press.

Gwartney, James, and Robert Lawson. 2007. *Economic Freedom of the World: 2007 Annual Report*. Vancouver: Fraser Institute.

Haber, Stephen H., Armando Razo, and Noel Maurer. 2003. *The Politics of Property Rights: Political Instability, Credible Commitments and Economic Growth in Mexico*. New York: Cambridge University Press.

Haggard, Stephan. 1990. *Pathways from the Periphery*. Ithaca, NY: Cornell University Press.

References

Hall Peter, and David Soskice, eds. 1999. *Varieties of Capitalism*. New York: Oxford University Press.

Hamilton, Gary, and Robert Feenstra. 2006. "Devil in the Details." Paper presented at Observing Trade Conference. Princeton, NJ: Observing Trade Conference.

Hardin, Garrett. 1968. "The Tragedy of the Commons." *Science* 162/3859: 1243–8.

Harrison, Lawrence, and Samuel Huntington. 2001. *Culture Matters*. New York: Basic Books.

Harvey, David. 2005. *A Brief History of Neoliberalism*. New York: Oxford University Press.

Hasenfeld, Yeheskel, and Jane A. Rafferty. 1989. "The Determinants of Public Attitudes toward the Welfare State." *Social Forces* 67: 1028–48.

Hassan, Salah S., and Lea Pravel Katsanis. 1994. "Global Market Segmentation Strategies and Trends." In S. S. Hassan and E. Kaynak, eds, *Globalization of Consumer Markets*. New York: Howarth Press, pp. 47–62.

Haupt, Heinz-Gerhard. 2004. "The History of Consumption in Western Europe in the Nineteenth and Twentieth Centuries: Some Questions and Perspectives for Comparative Studies." In H. Kaelble, ed., *The European Way: European Societies in the 19th and 20th Centuries*. New York: Berghahn Books, pp. 68–89.

Hawley, James P., and Andrew T. Williams. 2000. *The Rise of Fiduciary Capitalism: How Institutional Investors Can Make Corporate America More Democratic*. Philadelphia, PA: University of Pennsylvania Press.

Hayek, Friedrich A. 1944. *The Road to Serfdom*. London: G. Routledge & Sons.

Hayek, Friedrich A. 1945. "The Uses of Knowledge in Society." *American Economic Review* 35: 519–30.

Healy, Paul M., and Krisha G. Palepu. 2003. "The Fall of Enron." *Journal of Economic Perspectives* 17: 3–26.

Held, David. 1998. *Global Transformations: Politics, Economics, and Culture*. Stanford, CA: Stanford University Press.

Held, D., A. G. McGrew, et al. 1999. *Global Transformations: Politics, Economics, and Culture*. Stanford, CA: Stanford University Press.

Held, David, and Ayse Kaya, eds. 2007. *Global Inequality*. Cambridge: Polity.

Helleiner, Eric. 1994. *States and the Reemergence of Global Finance: From Bretton Woods to the 1990s*. Ithaca, NY: Cornell University Press.

Heritage Foundation. 2008. *Index of Economic Freedom*. Washington, DC: Heritage Foundation and Wall Street Journal.

Hirschman, A. O. 1977. *The Passions and the Interests: Political Arguments for Capitalism before Its Triumph*. Princeton, NJ: Princeton University Press.

Hirshleifer, David, and Siew Hong Teoh. 2003. "Herd Behavior and Cascading in Capital Markets: a Review and Synthesis." *European Financial Management* 9: 25–66.

References

Hirst, Paul, and Grahame Thompson. 1996. *Globalization in Question: The International Economy and the Possibilities of Governance*. Oxford: Blackwell.

Hobsbawm, E. J. 1969. *The Age of Revolution: Europe 1789–1848*. New York: Praeger Publishers.

Hobsbawm, E. J. 1975. *The Age of Capital, 1848–1875*. New York: Scribner.

Hobsbawm, E. J. 1987. *The Age of Empire, 1875–1914*. New York: Pantheon Books.

Hobsbawm, E. J. 1994. *The Age of Extremes: A History of the World, 1914–1991*. New York: Pantheon Books.

Hodess, Robin. 2004. "Introduction." In *Global Corruption Report 2004*, edited by Transparency International. Sterling, VA: Pluto Press.

Hoppit, Julian. 1986. "Financial Crises in Eighteenth-Century England." *Economic History Review* 39: 39–58.

Hout, Michael. 2006. "Economic Change and Social Mobility." In Therborn, *Inequalities in the World*.

Interbrand and *BusinessWeek*. 2007a. "All Brands Are Not Created Equal: Best Global Brands 2007." *Interbrand* and *BusinessWeek*. Available at: <www.interbrand.com/best_global_brands.aspx>.

Interbrand and *BusinessWeek*. 2007b. "Best Chinese Brands 2006: A Ranking by Brand Value." *Interbrand* and *BusinessWeek*. Available at: <www.interbrand.com/images/studies/07BCB071206.pdf>.

International Energy Agency. 2008. *World Energy Outlook, 2008*. Paris: IEA.

International Monetary Fund. 2007. *World Economic Outlook: Spillovers and Cycles in the Global Economy*. Washington, DC: IMF, April.

International Monetary Fund. 2008. *Time Series Data on International Reserves and Foreign Currency Liquidity: Official Reserve Assets*. Washington, DC: International Monetary Fund.

International Organization for Migration. 2008. *World Migration 2008: Managing Labor Mobility in the Evolving Global Economy*. Geneva: International Organization for Migration.

Isard, Peter. 2005. *Globalization and the International Financial System: What's Wrong and What Can Be Done*. New York: Cambridge University Press.

Johns, Jennifer. 2006. "Video Games Production Networks: Value Capture, Power Relations and Embededness." *Journal of Economic Geography* 6: 151–80.

Jones, Geoffrey. 2005. "Multinationals from the 1930s to the 1980s." In Alfred D. Chandler, Jr., and Bruce Mazlish, eds, *Leviathans: Multinational Corporations and the New Global History*. Cambridge: Cambridge University Press.

Judt, Tony. 2005. *Postwar*. New York: Penguin.

Kaminsky, Graciela, and Carmen Reinhart. 2000. "On Crises, Contagion and Confusion." *Journal of International Economics* 51: 145–68.

Kanbur, Ravi, and Anthony Venables. 2007. "Spatial Disparities and Economic Development." In Held and Kaya, *Global Inequality*, pp. 204–16.

References

Katz, Elihu, and Paul Felix Lazarsfeld. 2006 [1955]. *Personal Influence: The Part Played by People in the Flow of Mass Communications*. New Brunswick, NJ: Transaction Publishers.

Kaufmann, Daniel, Aart Kraay, and Massimo Mastruzzi. 2005. "Governance Matters IV: Governance Indicators for 1996–2004." *World Bank Policy Research Working Paper 3630*, June 2005. Washington, DC: World Bank.

Kaufmann, Daniel, Aart Kraay, and Massimo Mastruzzi. 2007. "Governance Matters IV: Governance Indicators for 1996–2006." *World Bank Policy Research Working Paper 3630*, June 2007. Washington, DC: World Bank.

Keohane, Robert. 1984. *After Hegemony*. Princeton, NJ: Princeton University Press.

Keynes, John Maynard. 1920. *The Economic Consequences of the Peace*. New York: Harcourt, Brace, and Howe.

Keynes, John Maynard. 1997 [1936]. *The General Theory of Employment, Interest, and Money*. Amherst, NY: Prometheus Books.

Kick, Edward, and Byron L. Davis. 2001. "World System Structure and Change: An Analysis of Global Networks and Economic Growth Across Two Time Periods." *American Behavioral Scientist* 44 10: 1567–78.

Kim, Sangmoon, and Eui-Hang Shin. 2002. "A Longitudinal Analysis of Globalization and Regionalization in International Trade: A Social Network Approach." *Social Forces* 812: 445–71.

Kindleberger, Charles P. 2000 [1978]. *Manias, Panics and Crashes: A History of Financial Crises*. New York: John Wiley & Sons.

King, Anthony D. 2004. *Spaces of Global Cultures: Architecture, Urbanism, Identity*. London/New York: Routledge.

Klein, Daniel B., and Charlotta Stern. 2007. "Is There a Free-Market Economist in the House? The Policy Views of American Economic Association Members." *American Journal of Economics and Sociology* 66: 309–34.

Klein, Naomi. 2000. *No Logo: Taking Aim at the Brand Bullies*. New York: Picador.

Kohli, Atul. Forthcoming. "Nationalist versus Dependent Capitalist Development: Alternate Pathways of Asia and Latin America in a Globalized World." *Studies in Comparative International Development*.

Kohn, Margaret. 2004. *Brave New Neighborhoods*. New York: Routledge.

Kohn, Meir. 2004. *Financial Institutions and Markets*. New York: Oxford University Press.

Korzeniewicz, Roberto-Patricio, and Timothy Moran. 1996. "World-Economic Trends in the Distribution of Income, 1965–1992." *American Journal of Sociology* 102: 1000–39.

Kose, M. Ayhan, Eswar Prasad, Kenneth Rogoff, and Shang-Jin Wei. 2006. "Financial Globalization: A Reappraisal." In *IMF Staff Papers WP/06/189*. Washington, DC: International Monetary Fund.

Kramper, Pierre. 2000. "From Economic Convergence to Convergence in

References

Affluence? Income Growth, Household Expenditure and the Rise of Mass Consumption in Britain and West Germany, 1950–175." In *London School of Economics Department of History Working Paper No. 56/00*. London: London School of Economics.

Krueger, Anne O. 1974. "The Political Economy of the Rent-Seeking Society." *American Economic Review* 64: 291–303.

Krugman, P. R. 1994. *Peddling Prosperity: Economic Sense and Nonsense in the Age of Diminished Expectations*. New York: W.W. Norton.

Kuczynski, Pedro-Pablo. 2003. "Setting the Stage." In Pedro-Pablo Kuczynski and John Williamson, eds, *After the Washington Consensus: Restarting Growth and Reform in Latin America*. Washington, DC: Institute for International Economics, pp. 21–32.

Kuhn, Thomas. 1962. *The Structure of Scientific Revolutions*. Chicago, IL: University of Chicago Press.

Kuznets, Simon. 1955. "Economic Growth and Income Inequality." *American Economic Review* 45: 1–28.

LaFeber, Walter. 1999. *Michael Jordan and the New Global Capitalism*. New York: Norton.

Landes, David S. 1999. *The Wealth and Poverty of Nations*. New York: Norton.

Lewis-Beck, Michael S., and Mary Stegmaier. 2000. "Economic Determinants of Electoral Outcomes." *Annual Review of Political Science* 2000: 183–219.

Lewis-Beck, Michael S., R. Nadeau, and E. Belanger. 2004. "General Election Forecasts in the United Kingdom: A Political-Economy Model." *Electoral Studies* 23: 279–90.

Logemann, Jan. 2008. "Different Paths to Mass Consumption: Consumer Credit in the United States and West Germany during the 1950s and 1960s." *Journal of Social History* 41: 525–59.

Lowenstein, Roger. 2000. *When Genius Failed: The Rise and Fall of Long-Term Capital Management*. New York: Random House.

McNeil, J. R. 2000. *Something New under the Sun*. New York: W. W. Norton.

Maddison, Angus. 2001. *The World Economy: A Millennial Perspective*. Paris: OECD.

Mahutga, Matthew. 2006. "The Persistence of Structural Inequality? A Network Analysis of International Trade, 1965–2000." *Social Forces* 84/4: 1863–89.

Maddison, Angus. 2007. *Contours of the World Economy, 1–2030 AD*. New York: Oxford University Press.

Malthus, T. R. 1986 [1798]. *An Essay on the Principle of Population*. London, W. Pickering.

Mansvelt, Juliana. 2005. *Geographies of Consumption*. London/Thousand Oaks: Sage.

Marglin, Stephen. 1974/1975. "What Do Bosses Do?" *Review of Radical Political Economics* (summer 1974) 6/2: 50–112; (winter 1975) 7/1: 20–37.

References

Martin, John Levy. 1999. "The Myth of the Consumption-Oriented Economy and the Rise of the Desiring Subject." *Theory and Society* 28: 425–53.

Marx, Karl. 2002 [1848]. *The Communist Manifesto*. New York: Penguin Books.

Marx, K. 1981 [1867]. *Capital: A Critique of Political Economy*. New York: Penguin Books.

Matthews, Emily, et. al. 2000. *The Weight of Nations*. Washington, DC: World Resources Institute.

Meadows, Donella, Jorgen Rander, and Dennis Meadows. 2004. *Limits to Growth: The 30 Year Update*. White River Junction, VT: Chelsea Green Publishing.

Megginson, William L., and Jeffry M. Netter. 2001. "From State to Market: A Survey of Empirical Studies on Privatization." *Journal of Economic Literature* 39: 321–89.

Menkhoff, Lukas. 2002. "Institutional Investors: The External Costs of a Successful Innovation." *Journal of Economic Issues* 36: 907–33.

Menkhoff, Lukas, and Norbert Tolksdorf. 2000. *Financial Market Drift: Decoupling of the Financial Sector from the Real Economy?* New York: Springer.

Michels, Robert. 1999 [1915]. *Political Parties: A Sociological Study of the Oligarchical Tendencies of Modern Democracy*. New Brunswick, NJ: Transaction Publishers.

Milanovic, Branko. 2006. "Global Income Inequality: What It is and Why It Matters." *DESA Working Paper, No. 26*, August. Washington, DC: World Bank.

Mitchell, Don. 2003. *The Right to the City: Social Justice and the Fight for Public Space*. New York: Guilford Press.

Mokyr, Joel. 1988. "Is There Still Life in the Pessimist Case? Consumption During the Industrial Revolution, 1790–1850." *Journal of Economic History* 48: 69–92.

Montiel, Peter, and Carmen Reinhart. 1999. "Do Capital Controls and Macroeconomic Policies Influence the Volume and Composition of Capital Flows? Evidence from the 1990s." *Journal of International Money and Finance* 18: 619–35.

Mooney, Alexander. 2008. "Poll: Majority against Free Trade." CNN. <http://www.cnn.com/2008/POLITICS/07/01/cnn.poll/index.html>.

Morales, Juan Antonio, and Jeffrey Sachs. 1989. "Bolivia's Economic Crisis." In Jeffrey Sachs, ed., *Developing Country Debt and the World Economy*. Chicago, IL: University of Chicago Press, pp. 57–80.

Muller, Jerry Z. 1994. *Adam Smith in His Time and Ours: Designing the Decent Society*. Princeton, NJ: Princeton University Press.

Muller, Katharina. 2000. "Pension Privatization in Latin America." *Journal of International Development* 12: 507–18.

References

Munshi, Kaivan and Mark Rosenzweig. 2006. "Traditional Institutions Meet the Modern World: Caste, Gender, and Schooling Choice in a Globalizing Economy." *The American Economic Review* 96/4: 1225–52.

Murrell, Peter. 1993. "What is Shock Therapy? What Did It Do in Poland and Russia?" *Post-Soviet Affairs* 9: 111–40.

Neckerman, Kathryn, and Florencia Torche. 2007. *Annual Review of Sociology.* 33: 335–57.

Neumark, David, Junfu Zhang, and Stephen Ciccarella. 2007. "The Effects of Wal-Mart on Local Labor Markets." *Journal of Urban Economics* 63: 405–30.

Nofsinger, John R., and Richard W. Sias. 1999. "Herding and Feedback Trading by Institutional and Individual Investors." *Journal of Finance* 54: 2263–95.

North, D. C. 1981. *Structure and Change in Economic History.* New York: W. W. Norton.

North, D. C., and R. P. Thomas 1973. *The Rise of the Western World; A New Economic History.* Cambridge: Cambridge University Press.

Obstfeld, Maurice. 1996. "Models of Currency Crises with Self-Fulfilling Features." *European Economic Review* 40/3–5: 1037–47.

Olson, Mancur. 1982. *The Rise and Decline of Nations: Economic Growth, Stagflation, and Social Rigidities.* New Haven, CT: Yale University Press.

Organization for Economic Cooperation and Development. 2009. News Release, February 18: "GDP in OECD area fell by a record 1.5% in fourth quarter of 2008." Paris: OECD.

Overton, Mark. 1996. *Agricultural Revolution in England.* Cambridge: Cambridge University Press.

Peacock, Alan, and Alex Scott. 2000. "The Curious Attraction of Wagner's Law." *Public Choice* 102: 1–17.

Perrow, Charles. 1984. *Normal Accidents.* New York: Basic Books.

Perrow, Charles. 2005. *Organizing America.* Princeton, NJ: Princeton University Press.

Pew Global Attitudes Project. 2007. "Global Views on Life Satisfaction, National Conditions, and the Global Economy." Washington, DC: Pew Research Center.

Piana, Valentino. 2006. "Centers and Peripheries: Trade Network Hierarchies", paper presented. Princeton, NJ: Observing Trade Conference.

Piketty, Thomas, and Emmanuel Saez. 2003. "Income Inequality in the United States, 1913–1998." *Quarterly Journal of Economics* 118/1: 1–39.

Piore, M. J., and C. F. Sabel. 1984. *The Second Industrial Divide: Possibilities for Prosperity.* New York: Basic Books.

Plato. 1908. *The Republic.* Oxford: Clarendon Press.

Pogge, Thomas. 2007. "Why Inequality Matters." In Held and Kaya, *Global Inequality,* 2007.

Polanyi, Karl. 1944. *The Great Transformation.* New York/Toronto: Farrar & Rinehart.

References

Pomeranz, K. 2000. *The Great Divergence: China, Europe, and the Making of the Modern World Economy*. Princeton, NJ: Princeton University Press.

Pomeranz, Kenneth, and Stephen Topik. 2005. *The World That Trade Created*. Armonk, NY: M. E. Sharpe.

Ponting, Clive. 1991. *A Green History of the World*. New York: Penguin.

Portes, Alejandro. 1997. "Neoliberalism and the Sociology of Development: Emerging Trends and Unanticipated Facts." *Population and Development Review* 23: 229–59

Przeworski, Adam, and Fernando Limongi. 1993. "Political Regimes and Economic Growth." *Journal of Economic Perspectives* 7: 51–69.

Quintin, Erwan. 2004. "Mexico's Export Woes Not All China-Induced." December 6. *Southwest Economy*. Texas: Federal Reserve Bank of Dallas: 9–10.

Radetzki, Marian. 2006. "The Anatomy of Three Commodity Booms." *Resources Policy* 31/1 (March): 56–64.

Rands, Tania, and Miguel Centeno. 1996. "The World They Have Lost." *Social Research* 63/2: 369–402.

Ricardo, David. 1996 [1817]. *On the Theory of Political Economy and Taxation*. Amherst, NY: Prometheus Books.

Robinson, William I. 2004. *A Theory of Global Capitalism*. Baltimore, MD: Johns Hopkins Press.

Rock, David. 1987. *Argentina, 1516–1987: From Spanish Colonization to the Falklands War*. Berkeley, CA: University of California Press.

Rodrik, Dani. 1996. "Understanding Economic Policy Reform." *Journal of Economic Literature* 34: 9–41.

Rodrik, Dani. 2006. "The Social Cost of Foreign Exchange Reserves." in *NBER Working Paper No. 11952*. Cambridge, MA: National Bureau of Economic Research.

Rodrik, Dani. 2007. *One Economics, Many Recipes*. Princeton, NJ: Princeton University Press.

Rodrik, Dani, and Arvind Subramanian. 2008. *Why Did Financial Globalization Disappoint?* Cambridge, MA: Harvard University Press.

Ross, Michael. 1999. "The Political Economy of the Resource Curse," *World Politics* 51 (January): 297–322.

Ruggie, John Gerard. 1982. "International Regimes, Transactions, and Change: Embedded Liberalism in the Postwar Economic Order." *International Organization* 36: 379–415.

Sachs, Jeffrey D. 1989. *Developing Country Debt and the World Economy*. Chicago, IL: University of Chicago Press.

Sala-i-Martin, Xavier. 2007. "Global Inequality Fades as the Global Economy Grows." *Index of Economic Freedom*. Washington, DC: American Enterprise Institute.

Schnaiberg, Allan. 2005. "The Economy and the Environment." In *The Handbook of Economic Sociology*. Neil Smelser and Richard Swedberg, eds. Princeton, NJ: Princeton University Press, pp. 703–25.

Schumpeter, Joseph Alois. 1942. *Capitalism, Socialism, and Democracy*. New York and London: Harper & Brothers.

Schwartz, Herman. 2007. "Dependency or Institutions? Economic Geography, Causal Mechanisms, and the Logic of Understanding Development." *Studies in Comparative International Development* 42: 115–35.

Scott, Allen. 2006. "The Changing Global Geography of Low-technology, Labor Intensive Industry." *World Development* 34/9: 1517–36.

Seis, Mark. 2001. "Confronting the Contradiction: Global Capitalism and Environmental Health." *International Journal of Comparative Sociology* 42: 123–44.

Sen, Amartya. 2001. *Development as Freedom*. New York: Oxford University Press.

Shanahan, James, and Michael Morgan. 1999. *Television and Its Viewers: Cultivation Theory and Research*. New York: Cambridge University Press.

Shiller, Robert J. 2000. *Irrational Exuberance*. Princeton, NJ: Princeton University Press.

Sias, Richard W. 2004. "Institutional Herding." *Review of Financial Studies* 17: 165–206.

Simmons, Beth A., Frank Dobbin, and Geoffrey Garrett, eds. 2007. *The Global Diffusion of Markets and Democracy*. New York: Cambridge University Press.

Singer, Peter. 2002. *One World: The Ethics of Globalization*. New Haven, CT: Yale University Press.

Smeeding, Timothy. "Globalization, Inequality, and the Rich Countries of the G-20: Evidence from the Luxembourg Income Study." Syracuse, NY: Miemo, Maxwell School, Syracuse University, 2002.

Smelser, Neil, and Richard Swedberg. 2005. *The Handbook of Economic Sociology*, 2nd edn. Princeton, NJ: Princeton University Press.

Smith, Adam. 1994 [1776]. *An Inquiry into the Nature and Causes of the Wealth of Nations*. New York: Modern Library.

Snowdon, Brian, Howard R. Vane, and Peter Wynarczyk. 1994. *A Modern Guide to Macroeconomics: An Introduction to Competing Schools of Thought*. Brookfield, VT: Edward Elgar.

Soederberg, Susanne. 2008. "Deconstructing the Official Treatment for 'Enronitis': The Sarbanes-Oxley Act and the Neoliberal Governance of Corporate America." *Critical Sociology* 34: 657–80.

Stearns, Peter N. 2006. *Consumerism in World History: The Global Transformation of Desire*. New York: Routledge.

Stiglitz, Joseph E. 2000. "Capital Market Liberalization, Economic Growth, and Instability." *World Development* 28: 1075–86.

Stiglitz, Joseph E. 2002. *Globalization and Its Discontents*. New York: W. W. Norton.

References

Story, Louise. 2007. "Anywhere the Eye Can See, It's Likely to See an Ad." In *New York Times*. New York: New York Times.

Strasser, Susan. 1989. *Satisfaction Guaranteed: The Making of the American Mass Market*. New York: Pantheon Books.

Surowiecki, James. 2004. *The Wisdom of Crowds: Why the Many are Smarter than the Few and How Collective Wisdom Shapes Business, Economies, Societies, and Nations*. New York: Doubleday.

Sutcliffe, Bob. "The Unequalled and Unequal Twentieth Century." In Held and Kaya, *Global Inequality*, 2007.

Suzuki, Reiko. 2004. "Globalization of Production of Electronic Machinery". *JCER Researcher Report* 37 (July): 1–3.

Tainter, Joseph A. 1988. *The Collapse of Complex Societies*. Cambridge: Cambridge University Press.

Taylor, Lance. 2006. "External Liberalization in Asia, Post-Socialist Europe, and Brazil." In Lance Taylor, ed., *External Liberalization in Asia, Post-Socialist Europe, and Brazil*. New York: Oxford University Press, pp. 1–42.

Tedlow, Richard S. 1990. *New and Improved: The Story of Mass Marketing in America*. New York: Basic Books.

Tedlow, Richard S. 1993. "The Fourth Phase of Marketing: Marketing History and the Business World Today." In R. S. Tedlow and G. Jones, eds, *The Rise and Fall of Mass Marketing*. New York: Routledge, pp. 8–35.

Therborn, Göran. 2006. *Inequalities of the World*. London: Verso.

Thirsk, Joan. 1978. *Economic Policy and Projects: The Development of a Consumer Society in Early Modern England*. Oxford: Clarendon Press.

Tilly, Charles. 1990. *Coercion, Capital, and European States, AD 990–1990*. Cambridge, MA: Blackwell.

Tilly, Charles. 1998. *Durable Inequality*. Berkeley, CA: University of California Press.

Tullock, Gordon. 1993. "Government Spending." In David R. Henderson, ed., *The Concise Encyclopedia of Economics*. Library of Economics and Liberty. Available at: <http://www.econlib.org/library/Enc1/GovernmentSpending.html>.

Tziralis, Georgios, and Ilias Tatsiopoulos. 2007. "Prediction Markets: An Extended Literature Review." *Journal of Prediction Markets* 1: 75–91.

United Nations Environmental Program. 2007. *Geo4 Environment for Development*. Nairobi: UNEP.

United States Bureau of Labor Statistics. 2006. "100 Years of U.S. Consumer Spending: Data for the Nation, New York City, and Boston." Washington, DC: Bureau of Labor Statistics.

Veblen, Thorstein. 2001 [1899]. *The Theory of the Leisure Class*. New York: Modern Library.

Viser, Victor J. 2001. "Winning the Peace: American Planning for a Profitable Post-War World." *Journal of American Studies* 35: 111–26.

References

Wacziarg, Romain. 2002. "Review of Easterly's the Elusive Quest for Growth." *Journal of Economic Literature* XL: 907–18.

Wade, Robert. 2003. *Governing the Market*. Princeton, NJ: Princeton University Press.

Wade, Robert. 2004. "Inequality and Globalization: A Comment on Firebaugh and Goesling." UC Atlas of Global Inequality. California: University of California. Available at: <www.ucatlas.ucsc.edu>.

Wallerstein, I. M. 1974. *The Modern World-System*. New York: Academic Press.

Wallerstein, I. M. 1996 *Historical Capitalism with Capitalist Civilization*. London: Verso.

Warde, Alan. 2005. "Consumption and Theories of Practice." *Journal of Consumer Culture* 5: 131–53.

Weber, Max. 1949. *The Methodology of the Social Sciences*. Glencoe, IL: Free Press.

Weber, M. 1978. *Economy and Society: An Outline of Interpretive Sociology*. Berkeley, CA: University of California Press.

Weber, Max. 1981 [1914]. *General Economic History*. New Brunswick, NJ: Transaction Books.

Weeks, John. 2005. "Inequality Trends in Some Developed OECD Countries." DESA Working Paper No. 6. ST/ESA/2005/DWP/6, October.

Weir, Margaret. 2001. "The Political Collapse of Bill Clinton's Third Way." In Stuart White and Susan Giaimo, eds, *New Labor and the Future of Progressive Politics*. New York: Macmillan: 137–49.

Weiss, Michael J. 1994. *Latitudes & Attitudes*. New York: Little Brown.

Wilkins, Mira. 2005. "Multinational Enterprise to 1930." In Alfred D. Chandler, Jr., and Bruce Mazlish, eds, *Leviathans: Multinational Corporations and the New Global History*. Cambidge: Cambridge University Press.

Williamson, John. 1990a. *Latin American Adjustment: How Much Has Happened?* Washington, DC: Institute for International Economics.

Williamson, John. 1990b. "What Washington Means by Policy Reform." In John Williamson, ed., *Latin American Adjustment: How Much Has Happened?* Washington, DC: Institute for International Economics.

Williamson, J. G. 2005. *The Political Economy of World Mass Migration: Comparing Two Global Centuries*. Washington, DC: AEI Press.

Wise, Carol. 2007. "Unfulfilled Promise. Economic Convergence under NAFTA." In Isabel Studer and Carol Wise, eds, *Requiem or Revival: The Promise of North American Integration*. Washington, DC: Brookings Institution, pp. 27–52.

Wood, Adrian. 2002. "Globalization and Wage Inequalities: A Synthesis of Three Theories." *Review of World Economics* 138: 54–82.

Wood, Geoffrey E. 1999. "Great Crashes in History: Have They Lessons for Today?" *Oxford Review of Economic Policy* 15: 98–109.

References

World Bank. 2007. "World Development Indicators Online." Washington, DC: World Bank Group. Available at: <http://devdata.worldbank.org/wdi2006/contents/Section1.htm>.

Yellen, Janet L. 2006. "Economic Inequality in the U.S." *Federal Reserve Bank of San Francisisco, Economic Letter*, December, Available at: <http://www.frbsf.org/publications/economics/letter/2006/el2006-33-34.html>.

Yergin, Daniel, and Joseph Stanislaw. 1998. *The Commanding Heights: The Battle between Government and the Marketplace That Is Remaking the Modern World*. New York: Simon & Schuster.

Young, Nick. 2007. "How Much Inequality Can China Stand?" Special report from China Development Brief. Available at: <http://www.chinadevelopment-brief.com/node/1001>.

Zelizer, V. 1994. *The Social Meaning of Money*. New York: Basic Books.

Index

Index

Index

Index

Index

Index

Index

Index

Index

Index

Index

Index